WARD, Charlotte

Why am I always
the one before 'the one'?

Why Am I Always the One Before 'The One'?

CHARLOTTE WARD

headline

First published in 2008
by HEADLINE PUBLISHING GROUP

1

978 0 7553 1815 5

Typeset in Cochin by Avon DataSet Ltd,
Bidford-on-Avon, Warwickshire

Printed and bound in Great Britain by
Mackays of Chatham plc, Chatham, Kent

HEADLINE PUBLISHING GROUP
An Hachette Livre UK Company
338 Euston Road
London NW1 3BH

www.headline.co.uk
www.hachettelivre.co.uk

Names, places and situations have been changed to avoid identifying the innocent who've helpfully given me their stories

For my Beau, the most patient man I know

Introduction

'*I'm 27 years old. I've* no money and no prospects. I'm already a burden to my parents. And I'm frightened.'

My jaw dropped as the scene from the film *Pride and Prejudice* echoed round the cinema.

In it Charlotte Lucas was 'fessing up to her friend Lizzie Bennett that she would be marrying her odious cousin Mr Collins because, being of spinster age, she didn't want to be left on the shelf.

My sister Sofie and I turned to look at one another. I was grimacing. Sofie was giggling. Exactly the same thought racing through our minds.

My name was Charlotte. I was 27. And I too, in Jane Austen speak, was yet to 'command a high price in the marriage market'. It was almost as if the film was talking to me.

Shoulders shaking, my 19-year-old sibling let out a snort.

But then, at eight years my junior and with all of her 20s stretched out in front of her, as alluring and inviting as the Yellow Brick Road, she bloody well would do.

'Just you wait,' I whispered crossly. 'Your twenties will pass by in a twinkling, just like with me.'

'Yeah, but you'll be nearly forty then,' she sniggered.

She had a point. It seemed time was running out and it made me think.

Throughout my 20s, I'd gone out with two serious boyfriends. But here I was again, single at 27, my biological clock ticking (well, according to every health article I read anyway) and not a potential husband in sight.

When I boarded the train plodding its way through my 20s, I assumed I had all the time in the world to get my life sorted.

Somewhere in the far, far distance was a well-signposted destination called 'The One' – conveniently located around my late 20s.

But I didn't have to worry about that for a long time. I had an open ticket with as many stops thrown in as I wanted. I could jump off for parties, I had time to meet unsuitable men, enjoy drunken and even comedy snogs, be relentlessly single and bounce back if my heart was broken.

As the train trundled along through my mid-20s, I'd find a great bloke, no sweat. He'd tick all the boxes and of course I'd know instantly he was the chosen one. Naturally, after a whirlwind romance, he'd propose and I'd get a rock that made Victoria Beckham's pale in comparison.

Cue marriage, babies and bliss. After all, it's not like I'm a freak or anything.

However, my path to happiness wasn't exactly lined with gold. By the time my mid-20s were well underway, it dawned on me that finding 'The One' was actually pretty tricky. And the more I panicked about it, the harder it got.

All around me friends were seamlessly meeting great men, tying the knot and producing offspring. Yet I would repeat the same pattern of spending ages with a boyfriend I wasn't destined to marry time and time again. The pressure was on.

I realised that although you can try to take the scenic route, meandering through your carefree days on a slow, old-fashioned steam train, sometimes you accidentally board the express train and then you're stuffed.

So what caused this hysteria? I'm not the type of girl who spends her life reading books like *The Rules* or *He's Just Not That Into You* and following them to the letter. To be honest, I'm just not that arsed.

While there is an element of logic in such guides, they are all a bit serious and it's important to be sceptical. No two men are the same and where's the romance in following a manual?

It's not like I hated being single either. My single spells were some of the most fun-packed times of my life. The unpredictability and excitement of going out and meeting different people is fab.

Undoubtedly, one of the most rewarding things that being single can bring is being able to plough all your energy into nurturing your great female friendships that are there through thick and thin. Although we'd all be loath to admit it, time with good friends can so often get a tad neglected when a man is on the scene.

No, the hysteria began with the realisation that ever since I met my first serious boyfriend, almost half my life ago, every single man I've dated long-term has settled down very quickly with the girlfriend after me.

While I've drifted on searching for a soul mate, I have routinely and unwaveringly become the one before 'The One'.

Although I've only stayed in touch with half of my significant exes, word-of-mouth, seasonal correspondence with family members and some bored Facebooking and Googling has kept me abreast of their romantic lives.

Fairly soon after the Charlotte Lucas episode, the startling and terrifying truth dawned on me – every past love had a life partner, was smitten and settled, happily cohabitating or procreating.

But where were my rewards? I'd earned my stripes spending many a weary hour trying to kick these, often wayward, boyfriends into shape. Then off they'd trot with their new-found man skills to enjoy some kind of happy ever after with another lady. *How selfish*.

In I'd breezed, like Supernanny, cracking the whip and setting the rules, until eventually we'd parted company and they'd gone off to be a model citizen for the next girlfriend.

It hadn't been an easy journey. During each individual's own personal 'naughty step' experience there were whisperings of malcontent. Words such as 'high maintenance', 'wears the trousers' and 'control freak' may have been bandied about. However, after resisting at first, they'd listened carefully, and the knowledge I installed had obviously set them up for life . . . but not life with me.

Recently, when I shared this revelation with friends on a night out, it was met with amusement.

I drunkenly recounted how my eagerness to change chaps, hopefully for the better, could be sourced from the fallout of the failed relationship I'd had with my first serious boyfriend, Patrick, who had been very over-bearing and had left me feeling deeply insecure.

From quite early on, I was paranoid he'd cheated on me. It was pretty obvious that he had his eye on other girls and he regularly belittled me. As the relationship progressed and I grew more and more suspicious, I'd lowered myself to snooping.

I examined his phone bill, read letters he'd hidden away and questioned his housemates.

Trying desperately to rein in his wandering eye, I frequently confronted him with what I'd discovered, in the hope I could catch him out before he even considered straying.

But my self-esteem finally hit rock bottom after he chatted up a girl in front of me in a nightclub, took her phone number and told me to get over it.

He claimed pathetically that he was setting her up with his friend. But when he, despite my protests, invited her and her friend back to his home, I caught him and this girl having what looked rather like 'a moment' as they made eyes at each other in the back garden.

We broke up soon after and it eventually filtered back to me that he was sleeping with the girl, just as I'd feared.

I was inconsolable and convinced I'd never get over it. But eventually my broken heart healed and I vowed never to let a man have a hold over me like that again. From then on I had a zero tolerance approach to relationships.

When I met Jack, a lad I went to college with, he had a novel attitude to dating.

'There's time spent with the bird and time with the lads,' he told me, romantically. 'Never shall the two meet.'

I was instructed that if he ever caught me frequenting the same drinking establishment that he was in with the boys, all hell would break loose.

The rules were unshakeable. 'What if I unwittingly stumble in there, not knowing that's where you are?' I enquired. We'd both go out with our respective friends in a town centre with about ten pubs, so it was possible.

Jack's steely gaze said it all, warning me, in no uncertain terms, that it should never happen.

I had my work cut out. There was going to be a power struggle. After all, this was the man who also announced he'd never spend New Year's Eve with 'any bird'.

But while I listened to his rules at first, I was already hatching a plot to shift the balance of power.

So I started playing some games of my own. I countered Jack's boys' nights out with my own girls' shindigs. My friends and I took it in turns driving all over the West Country to different clubs for raucous nights out.

Now Jack would have to vie for my time and, as I'd hoped, he didn't like it one little bit.

To my satisfaction his attitude began to change and soon his priority revolved largely around 'us'. The boys' nights out became infrequent as he opted for romantic nights with me instead.

When he mentioned New Year's Eve plans I scoffed: 'I'm not invited though, am I?'

'I've changed my mind, I want you to come,' he told me sheepishly.

However, ironically, just as I became the most important thing in Jack's world, I buggered off to university 300 miles from home.

Because of the geography, my interest in keeping up a long-distance romance wavered, and like a complete cow I unceremoniously dumped Jack just when he'd become his most dedicated.

Despite my cruelty, we stayed in touch and within a year he told me he'd met someone new – and it was serious. It seemed that after all my efforts to beat the laddishness out of Jack, he was now getting there of his own accord.

He dated the next girl for yonks and they are now happily married with a daughter.

Again, it was a similar scenario with Tom, my boyfriend throughout university. At the start he'd insisted on heading home to Manchester every weekend for hedonistic nights out, only to return to our university accommodation on a Sunday night tetchy and exhausted, with me bearing the brunt of it.

After being in the firing line one too many times, I told him either his lifestyle changed or we were over. Thankfully, Tom recognised that I was now so weary of the situation that I was teetering dangerously on the clifftop of indifference and a sudden maturity kicked in.

But, mirroring the relationships before, after Tom changed, we eventually and amicably headed our separate ways. Like his predecessors, Tom met someone else soon after and several years down the line they've bought a house together.

It was the same with the next boyfriend, Adam. During the course of our romance I'd curtailed his penchant for casinos, bookies and boozers and we'd settled into domestic bliss until the inevitable break-up. It had come down to one thing: I'd invested years, but I didn't want to marry him. The girl after me thought differently though. Within a year they'd bought a flat together and marriage may soon be on the cards.

How many times would I repeat this cycle?

The tale of my exes tickled my friend Caroline somewhat. 'You know what you are?' she concluded. 'You're a wedding fluffer!'

A fluffer, to explain to the more innocent among us, is a term used in the porn industry for someone who – how can I put this politely? – has the sole purpose of ensuring the 'adult entertainers' are, er, standing to attention before their big performance.

So, in other words, I was there, at the side of the stage, warming my ex-boyfriends up for the main show.

But where was *my* moment in the limelight?

I'd always assumed that having the strength of character to tell boyfriends to shape up or ship out was a good thing. But had I been too demanding and militant? Did I make every relationship that followed my reign of terror seem like a walk in the park for my poor henpecked victims? Equally, maybe my search for perfection meant ultimately I'd be the one who'd end up lonely and bitter?

I was worried that the answer might be yes, but then I was offered a reprieve.

I met a chap, The Beau – my man du jour.

We started seeing each other seriously a few months after the Charlotte Lucas episode. He seemed lovely, and, during these early stages, I wasn't sure whether The Beau was 'The One' or not. Indeed, I tried desperately not to obsess about it.

However I was feeling pleasantly optimistic and was certainly looking forward to going on lots of nice dates with him to find out.

I just hoped that this time I wouldn't make a complete pig's ear of it – and here lieth the foundations of this book.

Let's cut to the chase: show me a woman who claims she has a perfect dating history and I'll show you a pathological liar.

Quite frankly, I don't have all the answers and I'm not a dating guru. In fact, I'm the polar opposite.

I shell out the advice to my friends, but do I have the same unwavering willpower I ask them to summon up in times of crises? Sadly not – I have all the self-control of an obese, PE-hating, gluttonous kid in a sweet shop.

But either way, I'm not sure I believe in quick fixes, methods and rules.

Dating is more like your ghastly maths homework. Once you've made enough errors, you'd think you could finally get the hang of it. But it's all too easy to forget what you've learned and find a brand-new tricky equation that you have no idea how to solve.

Over the years, my friends and I have made some colossal mistakes and found ourselves in some ridiculous situations. We've been there, crying bitter tears of humiliation, and occasionally, along the way, we've been responsible for hurting someone else too.

If you're looking for a kindred spirit, you've found one. Once you've read some of life's most excruciating dating stories, you'll feel like the most empowered woman on earth.

If you think you've ever embarrassed yourself, you have no idea. By the time you finish this book, you'll feel like the sanest person ever and the biggest romantic success story IN THE WORLD.

Chapter One

Single v. Settled

I can pinpoint the exact moment I first felt The Fear. I was 26 and had spent the weekend at home with my family.

While out running errands with my mother, we bumped into a friend of hers, who invited us into her home for a quick cuppa. As we tucked into tea and lemon cake, the lady proudly announced her daughter was expecting a baby any day.

Mum and I did the obligatory cooing as she filled us in. But then the grandmother-to-be turned to me.

'What about you, Charlotte?' she smiled. 'Do you have a boyfriend?'

I should have seen it coming.

'No,' I answered absentmindedly, wiping crumbs from my chin. 'I'm not really worried. I'm only twenty-six, I'm a bit young for all that. I'm just having fun at the moment.'

'Only twenty-six?' the lady frowned, wrinkles appearing in her forehead. 'Too young? I was married and had children at your age. You better get a move on!'

Up until that point, the dictionary definition of Charlotte would have been:

Party-loving, opening-of-an-envelope-attending, boozer-frequenting, bad-dancing, karaoke-obsessing, gym-shirking, junk food-binging and hangover-suffering young person. Often in need of weekends of TLC at home with Mother, who force-feeds fruit and vegetables, while emitting the following sentence in a frustrated voice: 'You've been burning the candle at both ends again, haven't you?'

She is nowhere, I repeat NOWHERE, near marrying age.

Suddenly the dictionary had been updated. Now it read:

Charlotte: a childless, fiancé-less spinster. (Oh and a dessert of many varieties.)

Like an awkward 11-year-old learning they'd have to leave the comfortable folds of their junior playground to be thrown into the bear pit of big school, I suddenly grasped that a new era was approaching.

Girls my age were expected to begin the scary process of 'settling down'. Time dictates: 'You've had your fun. Now off you trot and find a husband.'

'How did I get here?' I screamed inwardly. 'What on earth happened to my carefree youth?'

If it was time for the main performance, I hadn't rehearsed enough. I was still fluffing my lines. I wanted more time to practise, but time was running out. Was I now going to have to settle for a mediocre repertoire?

From the word go, my dating life had been troublesome, blundering and at times humiliating.

Like a lot of teenagers, I was awkward, lacking in confidence and wore braces. On top of this, I'd gone to an all-girls school and was subsequently completely clueless when it came to boys.

If I found myself within a four-mile radius of a male my own age, my face would quickly become the colour of beetroot and I'd start giggling like a maniac.

Despite all this, at the age of 13, I managed to secure my very first boyfriend – for a grand total of three weeks.

He was a friend of my cousin, two years older than me and 'gorgeous'. But while I was happy to partake in hand-holding and giggling, I was terrified to kiss him. Hence he quickly became bored with me.

The first I knew about being dumped was when I received a letter telling me not only that our childish romance was over, but also that his new girlfriend was called Heidi. Yeah, thanks for that!

Oh and to add insult to injury, he'd included a cassette single of 'Everything I Do' by Bryan Adams. Did he want me to kill myself?

But, like a true, changeable teenager, although it seemed like the end of the world for about five minutes, I soon got over it. Looking back at the cringeworthy diaries I wrote at that age, I was about as fickle as Mr Wickham when it came to deciding where my affections lay.

One day Richard was 'lush', the next David was 'amazing', and don't even get me started on 'horny' Mark Owen. (While I'm mortified by the vocabulary of my teenage self, at least I didn't use text speak like the youth of today.)

One of my big crushes was on now-well-known Radio 1 DJ Scott Mills, who back then was a local radio presenter. Cultivating my stalking skills from a young age, I cunningly managed to blag myself work experience with him.

To my delight, I was soon answering the phones for Scott and popping in and out of the studio whenever I could to appear 'helpful'. While the records were playing, I'd precociously try to impress him with my, ahem, sparkling 14-year-old wit.

It was with some dismay that I later learnt my efforts would always remain fruitless – I'd never be his type. EVER. Ironically, just like me, Scott was wild about boys. Shite.

After about ten thousand adolescent crushes, I went on to have my first 'real relationship' at the age of 16 with the vastly unsuitable Patrick. I say 'real', but in hindsight it is desperately sad to think that this ordeal was my introduction to 'love'.

He was six years older than me and it wasn't a good match. When I wasn't being labelled 'dull', 'boring' and 'clingy' ('Charlotte, all this holding hands is so passé, I've been there, done that ...'), he would be very over-protective and I was shouted at for not checking in with him on rare nights out.

Once when I forgot to call and say I'd arrived to meet my friends for a night out, he called the train company and then my mum to see if I was dead.

Then when I went on a two-week holiday to San Francisco, he'd call me in the middle of the night saying he could only sleep when I was sleeping and America was dangerous and I'd probably get stabbed.

Ironically, despite his declarations of everlasting love, he kindly gave me the heave-ho – leaving me to scrape what was left of my self-esteem off the floor. It was my first proper heartbreak and I was devastated.

Of course, whenever I did feel I was making progress and beginning to forget him, I'd get the inevitable ranting phone call, but thankfully, I did eventually manage to sever all ties and went on to meet gentle Jack. While he was possessive over his nights out with the lads, it was in many ways the perfect teenage romance.

When I stayed over at his, I slept in his younger sister's room and I'd spend many a happy evening hanging out with his lovely family. He was mad about motor sport, so I'd devotedly accompany him to race days and even the British Grand Prix at Silverstone. We'd go clothes shopping on Saturdays, spending our wages from Sunday jobs at Sainsbury's.

But then Jack was cruelly dispatched as the bright lights of higher education beckoned.

At university in the north-east, I rented a room in a house belonging to a couple that had two young children. They were both about 30 and in my mind bloody ancient. Their lives seemed to revolve around kids, school runs, work and mortgages. In contrast, my life was a heady mix of alcohol, clubbing and coursework – pretty much in that order.

By then I had a new boyfriend, Tom – we were together on and off for over three years – but at that age the thought of weddings and children was laughable. With more than a decade to sort myself out, being 30 was so far removed from where I was.

'When I'm 30 I'll probably be married with two kids as well,' I told myself, observing my landlord attempting to stop his young daughter from clambering up on to the dinner table, fish finger in hand.

Back then, teenagers weren't connected to thirty-year-olds. It seemed like another lifetime. So that was the benchmark for me. About 28 or 29 would be the point when I'd finally be a grown-up. I'd have a great job, a fiancé, I'd be married by 30 and my first child would be on the way by 31. But at 18, I had years and years to go before I had to worry about all that grown-up stuff.

I adopted pretty much the same attitude as I began my early 20s.

I'd seen friends at university proposed to after five minutes and still found it all very silly. What was the point of getting serious so soon when you still had all sorts of life to live first? There was no way I was going to marry my university boyfriend. Well, not unless we both got jobs in the same city and neither of us changed. But at the back of my mind I knew we both had a lot of growing up to do and not necessarily at the same pace.

One young couple I knew got engaged after just a few months, marking their commitment with a cheap ring purchased on credit from a crap high street jewellers.

They spent the night of their engagement wandering the streets of our university town, wondering what to do with themselves. Finally, they arrived at the grotty student house I shared with two friends and my boyfriend and we toasted their impending nuptials with Lambrusco.

Then, rather meanly, I got my camera out and made them re-enact the moment he had got down on one knee. They dutifully did as I snapped the process and my housemate sniggered. We later mocked up a 'My Guy'-style photo casebook of their engagement, complete with stupid captions.

In hindsight, it was pretty cruel of us to laugh at what was obviously a very heartfelt and sweet gesture at the time. But as it happens, our cynicism was right and it didn't last.

I just couldn't understand why my friends were in such a hurry to grow up, and as the years passed my attitude didn't alter much.

A little while after we'd completed our degrees, Tom and I broke up.

I'd moved to Liverpool and for the first time in ages I was single – and it really was a jungle out there. Like so many single girls, my self-esteem took a pounding as I went through a terrible spell of meeting men who fell into the 'stalker' or 'wanker' categories.

I began to despair that I'd never find a nice fella who was, well, normal. There were plenty of flaky, fickle chaps I'd enjoy a date or two with, only for them to go cold on me or cut all contact.

Regrettably, many of the wankers I had the misfortune to meet were deemed so because they already had girlfriends.

This was largely to be my boyfriend-distracting phase.

I say 'distracting', as I didn't actually steal anyone's boyfriend (note the desperate attempt to justify oneself), but during this time I did briefly tempt them elsewhere.

In my defence, I am not the sort of hateful cow who deliberately sets out to pursue an attached man – it's just that at this time unavailable men seemed compelled to try it on with me, while failing to mention their relationship status.

On one such occasion, I convinced myself I was immune from morality judgements because I hadn't known about the girlfriend when we first started up (yeah, right). Plus, I'd never met the girl so therefore she wasn't a real person, capable of being hurt by my actions.

So instead of viewing myself as a boyfriend-nicking ho-bag, I felt a constant inner rage at her. My logic knew no bounds. I wanted him to myself, so in my head I vilified the girlfriend. She was the problem, not him. She was the reason preventing us from being together, end of. It was weak and deluded.

Anyway, back to my crime. One day, in an excruciating moment, I stumbled across him and her together at the local swimming pool.

I was doing laps and my stomach churned as I spotted them heading my way. To my horror, she wasn't what I expected at all. Truth be told, she looked lovely. She wasn't the troll I'd imagined, but a pretty girl with a good figure (well, wadda ya know).

And there she was, splashing around in the water with his brother's kids (I'd seen pictures). They appeared to adore her. Oh Gawd, she was obviously a nice person.

While this was going on, lover boy was swimming past me smirking. It was at that moment that I realised what a silly mare I'd been to pursue him and what a heartless piece of work he was. Rather than being fearful that his girlfriend and I were in such close proximity, he actually found it exhilarating. He obviously wasn't feeling guilty about his indiscretions or worried about her rumbling us.

Or perhaps he just knew, quite rightly, that I'd never say anything.

Later, when I saw her in the changing room drying her hair, she caught me staring, but I looked away, ashamed of myself. I felt like the biggest scuzzer on earth. I'd love to say that was the point I learnt my lesson. But sadly that wasn't to be the end of the boyfriend-bothering.

When history repeated itself, with yet another potential love interest finally admitting he was already attached, it left me fretting over what sort of signals I was giving out. Those of an immoral scrubber?

So on I tiptoed through single life, trying to avoid any more infidelity landmines – and it was then that I found myself in stalker territory. Maybe it was karma.

These men were unattached (hurrah!), but blimey did they want a girlfriend.

There was the marketing executive that I foolishly took to a friend's barbecue on our first (and only) date. He soon unnerved me by gazing at me adoringly as I played with a friend's kids and cooing, 'You'd be a great mum.' Then, after a few too many Stellas, he announced, in all seriousness, that he'd 'kick off' if I talked to any other men. I was really quite scared.

On another occasion, I met a chap in a nightclub. He seemed nice so we swapped numbers, even though we lived in different cities, two hours apart. He called me the very next day and a week later he came to visit.

The date was perfectly jolly, although he was a little on

the quiet side, and it ended with plans for us to meet again. However, before date two something changed. The young man in question phoned with some astonishing news.

'I've borrowed some money and bought a car so I can come and see you,' he said excitedly. Immediately I felt a little bit sick. I'd only met him a little over a week previously, but already there was an enormous pressure for things to work out.

Still, I agreed to see him, and he rolled up in his new car.

Again, we were getting on fine until he dropped another bombshell. 'I'm thinking of moving here,' he announced. 'I think I'd really like it.'

Unsurprisingly, I didn't see him again. While it was nice to meet a man who didn't believe in playing games, it was just too much too soon and I found his haste completely unnerving.

Without meaning to come over all Gollum-like – just to play devil's advocate with myself – a cynic would argue: 'Well, yes, it was a little OTT, but you were quick to complain when they treated you badly, and when they treat you nice you're not interested either. What's that all about?'

It is true that often girls are compelled to date losers or chaps who make them unhappy. Perhaps we can't help but love baddies. So, yes, if they give us the runaround we are hooked, yet if they are plain nice and keen from day one, it's viewed as a bit weird.

A friend, Erika, has had such a bad run of luck when it comes to meeting chaps, she now believes she's programmed to date wrong 'uns.

'When a good one came along recently, I had no idea how to handle it and in the end I treated him dreadfully,' she admitted. 'I cheated on him with his pal at a bar we were all in because I thought he wasn't interested.

'Then I moaned at work every day to my mate who'd set him up with me in the first place.

'Despite the chants of "Give him a chance, Erika," I was expecting calls and texts ten times a day. Little did I know he'd been playing it cool because he really liked me and was a decent man.'

After the boyfriend-bothering and the stalker-shirking, I, like Erika, became deeply embedded in a similar circle of gloom.

I let rogue after rogue give me the runaround, I had no self-esteem, I was giving off an air of desperation. But then, after yet more failed infatuations, I found love in an unlikely place. I started hanging out more and more with Adam, a friend who constantly laughed at my stupidity when it came to relationships.

We worked in the same office, became good friends and one evening shared a drunken snog. But instead of feeling mortified the next day, we realised it hadn't been an embarrassing mistake. Instead, to our surprise and that of our friends, love blossomed.

We moved into a one-bed flat, and although we talked about buying a house together, that was as far as our 'commitment chats' went. I liked being in a relationship, but also missed some of the independence being single had brought me.

Now there was another person to consider. I couldn't just get pissed and roll in whenever I liked without a second thought. If I greedily drank all the orange juice, he'd complain. It also meant I couldn't wander round the flat in my worst T-shirt and pants, with hair-removing cream smeared attractively across my top lip.

THE PROS AND CONS
OF SINGLE V. SETTLED

Single

- You get a whole double bed to yourself and can lie in at the weekend for as long as you like. You will not be disturbed by snoring, or someone hogging the duvet or breaking wind.
- No man is going to moan that you are neglecting him if you decide to devote the majority of your week to partying, shopping or hanging out with friends.
- Living alone means a discount on your council tax.
- There's no obligation to buy Christmas/birthday presents for a second set of family/friends. That's more money for shoes.
- You can flirt outrageously (or even just chat) with any man you like without being branded a trollop by your jealous partner.
- You can gorge on *Friends*, *Desperate Housewives* or *Streetmate* without someone tutting and turning over to Sky Sports whenever you leave the room.

Settled

- Unconditional love dictates that your man will put up with even the most futile bouts of whinging, PMT and self-loathing because he loves you.
- When you're hungover you can lie pitifully in bed, smiling weakly (but bravely) at your better half and hopefully he'll bring you tea and toast or rush to the shops to buy you a pain au chocolat.
- Your knight in shining armour is duty bound to check your wellbeing at regular intervals, so if you happen to get locked in the lavatory you'll be discovered well before you have to start snacking on spiders.
- As a couple you are immune from the 'Odds and Sods' table at weddings.
- You can blackmail him into letting you watch *Strictly Come Dancing* with the threat of a suspension of all carnal privileges.
- When you're standing shivering at the bus stop late at night in a silly little dress and stilettos he'll give up his coat and take the cold like a man.

My birthdays came and went – 24, 25 – but that still seemed pretty young.

Adam and I were happy for a while – but were we happy enough? At 26 doubts began to set in. We'd recently moved to London and Adam's anti-social working hours meant we hardly ever saw each other.

Our friends were beginning to get engaged and married. It scared me shitless. Deep down I knew I had itchy feet; I wasn't the same smitten girl I'd been when we'd got together.

So, reluctantly, we parted company, I embraced single life – for all of about five minutes – and then my mum's friend branded me a spinster. Thanks to the proud grandma-to-be's words, I had a newly acquired, and frankly unwanted, epiphany to muse upon.

So by the time my 27th birthday arrived, I was feeling blue.

A dark cloud descended on me as it occurred to me that my life plan was completely unrealistic. Although I had lived with boyfriends in the past, now single and with the looming realisation that I was forced to start all over again, the thought of joint mortgages, marriage and kids freaked me out.

Yes, I had friends who were settled, engaged and even married, but I also had plenty who, like me, were unattached, renting and carefree. But turning 27 definitely triggered something. From then on in, I was acutely more aware of how everyone else my age was doing in the commitment stakes.

So when I first set eyes on my long-suffering beloved in a hotel bar in Shepherd's Bush, I was immediately carefully considering his long-term credentials.

The Beau was instantly appealing – tall, friendly and charming, with kind eyes and a chiselled jawline.

For some reason, that night I was pretending I worked for Karen Millen. (I was drunk. Sometimes I like to make up little stories.) Eventually I sobered up a bit and confessed my deception. Luckily he laughed. So far, so good.

I gave The Beau my number and he dispatched me

home with a gentlemanly kiss on the hand. He sent me a text the very next day, but to my frustration it was to be almost a month before we were to actually go out.

The Beau expertly juggled chivalry with playing it cool and I was quickly smitten. Almost three years later, I still am.

Now, as I begin my thirties, I still try to tell myself I have time on my side. The other day I read that the average age for marriage is now 32, so at least that buys me a bit of time (The Beau will be relieved).

However, project us back 60 years and it would be a very different story.

In my grandmothers' day, women were often married off in their late teens or early 20s and had a whole different set of priorities. With a country at war and sex before marriage frowned upon, emotions ran high, with men all over the country popping the question to their teenage sweethearts.

These days it is very easy to sit down and whine about how hard we all have it, but imagine if you'd just met your perfect man only for him to be called off to war?

The odds were this fabulous young fella might never return and you'd spend your life devastated and wondering what might have been if you'd just been allowed that chance of happiness.

Without text messages and emails to complicate matters, you'd pretty much have full clarity on whether you liked someone or not. But if you think waiting for a phone call is agonising, imagine the torment for the girls back home waiting for letters from their loves and dreading the day the arrival of a telegram would bring them the news they feared so much.

My grandparents actually became engaged while my grandfather was a soldier in World War II. They had started courting when they were both 17, having known each other for years through their families. Six months after the romance began, my late grandfather, Roger, headed off to Australia to work on a farm. He expected to return two years later, and the pair kept up their romance with frequent letters.

But while he was out there, war broke out. Despite being underage, Roger, who could never sit still at the best of times, decided to join the New Zealand army and headed off to fight. Meanwhile, back in Wiltshire, my grandmother, Mary, joined the Land Army, mucking in with all the traditional men's work.

The only contact she had with her future husband was by letter, so for years she did not see him or hear his voice.

Indeed, as Roger later chronicled in his personal memoirs, a letter, wishing him luck, arrived from Mary on his 21st birthday. That day, fighting in the Libyan Desert, he was almost killed when his platoon was ordered to undergo a kamikaze mission. They were instructed to plough into the path of enemy troops. It would have meant certain death if a last-minute halt to the mission had not been ordered.

It was during Roger's duty in Egypt that he posted Mary a £7 engagement ring. He had painstakingly picked it out in Cairo, and had spent a weeks army wage on it.

While she was ecstatic to be engaged, my grandmother could not rest until her fiancé returned safe and well. Usually she'd receive a letter from him once a week, but the postal service was erratic to say the least.

'Sometimes six weeks would go past without any news and you'd begin to wonder,' she told me.

Thankfully, Roger was one of the lucky ones to return unscathed from the war. He arrived back to the sweetheart he had not seen or spoken to for seven long years and married her soon after.

And to think we worry about text messages.

'It's a different world now,' my grandmother agreed. 'Girls today have so much more than we did.'

In her day, although clandestine affairs did go on, it was a risky business. There was no pill, and you were expected to be a virgin bride. Woe betide the young woman who had a baby out of wedlock.

When my own mother was in her late teens, an unmarried friend of hers fell pregnant. She managed to keep her dilemma a secret for five months, but then tearfully confessed all to her parents.

It was decided that she would give up her job at once under the pretence that she was moving to London. She asked my mother to go with her, to offer some support and company, but although my mother was willing, she was forbidden to by her parents. So, accompanied by her mother, the 19-year-old friend travelled down to London to start a secret life.

As soon as they arrived at Paddington Station, they went to a jeweller on Platform One and bought a cheap gold wedding band. This was to add credibility to her story that she was an army wife whose husband was abroad. She stayed with her aunt, before eventually moving into cheap accommodation with another unmarried mother-to-be.

When she eventually gave birth by caesarean section,

she had little recollection of it all and her baby was soon whisked off. When she woke she overheard one of the nurses asking what she'd had.

Another nurse replied swiftly, 'Ssh! She's not married and it's being adopted. She had a boy.'

A week later she had to kiss her baby goodbye, as he was off to be adopted.

My mother's friend went on to marry and have two more sons, and in a lovely conclusion, many years later, her first born, now all grown up, tracked her down and they have remained in contact ever since.

Giving up a baby could be a harrowing ordeal, but back then the alternative often seemed worse.

Going for a backstreet abortion was like playing Russian roulette, with young women putting their health at risk, with some being left infertile due to complications or, even worse, not making it at all.

No wonder many girls were content to find a husband, settle down and have children at the earliest opportunity.

Although, while some girls were happy to settle near to their parents, others went in search of life experiences. My mother was fortunate to have had the opportunities to travel abroad, work in London and enjoy life before settling down.

While her family teased her for her singleton status – when she eventually married my father, at 27, her younger brother and older sister were already wed – it was generally very light-hearted. Apart, that is, from an ageing aunt on my dad's side of the family (there's always one) who observed my mum's first visit to his native Australia with some interest.

'What I want to know is how many times she's been jilted?' she enquired of his grandmother. ('Jilted' – what a lovely expression. It's right up there with 'spinster', 'old maid' and 'on the shelf'.)

While my mother may have recounted these stories to me, with mock horror, she's been guilty of teasing me in the same manner and I am acutely aware that she would like to be a granny.

A few weeks ago I overheard her on the phone catching up with a family friend.

'How are your grandchildren?' she asked, and then I heard an ominous sigh.

'No, I don't have any yet,' she said, her voice flat with disappointment. 'They're all too busy unfortunately…'

While she'd hold off from actually demanding a grandchild, I know the score. I can see the longing in her eyes whenever I nurse one of my cousins' children. I need to produce an heir pronto.

As the eldest child, all the pressure is on me. My brother and sister have it easy. In fact, it is me who has now taken on the role of being the butt of the family's jokes.

On a holiday to Kefalonia last summer, we visited a picturesque town called Sami. While walking around the harbour, my mother took my arm and whispered affectionately, 'The last time I was here, I was 29 and pregnant with you. Isn't it funny that you've visited at the same age?'

'Yes, Mum, very funny,' I replied, predicting where this would be leading.

'You're not pregnant, are you, Charlotte?' my dad chirped.

'No,' I sighed. 'I'm not.'

The ridicule continued all afternoon, with my dad confessing that a few years earlier, during a visit to a freshwater lake in Malaysia, he'd lied when telling me local legend dictated that swimming in the water aided fertility. Being extremely gullible, and not wanting to be cursed 'with child', I'd retreated from the water with the speed of someone who'd been bathing in sewage.

This is what life is like from the late 20s onwards, and it only gets more incessant.

Pick up a baby or look lovingly at one and you get a knowing smile and the comment, 'Feeling broody are we?' Go to a wedding and you hear, 'You'll be next,' or 'Don't worry, you'll meet someone.' Admit you've had a boyfriend for longer than six months and it's guaranteed you'll be asked, 'Do you think you'll marry him?'

Horrifically, you'll even be asked this in front of him, causing you to glance red-faced at each other, while mumbling, 'Erm, we've not really discussed that yet.'

And if you are hoping to sail through your 20s whistling to your own tune, then DO NOT join Facebook. Every time a new acquaintance request comes through, you just know it'll be an old friend from home/school/college/uni/work, and boy are they about to make you feel shit about yourself.

Even the most boring, geekiest and unlikely people in the world are procreating.

'Now wait just one minute,' you shout at your computer screen. 'I thought you were gay. Now you have a wife and baby? How on earth did that happen? Is this some kind of sick joke?'

Remember how that dowdy girl from school was always unlucky in love while you had your pick of boyfriends? At the time you were always sympathetic, but secretly her misfortune made you feel good about yourself.

Well look at that beaming little face on her wedding day. There's been a role reversal, my friend!

Suddenly you've become Sarah Michelle Gellar in *Cruel Intentions*. Your evil glee over her misfortune has clearly led to your own downfall. (Only in real life Sarah is married to Freddie Prinze Jr, so that makes you even more of a husbandless saddo.)

You can guarantee all these 'happily marrieds' will have a profile snap featuring a smug picture of either 'Me on my wedding day. The happiest day of my life' or 'Me with my darling daughter Ava. The most precious thing in my life.'

Instead, your profile is: 'Me drinking G&T! On My Own! (weeping into my glass)'

And it gets worse.

I was disturbed to hear recently that my stunning 24-year-old cousin has been nicknamed 'Shelfy' by her work colleagues because she has been boyfriendless for, oh, about six months.

This struck me as completely ridiculous. Apparently when she comes into work on a Friday or after the weekend, she gets asked, 'Ooh did you get lucky last night?' I was infuriated to hear this.

One of my pet hates is the way that single girls are viewed as a bit craven, desperate or promiscuous. You are more likely to have spent your Friday evening in watching *Sex and the City* than actually making that title a reality.

Yet a single man of the same age is just allowed to be a bachelor and get on with it. No pressures, no worries, no dramas and lots of back-patting.

The fact that he may have been out and bedded two girls in one weekend is positively encouraged with a hearty cry of 'You player!'

Even girls are guilty of flocking to men like this. Every office has its cute, loveable rogue with hordes of ladies falling over themselves to rescue his poor misunderstood soul and ending up just another notch on his bed post.

But can you imagine if a girl came into work and made the same frank revelations about her love life? Her colleagues would embark on a bitching fest behind the water cooler in no time at all.

So if we're getting it, we're slags, and if we're not, we're spinsters.

But why shouldn't a single girl be able to crow about enjoying the occasional no-strings dalliance? Sometimes a casual encounter can do wonders for a girl's self-esteem.

A friend recently turned up for lunch with a ruddy complexion and a grin that stretched from ear to ear.

'What have you been up to?' I enquired.

The perma-grin didn't leave her face for a second as she recounted how she'd struck up an 'arrangement' with a handsome young man she'd met through another friend. Neither one of them was interested in anything serious, but they were having fun together – judging by that smile on her face, a LOT of fun.

I was glad for her. She'd come out of a long-term

relationship a few months before and had been left feeling low. A bit of light mischief was just the tonic to make her feel empowered and sexy once more.

She told me she'd chucked away all her old, greying undies and had splashed out on some racy new lingerie from Agent Provocateur.

'I've never felt so confident,' she laughed.

And casual (but safe) sex seems to have become a bit of a hobby for another red-blooded minx I know. We've even nicknamed her 'Samantha Jones' after the *SATC* nymph.

When she spies a man she likes the look of, she approaches him and offers to buy him a drink. Seeing her in action is quite breathtaking. It's particularly hilarious to see the reaction of the lucky man she has singled out. As this gorgeous, willowy brunette saunters up to them, they either eye her suspiciously like it's a wind-up or grin like all their Christmases have come at once.

'One-night stands are really intoxicating,' she told me. 'I love that moment when you're looking at each other intently and your pupils dilate as that electricity takes you over.

'You look at their lips, wondering if they're a good kisser, and then suddenly you can't get enough of each other . . . I think I'm addicted to lust.'

One day my gorgeous friend will settle down, but for now she says she is having way too much fun.

'There're so many fit men out there, why would I limit myself to one?' she laughs. 'I love being single.'

Another friend recounts the funniest story of her single days, the time she couldn't decide between two handsome men she got talking to in a bar while away for a hen weekend. So, feeling cocky, she cheekily suggested going home with both of them.

It was a wild night, but the next morning there was a farcical new twist when she was unfortunately involved in a car crash as one of the men gave her a lift to the train station.

Although, thankfully, she was left unhurt, the car was written off and she had to give a witness statement to the police. It was when they began to ask questions about how she knew the driver that things started to get embarrassing . . .

Stories like this never fail to amuse me, they also illustrate that life these days does not have to revolve around whether or not you've netted yourself a man. As one friend told me, it's all too easy to be a female commitment-phobe.

'The reason is simple,' she asserts. 'Being single is fun and you can be utterly selfish and self-absorbed.'

Sometimes there just isn't space in a busy social diary for a boyfriend, and while there are periods when girls obsess, often much of their time is taken up talking about current affairs, work, money, holidays, property and family rather than harping on about relationships.

This generation is very much about being independent and go-getting. There's so much more to enjoy out there, and it's important to embrace that.

As much as family/friends/strangers rib me about being of a marrying age, when I go home for weekends my mother (once she'd stopped pining for a grandchild) loves to hear all about my life and what I've been doing at work.

Years ago, it was my mother's dream to be a journalist,

yet when she visited the career adviser at the convent school she attended, her ambition was scoffed at.

'You'll probably get married, dear,' she was told. 'But there's always secretarial college.' Lacking the confidence to go against this advice, she dutifully did as she was told and has regretted abandoning her ambitions of writing ever since.

But the obstacles my mum faced have meant she goes out of her way to encourage me. Thankfully, she is also as supportive when it comes to my love life. I've never needed to censor my dating stories too much.

I think she can relate to my life a lot. After all, this is the lady who my godmother recalls was panicking when they first met as the two chaps she was dating were drinking in the same pub at the same time. Nice work, Mum!

Anyway, I digress. Young women today have arguably never had it better. We can have enormous amounts of fun without being tied down – well into our late 20s or 30s or for as long as we wish. The world is our oyster.

We have our own money, cars, jobs, flats and houses. We don't need to be kept women, finding a husband and producing offspring while attempting to run our households within the restraints of the kitty set aside by our master and provider.

If you want to have a career before thinking of children, that's fine. Women are now having babies well into their 30s and 40s and champion the fact that they've been able to live a little first before becoming a full-time mum.

Then there are the ones who decide not to have children at all, preferring instead to enjoy the fruits of their hard work and do all the things in life they've always wanted to do.

What a change from the guidance my mum was given from that very enlightened career adviser.

One genuinely child-phobic 30-something told me: 'I'm a bit weird about this one. I don't actively want them, and I'd happily never have any, but if you told me tomorrow that I couldn't have children, then I'd probably change my mind. I haven't quite worked this one out yet. But I never, ever imagine them in my future, which is probably quite telling.'

There is no right or wrong with this situation, but you should certainly have the conversation before you say 'I do'!

One couple I know both earn good money and have a happy married life together. They decided early on that kids were never on the cards and although she is permanently told by friends that are mothers that she'll change her mind, it still hasn't happened.

I, on the other hand, have been broody since day one.

I was changing Sofie's nappies aged eight and am always the first person offering to hold friends' babies. In recent years, this cluckiness has kicked in with gusto.

On a recent girls holiday to Ibiza, we spent a glorious day on the beach lying on sun-loungers and enjoying cocktails. As I basked in the sunshine, I was flicking through a copy of *Easy Living* magazine when I stopped on a page of household items just screaming to be bought: comfy cushions, colourful colanders and chic cutlery.

Inadvertently, I let out a satisfied sigh.

One of the other girls looked up.

'I love house stuff,' I admitted. 'I just want to nest.'

Another girl put down her magazine.

'Do you?' she asked, puzzled.

'Yes,' I carried on. 'I want to get married and have babies and a home in the country with a vegetable patch and chickens.'

Suddenly I had their full attention.

'When did this start to happen?' the first girl enquired. 'When did you start to feel like this?'

It suddenly occurred to me that, at 29, I was the old fogey of the trip. The rest of them were aged from 24 to 26.

They were the ones out raving 24/7 all holiday, while I struggled to keep up, preferring to have one night on, one night off. Of course they hadn't even thought about nesting yet.

Parties do not excite me any more. When people suggest going out for a night that I know will end in binge-drinking, I am overcome with a feeling of dread. I've had enough of abusing my body and fending off the advances of undesirables. In short, I want to be Felicity Kendal in *The Good Life*.

I try not to talk about it, yet I'm always talking about it. Hardly a day goes by without me expressing my pipedreams of cute babies and marital bliss. I permanently reside on The Beau's shoulder, pecking away.

'You've got marriage and babies Tourettes,' he remarked dryly.

'I just need to know you want it too,' I replied, defending myself.

Infuriatingly, he never gives an answer, just smiles and

says nothing. I could kick myself for applying so much pressure. Why don't I just leave him be? But I can't. I'm like a dog with a bone. Next I'll be playing him audio tapes with subliminal 'commitment' messages to hypnotise him in his sleep.

I was relieved to hear a friend went through a similar scenario with her bloke.

'I just woke up one morning and thought: "I want a baby and I want to get married. NOW,"' she admits.

This from the person who said she would never wed and would only have a baby in her 30s, during a well-timed career break. On top of this, she'd only just got back with her ex-boyfriend.

They were supposed to be taking things slowly, but suddenly she could see herself taking it slooooooowly for years and years, with him happily playing computer games and meeting his mates down the pub and her becoming all wrinkled, wizened and barren at home, crying in the middle of a heap of *Mother and Baby* magazines.

She kept it to herself for a few days because she thought he would run a mile if she even mentioned the B or M words to him. In fact, she was silently driving herself crazy thinking about it. A few days later, they were halfway through a romantic meal and two bottles of wine at a local restaurant.

'I just kind of blurted out that I wanted a baby or marriage or both,' she said. 'His face was a picture. Strangely, as soon as I said it, I realised that I did not really want those things right now, just some kind of assurance that he might possibly be in for the long haul.

That perhaps one day, maybe, we might have both of those things.'

Thankfully, without any more prompting, her lovely boyfriend told her that he too wanted those things and, even better, he thought he actually wanted them with her, but just not yet.

'I have not thought about marriage or babies since (much),' she smiles. 'I am now happy just taking things as they come.'

While there is the temptation to go hell for leather into commitment and taking things slowly sounds a bit boring, as the saying goes, 'Only fools rush in'.

Although it's easy to get caught up in the excitement of a brand-new relationship, sometimes it's better to take your time to discover whether this person is really as fabulous as you think they are.

A little bit inside all of us may crave a ridiculous whirlwind love affair, where you meet the man of your dreams, get engaged a week later and marry within months, but it's better to err on the side of caution.

If we want a modern-day tale to promote the perils of leaping in headfirst, we need look no further than Chantelle and Preston.

Chantelle Houghton, an unknown aspiring glamour model, was picked to go into the *Celebrity Big Brother* house to mix it up a bit. She immediately caught the eye of one Samuel Preston, lead singer of band The Ordinary Boys.

Preston, as he is nicknamed, already had a beautiful French girlfriend, Camille. After two weeks of unceremonious flirting with Chantelle on live TV, he left the reality show to face Camille.

Instead of apologising and trying to slowly regain her trust, he promptly proposed. Only he changed his mind and dumped her shortly afterwards (nice) for Chantelle (even nicer).

Within weeks, Preston and Chantelle were engaged and six months later they married, posing sweetly on their wedding day for a celebrity magazine. A year later and WOWZERS! Someone get the Dolly LP out sharpish. It's D-I-V-O-R-C-E.

Somewhere across the English Channel, I'm sure there's a very pretty French girl rewarding herself with a big chocolate croissant and hawheehawing about how she told him so. *C'est la vie*. Indeed, according to The Bible (that's *Heat* Magazine to the rest of us) Preston and Camille have been spotted together looking rather friendly of late . . . Blimey.

The point is, you don't need to tick off everything on your life checklist in one go. Sometimes it's more fun to pursue your goals on your own terms.

Buying a flat by myself was one of the most exciting things that has ever happened to me. Obviously completing the paperwork and sorting out the stamp duty, solicitor's fees and deposit were far from fun. In fact, when I received the zillionth phone call saying I needed yet another document/bank statement/credit check it was enough to make me abandon everything and set up an illegal camp on Hampstead Heath in north London.

But in the end, buying my own place was completely worth it.

As it happened, I'd started the process of buying

somewhere with my then boyfriend Adam, in Birmingham, years previously.

We'd started looking at two-bedroom houses, but eventually put it off after deciding to move to London for more work opportunities. Three months after arriving in the Big Smoke we split.

In hindsight, I realised I'd had a lucky escape.

Recalling a conversation Adam and I'd had about plans for our new abode, it was clear we'd never see eye to eye. We stood on the landing of one potential two-bedroom property, taking in a spacious downstairs room.

I already had it in mind for a tasteful dining area. Adam, it transpired, had quite different thoughts. The conversation went a bit like this:

Me: 'Ooh, this is really nice. We could really make it our own.'

Adam: 'Yeah! This would be perfect for a games room.'

Me: 'A what?'

Adam: 'A games room! A boys' haven. A place I can invite the lads round to enjoy.'

Me: 'Um . . .'

Adam [gibbering faster and faster]: 'I could get a fruit machine, a pool table and a forty-two-inch flat-screen plasma telly with surround sound so we can watch the *Star Wars* trilogy back to back . . .'

Me [growing paler by the minute]: 'Can you even get forty-two-inch televisions?'

Adam [not listening and eyes boggling with

excitement]: 'And I'll have to get a beer fridge, maybe a mini-bar in a globe, or even better one of those La-Z-Boy chairs like Chandler and Joey had in *Friends* with the beer fridge in the arm. I could set up my Nintendo in here and subscribe to Sky Sports and the Adult Channel! The lads would love it!'

Me [hyperventilating]: 'But . . .'

Adam: 'Ideally, I'd like a fish tank with piranhas under the floor, but that'll have to wait until I making a killing down the casino.'

Oh. My. Lord. No.

Thankfully the games room never came to pass (with me anyway) and years later I was in the privileged position of purchasing my own place – a sweet little flat in north London.

I bought it from a bachelor who ironically appeared to live in a state of playboy, hedonistic glory. Adam would have loved it.

Each time I'd viewed the flat, the curtains were closed, the air was musty with the scent of testosterone and the place was littered with the paraphernalia of a single man who worked and played hard. There were pants and cups strewn across the floor, books on finance, copies of *Arena* and Martin Johnson's autobiography on the table, the covers of microwave meals for one littered across the kitchen, and a lonesome piece of icy chicken in the freezer. Incidentally, that sad little chicken was kindly defrosted and left in the fridge for me when I eventually moved in a good four or five months later.

Taking my first tour of my newly purchased abode, I noticed, unsurprisingly, that the oven appeared never to have been used and the cupboards were covered in stale cereal which had spilled from a damp packet of Special K well beyond its sell-by date, lying alongside the ghastliest attempt at pottery I have ever seen (it was dispatched to the local charity shop pronto). The man may have left, but the whole place still had the aroma of eau de sock. The windows were stiff from being unopened and the floors filthy.

But after scrubbing my beloved home from top to bottom and adding a few licks of paint, I began to make the transformation from lads' pad to girlie haven.

I painted the bathroom from a vile turquoise colour to light pink and adorned it with white towels and furniture, delicate framed pictures following a French theme and pretty bottles of cosmetics. I quickly obliterated the revolting purple paint offending my eyes in the bedroom with a tasteful duck-egg blue and added white dainty drawers and wardrobes, pictures and paintings.

Next I decorated the living room with big prints of Audrey Hepburn and Marilyn Monroe, a bird cage, a bust of a demure-looking Victorian woman and dozens of photos, cushions and scented candles. And, no, I didn't give a stuff that I'd lived up to every single girlie cliché. The transformation was complete – and not a games room in sight. Bliss.

So flying solo was not only empowering, but also gratuitously satisfying. I soon realised that buying my own personal place was a once in a lifetime opportunity to make it everything I wanted – before games rooms, cupboards speckled with baby food and pictures of ugly godchildren became unavoidable.

Incidentally, Adam went on to buy his ultimate lads' pad with his best mate. However, much to his horror, his laddish paradise is presently being transformed now that his girlfriend has bought the friend out of the mortgage.

'She told me the *Men Behaving Badly* look has to go,' he told me sadly. 'I've had to sell my fruit machine and I have to make the bed every day and put cushions on it or I can't watch the football.'

I was just about to sympathise when he asked if he could tell me his new favourite joke.

'How do you get a fat girl into bed? A piece of cake. Brilliant isn't it!'

Suddenly I felt very sorry for his girlfriend.

But, ironically, while wide boy Adam was giving up the power to his lady, I was still struggling to share my independence.

Not long after I bought my pad, The Beau, by then my steady boyfriend, was becoming a more and more frequent visitor to my home. At times I longed for him to move in permanently, at others I was far too content spending nights in with my beloved scented candles, cushions and Ikea catalogues.

I'd successfully made the transition from Single to Settled, but my home was my castle. The question was: could I ever share it?

Chapter Two

Getting Started

*S*o *how do you find* a decent chap? It's the million-dollar question.

It's inspired endless *EastEnders* storylines, it's been discussed on *Trisha*, it's been agonised over through the medium of song (see Mariah Carey, Celine Dion and Leona Lewis).

But unfortunately it's all a bit of a tombola situation. You buy your ticket and hope for the best. You might scoop a bottle of vintage champagne or you could bag an out-of-date can of Strongbow.

SPOTTING THE CADS

The other day I picked up a card for a friend. It was illustrated with a retro-style illustration of a young lady and read: 'She threw herself into the paths of unsuitable men.'

When I presented it to her she laughed, as never has a truer word been spoken. However, it really isn't her fault.

The roads of Singledom are sadly paved with potholes

in the form of cads, bounders, mentalists and mummy's boys. Craftily hidden just beyond the break of a hill, they're almost impossible to spot until it's too late.

There's a screech of brakes and a nasty pop. Before you know it, your tyre has blown and there's nothing to do but sit around waiting for recovery. Then, when you feel brave enough, you set off down the rocky road of romance once more.

If only there were a few warning signs.

Peter Pan syndrome

For some reason, we often labour under a misconception that men hit 25 and suddenly start to mature.

But sadly not all commitment-phobes grow up. Alas, they can be found in their 30s and 40s, still relentlessly pursuing unwitting girls, aged about 23, with tales of their posh penthouse flats, sports cars and high-flying jobs.

I actually have a Peter Pan character as a friend. Despite rapidly approaching his 40s, he has the stamina to cane it like a 21-year-old. He has a high-pressure job, but is often out on a school night, partying and drinking until 6 a.m. Yet the morning after the night before, he always appears completely fresh-faced and on form. His secret? Five-minute power naps in the toilets.

You can always rely on him to bring you the most amusing stories of dates with highly-strung young ladies in their early 20s. But while he is one of the most entertaining people I have met, I would never in a million years allow any of my friends to date him.

A few years ago, a friend of mine embarked on a

disastrous relationship with a real ladies man. She met him at a party we'd attended together and they immediately hit it off.

From the word go he was flaky to the extreme. He would arrange dates only to cancel at the last minute and when they did meet she just wasn't that convinced he was a keeper. After several miserable months passed, they finally tried to get it on – only for him to put his back out while on the job.

Feeling completely frustrated by the whole sorry affair, she decided to break it off.

Recently I met another young lady and was stunned to hear that, in an amazing coincidence, she'd also dated the same lothario – and, remarkably, had met him at exactly the same party on exactly the same evening.

His treatment of her was also debatable, with the pivotal moment being when he invited her on a romantic break to his family's country hotel. Packing her best underwear and ridiculously excited, she set off with him for what she hoped would be the perfect mini-break.

Only when they arrived at the hotel he immediately put her to work in the kitchen. All weekend she found herself serving customers and running round like a headless chicken while he barked orders at her.

A few weeks later, her serious doubts were finally confirmed when she looked at his phone and discovered he was still attempting to worm his way back into his ex-girlfriend's affections.

That – and the revelation that he wore sequined jeans – finally convinced her the relationship was irreparable.

Banker Wankers

It's undoubtedly a little unfair to generalise, but I have quite an aversion to bankers.

I'm sure there are some nice ones out there, but in my experience the nature of their work – all that competitiveness and arrogance combined with passive aggression – means the nice ones are few and far between.

Plus I have a good reason to hate bankers, as I was feeling particularly vulnerable when I was badly burned by one.

At the time I had just broken up with Adam and I was considerably upset. Poignantly, our break-up coincided with the end of another great love story – that of Brad and Jen.

In a public statement they'd announced:

'This decision is the result of much thoughtful consideration.

'We happily remain committed and caring friends with great love and admiration for one another.

'We ask in advance for your kindness and sensitivity in the coming months.'

If I'd issued a statement about Adam and me, that's what I would have said too. Spooky. Jen and I were clearly cosmic twins. Obviously I wasn't married and world-famous with amazing flicky hair, but we were practically the same.

Thankfully, the demise of mine and Adam's three-year romance was not recorded for prosperity by the paparazzi, and Adam wasn't hanging around with Angelina Jolie, but I like to think it was just as dramatic.

In our case, after weeks of knowing it was on the cards, miserable silences and unspoken words, it was Adam who raised the possibility of going our separate ways.

In a late-night phone call from work (he was doing night shifts on a national newspaper), he suggested we break up.

Sobbing, I agreed and after a hysterical call to a friend, I necked a couple of Diazepam I'd been prescribed for my fear of flying in the hope that they would make me sleepy (they didn't really work) and tried to get some rest.

For several hours I tossed and turned, occasionally drifting off for a short-lived bout of fitful sleep. But then I'd wake, wondering why I felt sad for a minute before the full recollection of my despair hit me.

When Adam came in from work at 4 a.m. and climbed into our bed, I woke up and attached myself to him like a limpet, clinging on for dear life. In the darkness of night, the thought of being without him made me feel physically sick.

But in the morning when I got up for work, eyes looking like I'd gone ten rounds with Tyson, I felt strangely calm.

At work I sang along to songs on the radio a bit too merrily. My colleagues eyed me suspiciously. Something had to give and that evening, when I made the mistake of going for drinks after work, it did.

I was necking vino with gusto at a bar in Mayfair when Mr Banker Wanker sidled up to me smiling smugly.

'I think you and me would look really good together,' he announced without a hint of irony. Through my white-wine haze, I studied him intently. He was very pretty in a boyish way, but very short (why are short men always the cockiest?), shorter than me once I stumbled off the bar stool, I estimated.

Either way, in my post-break-up cloud of misery, I had absolutely no energy for anything like that.

'I'm sorry,' I smiled politely. 'I've got a boyfriend.'

Mr BW seemed to get the message and pissed off to bother someone else. But ten minutes later he was back.

'You lied to me,' he said accusingly. 'I've been talking to your friend and she says you just broke up with your boyfriend.'

I sighed before explaining truthfully that only 24 hours had passed and I was still feeling very upset.

Mr BW listened, then he looked at me scornfully.

'It's a shame, as we would look good together,' he repeated. 'Although there is one big difference between you and me [he paused here for effect] and that is the massive spot on your cheek.'

And with that, he verbally kicked a girl when she was already at her lowest.

It rendered me speechless and paranoid about the massive stress boil glowing like a beacon on my face. My apologetic friend told me later he'd been wearing a wedding band too. I hope his wife is a total bitch to him.

Anyhow, predictably, his callous comment opened the floodgates. It was quite literally the straw that broke the camel's back. By 10 p.m. I was on the verge of a breakdown when I met one of my best friends in a nearby pub.

The kindly chum took one look at my melancholy state and bundled me into a black cab. No sooner had the doors closed than I descended into a shaking, sobbing wreck.

I howled for the entire half an hour journey from Soho to Clapham. As my wails echoed round the taxi, the cabby closed the little window between him and us and turned up the radio.

When we arrived at our destination, my saint-like friend quickly rushed me into the house, to avoid disturbing the neighbours, and finally pacified my sobs with tea, chocolate and old episodes of *Friends* saved on her Sky Plus.

'Don't you worry,' she said, squeezing my hand. 'Everything will be OK and you can't really see that spot . . .'

Bless her lovely (lying) heart.

Ageing Lotharios

It was actually with the same friend, some months later (and in a slightly more composed state), that I found myself at the Met Bar, a pretentious London nightspot which I have no desire to frequent again.

Sitting at the bar, my friend and I decided it would be nice to record our night out with a photo.

'Will you take one please?' I asked the barman.

'You can't do that in here,' he said, shaking his head disapprovingly.

'Why not?' I asked.

'Because we get a lot of celebrities in here and they don't like pictures being taken in case they're in the background,' he replied snottily.

'But there aren't any celebrities in here,' I said, irritated, sweeping my arm round the half-empty room. 'Show me a celebrity.'

As I vented my spleen at the pompousness of it all, I felt a hand on the back of my neck.

'If you want a photo, you shall have a photo,' an authoritative male voice announced in my ear. The body belonging to the voice then leaned in to sandwich me between it and the bar.

I turned my head to see my knight-in-not-so-shining-armour. He was a grey-haired chap in his 60s.

'Now let's get you some champagne,' he simpered.

I tried to move, but he still had his hand on my neck, which he'd started unpleasantly kneading, like it was bread dough. My body immediately tensed as I tried frantically to think of a polite escape.

Thankfully, my friend saved the day. Not the least bit worried about being rude, she threw the man and his companion a filthy look and stormed off. Realising he was fighting a losing battle, the man at last released me from his vice-like grip and I was able to leg it after her.

I'm sorry to say this unpleasant experience wasn't the only time a man old enough to be my father has violated my personal space.

On holiday in New York with another friend, Clare, we got talking to a man in his 50s at the bar of a trendy joint.

He was an artist, and at first we really enjoyed chatting to him, as he seemed intelligent, interesting and passionate about his work. But then, to my disgust, after we'd accepted a couple of drinks, I felt a hand sliding onto my thigh. After the initial shock, I fidgeted in my seat until he removed it and then nudged my friend and we got up and left.

As before, I was shocked and outraged. It just made me

really angry that on both these occasions older men thought it was acceptable to manhandle me in such a bullish manner.

With youth no longer on their side, it seems this type of ageing male thinks he can get young women into bed with a mixture of pushiness and flashing the cash. It may make me squirm, but clearly there are ladies out there happy to grope a granddad.

The elderly obviously hold some appeal – Hugh Heffner and Peter Stringfellow always seem to clean up on the buxom blondes' front – but please allow me to remind you of one brilliant episode of *Sex and the City*.

When a 72-year-old millionaire propositions Samantha Jones, dollar signs are instantly ringing in her eyes. So much so that after he's presented her with diamond jewellery, she retires to his dimly lit bedroom to let the Viagra work its magic.

Sadly for her, once the deed is over and her elderly lover gets up to head for the bathroom, Samantha catches sight of the saggy skin drooping from his behind. Suddenly, all thoughts of material goods gone, she runs for the hills. Let that be your warning.

The Weirdo

In my teens, I once really liked a guy until he showed me his bedroom. He was maybe 18 or 19, but the ceiling was graced with pictures of Morton Harket from A-ha. Why he wanted to lie in bed and gaze up at the chiselled heartthrob was a mystery. A mystery I wasn't prepared to unravel.

But he was small fry compared to some of the letches and nutters I have encountered just embarking on my everyday life.

I don't know what it is, but I seem to have some sort of in-built homing device when it comes to attracting unwanted attention from weirdos. I also have an amazing ability to handle such situations so badly that they end up taking on farcical Benny Hill proportions.

During a trip to Austria, I had an encounter with a very unpleasant man at the hotel where I'd been staying. Ridiculously, the warped chain of events began when I booked in for a facial at the hotel health spa.

It was very nice. Apart from the fact that the over-zealous beauty therapist stole my eyebrows. And squeezed about twenty spots I didn't even know I had, until my face resembled the Elephant Man's.

Afterwards, somewhat woozy (I did have a little nap during the nice face-stroking bits), I asked where the toilet was. Before I knew it, she had bundled me through a door. How strange.

Suddenly I realised there were no loos in sight. I was in the sauna area. The NUDE sauna area. Out of the corner of my eye, I saw a flash of wild white hair and a big belly emerging from the jacuzzi. A grandpa's todger? That was something I didn't need to see. Frantically, I ran for the ladies' changing room.

I could have left at this point, but I didn't. For some stupid reason, the thought of having to face my militant beauty therapist and tell her I didn't want to be naked outweighed the fear of actually being naked.

I got chatting to two nude girls in the changing room.

They were English and liberal, I reasoned, maybe I could be too? I peeled off my clothes and sucked my tummy in, wrapping the towel round my exposed flesh. 'I can do this,' I told myself. 'It'll be really exhilarating.'

But suddenly the warning came. 'Watch out for the pervy guy.' I gripped my towel with panic.

'WHAT PERVY GUY?' I squealed.

'The northern guy,' they said. 'He invades your personal space and certainly doesn't stick to sauna etiquette about keeping your eyes on someone's face.'

My fear must have been obvious. 'You'll be alright with your towel in the sauna,' they soothed. 'But you're not allowed it in the steam room.'

Again my gut feeling told me to scarper. But I didn't.

Clinging onto my towel to preserve my modesty, eyes cast down, I quickly dashed past the jacuzzi and pool and into the first sauna I saw. Sighing with relief, I sat down. It was empty. It felt quite nice. Maybe I'll just remove this, see how it feels?

Before I could do anything, the door creaked open. In strolled a man in his late 30s. In all his naked glory.

'You're supposed to sit on your towel,' he informed me. In a northern accent. UH OH!

'I'm OK for now,' I replied.

'They'll tell you off for keeping your towel on,' he chastised, his eyes running up my legs.

'I've heard you're allowed it in here,' I replied.

Now this is the point where I definitely should have left. Did I? NO.

'Do you like menthol?' he asked.

'Yeah', I trembled. Not really thinking.

'Come in this next room,' he beckoned. Like a mug, I did as I was told.

The room did indeed smell of menthol and was all hazy with a light, misty spray coming from the ceiling. Eek! Yes, he'd got me in the steam room. The compulsory naked steam room.

'You've got to take your towel off in here,' he told me triumphantly. 'If the man catches you, he'll give you a stern telling off.'

'I'll risk it,' I stammered.

A minute passed. 'Your towel must be getting very wet,' he helpfully observed. I refused to move a muscle.

The stand-off continued.

'It's OK, I won't look if you take it off,' he said, moving closer to me.

Finally common sense prevailed. 'I'm just NOT comfortable being naked!' I snapped, standing up. 'I've got to go and phone my boyfriend.'

And with that, I legged it. To the sodding toilet.

Mr Vain

From the way my flashing friend paraded around that sauna, he obviously thought he was something very special. And there is something both amusing and unnerving about a man who clearly thinks he's God's gift to women.

Vanity in a chap is something I've never really got my head round. Years ago, I realised I was dating Mr Vain when I went out to a club. He seemed like a nice chap. He was handsome, a great dancer and I was enjoying a good old boogie when he stopped and whispered in my ear.

'Pretend you don't know me,' he instructed.

'Why?' I asked, puzzled.

'If we're both dancing on our own, we can see who gets the most attention,' he revealed, grinning. 'I used to do it all the time with my ex-girlfriend.'

'Did she love herself too?' I thought to myself, amazed by how odious their little amusement was.

Recently, a friend had even more misfortune when she began to date seemingly the vainest man in Britain.

It was clear that admiring his handsome charms took up a great deal of his time. She often caught him looking at himself in the bathroom mirror, pulling the kind of faces on a par to male model Derek's 'Blue Steel' pose in comedy film *Zoolander*.

But for her guy it was no joke. He took his looks very seriously. Soon her bathroom cupboards were cluttered with his cosmetics. Most disturbingly of all, her metrosexual man felt he could not spend a day away from home without applying his fake tan. So that appeared in her bathroom too.

'He checked his appearance dozens of times before leaving the house and even used to look at himself in shop windows as he walked down the street,' she huffed.

At the start, she was willing to forgive his weird hang-ups and found the fact that he would never dance at a party in case someone laughed at him endearing. But when he refused to have sex with her in case he wasn't up to scratch, it was the beginning of the end.

The main problem with men this vain is they are rarely as beautiful as they believe themselves to be and even if they are, in reality they are unlikely to stay that way.

I'd actually quite like to fast-forward 30 years when old age has set in. What will he look like when inevitably his looks fade? A bit like Michael Jackson or David Gest I like to imagine.

Mummy's Boys

Let's move from the overconfident to those in need of the ultimate approval – from their mothers.

While a bloke who looks after his mother is a good find indeed, if he's still attached to Mummy's apron strings at the age of 30, you've got to wonder.

A friend once went out with a guy who, along with his brother, had his own labelled bottle of coke in the fridge, so he didn't have too much sugar. Not. Normal.

Then there was the girl who got the shock of her life when she stayed over at her boyfriend's parents' for the first time. Like a good, respectable potential daughter-in-law she dutifully retired to the spare room after a night out. The next morning, having overslept and feeling slightly the worse for wear, she stumbled into the kitchen to see her boyfriend was already in there having breakfast with his mum and sister.

There, before her very eyes, was her man and his family, smiling toothy grins over their bowls of porridge – all three of them wearing exactly the same teddy-bear pyjamas. It was like some freaky version of *The Waltons*.

Another young lady went shopping with her man and was left amazed at the palaver it took to purchase him a pair of socks. Looking a bit overcome by the decision-making process, he took his phone from his pocket, and, to her astonishment, proceeded to phone his MUM to find out what size socks he should buy. HE WAS 27.

Which brings me to the 31-year-old who lived with his parents – despite owning his own house.

'He had absolutely no desire to move out,' a friend recalls. 'I used to visit him at his new house, and didn't really twig until a few weeks later that he wasn't actually living there.

'I finally realised when I commented that he smelled nice, and he said it was his dad's Lynx that he'd borrowed.' Lordy.

Mr Drippy

Often mummy's boys can be a little bit drippy too. The afflictions appear to go hand-in-hand, and neither one is a turn-on.

While it's nice to be adored, being stared at continually or constantly having your hair stroked can irritate even the most tactile of ladies. Likewise, a pained look just because you don't want to hold their hand every second of every day can really start to grate. You want to feel equal in a relationship, so being followed around by a little lovesick puppy is just not sexy.

Often the Mr Drippy in your life may be the male friend you've known for ten years plus. You're probably uncomfortably aware that this man has secretly had a thing for you for years, but has never had the backbone to pluck up the courage to tell you (not that you'd want him to).

Instead you catch him gazing at you, the tragic woes of

unrequited love written all over his face. He's always engulfing you in 'friendly hugs', during which time you're pretty sure he's sniffing your hair furtively.

When he gets a girlfriend you'll be very relieved.

The Toff Tosspot

While a man who's too chicken to speak his mind is horribly off-putting, the other extreme can be just as unattractive.

As with the banker I encountered after my break-up with Adam, I recently found the insulting advances of a posh, pompous man just as odious.

A friend and I were in a club in Fulham when we spied the crème de la crème of celeb sightings: Prince William. It became clear, much to our glee, that we'd gatecrashed some sort of Sandhurst shindig.

We were drunk and ridiculously excited, so shamelessly positioned ourselves on the dancefloor right next to the future king. Wills was downing shots and cutting some serious shapes to Justin Timberlake. Surreal is not the word.

But then, mid-dance, one of his army acquaintances marched up to us and asked if we'd come to the club to spy the future monarch.

'No,' we insisted innocently. 'Is he here?'

The man briefly introduced himself – he had one of those posh names like Hugo or Guy – and then, without a word, he grabbed me by the elbows and moved me across the dancefloor.

'You're quite good-looking,' he told me in his plummy

tones before staring at me, his demeanour serious, as if expecting a thank you.

When I protested that he'd rudely left my friend on her own, he barked, 'She'll be OK,' before telling me all about his properties in Fulham and France. Big wow.

Like the Banker Wankers of this world, I found this man's gloating about his wealth revolting, especially when he went to the bar and loudly ordered the most expensive champagne on the menu. While I, like most girls, am unlikely to turn down a glass of fine champagne, producing a bottle of bubbly won't make me drop my knickers.

While there are girls out there whose eyes go 'ker-ching' at the sight of a gold card, when men gratuitously flash the cash it has the opposite effect on me – as it does with many of my friends.

'While I've been out with tight men and there's nothing nice about that, I would hate to be with a rich man,' asserts a pal.

'It would just make me uncomfortable and make me feel that we were living in separate worlds. Essentially I want a man with roughly the same sort of salary as me, but who isn't afraid to put his hand in his pocket now and again to treat me to something fabulous!'

Sometimes a small, thoughtful gesture means so much more. Personally, I'm a sucker for a lovingly prepared mix-tape or a surprise home-cooked dinner. But that was something Major Rah, as I'd nicknamed my obnoxious admirer, would never have understood.

I released myself from his grip and found my friend, but Major Rah followed me round all night, becoming more and more detestable – and crude.

'You love it,' he slurred, curling his top lip. Actually I didn't.

Incidentally, my chum Louise refers to this sort of man as a Fugly.

'A f***ing ugly boy (not just in looks) and the type of stereotypical, arrogant shit who will harass you even if you are explicitly uninterested,' she explains. 'I'm always tempted to reach for my mace spray.'

'WHAT DID YOU JUST SAY TO ME?' THE CHAT-UP HALL OF SHAME

They never fail to make you groan, yet men will insist on using them.

From the not so original . . .

'Hey darling, is there a mirror in your underpants? I can see myself in them this evening.'

'Is that a ladder in your tights or a stairway to heaven?'

[Approaches girl, takes ice cube out of drink, drops it and stamps on it] 'There, I've broken the ice, now let's get to know each other better.'

'Is there a thief in your family? Someone stole the stars out of the sky and put them in your eyes.'

'I've lost my phone number, can I have yours?'

'Do you believe in love at first sight? No? Well, shall I walk past you again then?'

'If I told you that you had an amazing body, would you hold it against me?'

To the dire . . .

'You're not pretty like your friend, but you have a nice personality.'

'Hello, do you mind if I stand here?'

'If you've lost your virginity, can I have the box it came in?'

'What's got two thumbs, speaks French and loves blow jobs? [Points to himself with thumbs] Moi.'

'Hey babe, my rickshaw's outside, fancy a trip to the far, far east?'

'Hi, my name's Jon. Remember it, you'll be screaming it later.'

'Do you ride like you dance?'

To the frightening . . .

'I like those. Can I touch them?'

'Get your coat, I've got a knife . . .'

The Rebound

As a rule, rebound men are never a good bet. They can go one of two ways, as Louise, previously of Fugly fame, has categorised them:

The ghost dater

As soon as you start dating him, he treats you like his long-term ex-girlfriend, expecting intimacy like he had with her, expecting you to be on good terms with his family and immediately giving you your own pet name. Yikes.

Louise recalls how she snogged a rebound boy at a party, only for him to come on too strong.

'He took me out for drinks the next week and started stroking my arm after one minute,' she remembers. 'It was weird and creepy and in no way sexy. Then after dinner he asked me if he could introduce me to his parents on my way home. There was no second date.'

The ex addict

He seems keener than mustard, but then bottles out inexplicably to head back to his ex.

During her single days, another friend went on a hen night with a group of girls and got dancing with the most gorgeous bloke she had ever seen.

At the end of the night, she and the chap, who was called Tim, snogged and swapped numbers. Wistfully she wished him farewell, assuming someone of his calibre would never get in touch.

But lo and behold, the very next day she received a text from him saying he wanted to visit – that same day. So she invited the gorgeous boy out for drinks with her mates, who looked at her gobsmacked as she grinned from ear to ear.

But it got even better. Tim revealed he was a pilot and

had even brought his uniform with him, so he could go straight to work from her place.

'I nearly wet myself with excitement when I saw it hanging in my wardrobe,' she recalled. 'By this time, I was already visualising myself as Mrs. Pilot!'

Later that night, the gorgeous man was under her duvet and things were getting lively. However, not wanting to be seen as a one-night stand type of girl but more respectable wife material, she refused to have sex with him. So, instead, after a bit of a fumble, they went to sleep.

Next morning, my pal pretended to still be in a peaceful slumber as he dressed to leave for work. But sneaking a peek she almost squealed with delight at the sight of him in his uniform.

'He looked like something out of *Top Gun*!' she enthused.

So he kissed her goodbye and left, promising to call that night, leaving her to dream of wild adventures with her pilot hunk and tell EVERYONE – friends, family, the woman in the corner shop . . .

Only he didn't call. Instead she got a text two days later: 'Hi, really enjoyed spending time with you, but I've got back with my ex. Thanks for a great day, Tim.'

'I was furious,' she said. 'So I deliberated for a while, until I thought up the perfect, cool, couldn't-care-less reply: "Tim who?"

'It was futile, but it made me feel a lot better.'

The Marrieds

Like the ex-obsessed, married men are always a no no – if only they'd realise it!

Years ago, I was single and in a club with some friends when a handsome young man came up to me and started paying me attention. He bought me a drink, danced with me and complimented my outfit.

We'd been hanging out together for about an hour and were standing by the bar involved in some very flirty banter when suddenly our moment was interrupted by a cross-looking woman who barged past, hissing, 'I'm watching you . . .' at the man in question.

'What did she say that for?' I asked, confused.

The man gingerly held up his left hand and a shiny wedding band caught my eye. I was gobsmacked. It had been there right in front of me all night, but I hadn't seen it – mainly because him being married was the last thing I'd expected.

As I stood there, aghast, the man kissed me on the cheek and told me patronisingly that he was extremely flattered by *my* attention. As he walked away, I was apoplectic with rage. The cheek of him to try to make himself feel better by making out I was flirting with him, not the other way round.

But he, as married letches go, was small fry. I don't think he was actually planning to cheat, it was more of an ego thing. He obviously wanted to know that he still had it.

After that, my wedding band radar was permanently on high alert.

Obviously some men couldn't be trusted, so the minute I spotted a ring or a dent (in the case of the sly ones who take it off), I piped up.

On one occasion, the man then proceeded to tell me how much he loved his wife and kids and even showed me a photo. Yet he still begged me to go for dinner with him, until I politely told him to shove off.

My final example of a dastardly husband desperately seeking a bit of extra-marital comes courtesy of my friend Laura.

'After I clocked a wedding ring, he admitted, "OK, so I am married. But ... but ... [frantically searching for mitigating circumstances] she's dead!"'

The One To Be Really Scared Of: The Control Freak

While it's easy to laugh at stereotypical varieties of men, there are some unsavoury souls out there who just can't let go of the reins. According to a friend there are two types of control freak: the Driving Seat Control Freak and the Passenger Seat Control Freak.

She says there's no mistaking the Driving Seat Control Freak. He shamelessly controls every turn, skid and brake in the relationship – but then you knew he would before you climbed into his souped-up lifestyle wagon, so you really can't complain.

The Passenger Seat Control Freak is far more deadly because he takes a while to grab the wheel and when he does there's no letting go. Subsequently, the entire relationship crashes and burns because you certainly weren't expecting the backseat driving that he's hit you with.

During courtship and the early days of romance, most decisions were equal (or a great deal focused towards pleasing you). But once he's made a mental map of you and got you firmly tapped into his Tom Tom, it's full steam ahead to a one-track lifestyle.

The final destination is, unsurprisingly, all about him.

Get out fast, my friend warns. There is no room for a co-pilot in this dangerous vehicle.

When you are in a relationship with a control freak, friends and well-meaning acquaintances will often question why you put yourself through it. But as your self-esteem is subtly (and not so subtly) attacked, it is hard to escape unscathed.

Sadly, over the years, I have had several friends who have been in similar situations. Unless you have self-belief of Lara Croft proportions, it is very easy to be sucked in. Unfortunately, there are deeply insecure men out there who make themselves feel better by subtly manipulating and bullying their girlfriends.

Ironically, it is often the lovely, outgoing traits that first attracted him to her that he later tries to drain out of her. Instead of championing what he should see as the endearing quirks in her nature, he picks holes in them until she is a shadow of the girl she used to be. The manipulation is subtle but effective.

In my case, one ex would say to me: 'Are you wearing that skirt? If you like it, that's fine, but you do have really skinny legs and I think you'd look better in a long skirt.'

What he actually meant was: 'Cover up your body. I don't want any other man looking at it.'

Interestingly, during other relationships when I was

actually allowed to uncover my pins, I soon discovered they were the feature I received the most compliments about.

In the past I have watched a friend go from a confident, gorgeous girl to a self-doubting wreck, all because the bloke she was dating felt the constant need to belittle her. Her job was too low-rent, her conversation too dull and her aspirations too worthless. Thankfully, she finally saw the light, but not before her self-esteem had taken an absolute hammering.

The problem is that once you've put someone up on a pedestal, it's very humiliating to admit you were wrong. Instead I think a lot of girls (myself included) have been guilty of trying desperately to make a square peg fit a round hole.

You've come this far, invested all this time and energy and there's no turning back. If you focus on his few good points and avoid the overriding bad ones, perhaps he'll become the man you want him to be? Maybe, but sometimes you just have to admit defeat. When a man heaps that much control and criticism onto his girlfriend, it's scary. And so it should be. It's NOT NORMAL behaviour!

THE UNDESIRABLES:
THE WARNING SIGNS

Peter Pan Syndrome

- He refers to his home as his 'bachelor pad'.
- His last girlfriend was a model/studying for her A levels/in a girl band.
- He's got tickets for Babyshambles/The Kills/whichever 'of the moment' band that has a member Kate Moss is supposed to be screwing.

The Banker Wanker

- Within minutes of meeting him, he boasts about his annual bonus.
- He gets competitive about who lives in the better part of town – and you've only just met him.
- He belittles the bar staff and doesn't leave a tip.

The Ageing Lothario

- His botoxed forehead doesn't move and the hair is far too shiny and glossy. Just For Men anyone?
- He offers to pay for a boob job.
- He suggests you could try out for a pole-dancing job at his club.

The Weirdo

- He starts muttering to himself mid-date.

- He tells you all about the special relationship he has with his gerbil.
- He asks if you like guns.

Mr Vain

- You have to fight him to get into the bathroom.
- He's been using your hair dye/tweezers/moisturiser.
- You catch him looking at his reflection in shop windows and licking his finger to smooth down his eyebrows.

The Mummy's Boy

- He has to consult his mum about his outfit each morning.
- She smells his breath before he leaves the house.
- When you arrive back at his after a night out, she's on the doorstep in her nightclothes, hand on hip and looking at her watch crossly.

Mr Drippy

- He cries at the end of *Legally Blonde*.
- He sends you texts offering coffee and 'a hug'.
- If there's a noise in the night, YOU have to get up and investigate.

The Toff Tosspot

- He claims he dated Zara Phillips.
- In the bedroom, he playfully whacks you on the bottom with his polo stick calling you a 'dirty filly'.
- He tells you your breeding is questionable.

The Rebound

- When you do something perfectly normal like order a skinny cappuccino, he looks at you all confused and claims, 'That's not what my ex used to drink.'
- He cries about his lost love then begs you to be his girlfriend.
- When he goes to pay, several tear-stained photos of his ex fall out of his wallet.

The Marrieds

- His phone keeps ringing and he looks twitchy as he cancels the call.
- There's a suspicious looking tan line on the third finger of his left hand – and he isn't the type to wear fashion jewellery.
- There are kids toys in his car and he claims they belong to his niece.

The Control Freak

- He measures your hemline before you go out with the girls and anything above the knee is unacceptable.

- He screens your phone calls and fills in your diary.
- If you are a tiny bit late home from work, you are *blatantly* having an affair with your boss – even though he looks like Mr Bean.

Now you've seen the various type of men on offer, here's where *not* to go looking for them.

VENUE DILEMMAS

There's nothing quite like a night out dancing until the wee small hours. Only problem is, where's a girl to go?

The Club Tropicana

What is it about 80s music that attracts the most revolting, sweaty, overweight men?

They jump around thrusting their hips to 'Gold' by Spandau Ballet. Then they spill their pints of lager all over themselves and anyone unfortunate enough to cross their path as they recreate *Saturday Night Fever*, badly.

Before the smoking ban, their emissions were masked by the smell of cigarettes. Sadly, now you'd be lucky to last more than five minutes on the dancefloor, as the stench of body odour, beer-laced belches and eggy farts engulfs you.

Who you're likely to meet: Terry, who works in advertising, who's so drunk, he's dribbling. He gawps at your chest, while gibbering, 'My wife doesn't understand me.'

Most likely chat-up line: 'You've got amazing legs. They'd look great wrapped around my neck.'

The Crèche

Ah, the youth of today. They think they invented indie. The impertinent young fools.

Do you remember the days when you used to mosh along to 'Smells Like Teen Spirit' and 'Song 2'? Well, there's a whole new breed of teens getting down to Nirvana and the like. With all our favourite classic tracks mixed in with the new wave of indie rock, the music is great. But walk in wearing your spangly top and high heels and you'll immediately feel like an imposter.

The scene here is dyed black hair, piercings, eyeliner and Converse trainers. It's distinctly underage. Don't even think of telling them you're into Nu Rave, they'll only laugh at you.

Who you're likely to meet: Josh, who's 17 and claims he's in a punk band. He's wearing make-up to cover up his spots.

Most likely chat-up line: 'I've got a pierced tongue, do you want to see what else?'

The Trendy Club

You've made it through the door, well done you! Do you have ANY IDEA how privileged you are to grace these hallowed walls? You've been made to wait outside for an hour? Paid £20 on the door? Been belittled by the door staff? Lucky you! Don't you know this is where the trendiest, most beautiful people come? Christina Aguilera was here last week.

No, you can't request Girls Aloud. Our DJ has all the best R'n'B, please don't bother him with your terrible, inferior taste. And can I just say you're far too covered up, not to mention a little bit lardy, to be in here. We like our girls size eight and wearing as little as possible.

Who you're likely to meet: You were promised wall-to-wall celebs. Instead you've got Gaz who works in the Carphone Warehouse and boasts he sold Mark Ronson the latest Nokia the other day. He's pushy and flash. And an arse.

Most likely chat-up line: 'I'm setting up a business with Calum Best.'

The Bump 'n' Grind

As the slow jams blare out, if your hips don't grind, then you're falling behind. The guys line the walls, nodding appreciatively at the ladies and looking out for their next potential Dance Hall Queen. There she is, in the middle of the dancefloor, shaking her booty like a bad girl. Before you know it, she's surrounded by panting men, their pelvises rocking and dry-humping her into a frenzy. Now don't you go giving any of her gang-bang boys the eye. She might rough you up big styleee.

Who you're likely to meet: Dwayne, the rude boy. He's a wannabe producer, rapper and urban entrepreneur.

Most likely chat-up line: There's no time for polite chit chat! Let the grinding do the talking.

The Rah Bar

Are you called Verity, Arabella or Claudia? Well, you'll do nicely then. But you jolly well be careful; the chaps in hah (here) can be frightfully obnoxious. They really can't oblige crass girls with opinions, it shows bad breeding, yah.

They'll have floppy, foppish hair, wear brown suede loafers, chinos and pink, opened-necked shirts. Rah boys do love to dance, but for some reason they take great pleasure in pretending to roger each other on the dancefloor. It's an Eton thing, apparently.

Who you're likely to meet: Prince William, James Blunt or Hooray Henrys called Charlie, Freddie or Rupert.

Most likely chat-up line: 'Would you like to come back to one's palace?'

Druggie Paradise

Are you totally f***ed? Can you claim so in a raspy, husky voice? Are you LOVING this beat? You're right, it's massive. No, I can't stop my jaw from moving either.

What? You're narcotics free? Are you out of your f***ing mind? I've got some class gear, really intense. If you don't try it, you haven't f***ing lived.

Who you're likely to meet: Ketamine Tom. He really loves you – well, while he's high anyway.

Most likely chat-up line: 'Fancy a line back at mine?'

While trawling for Mr Right, never forget the 'five seconds to impress' rule.

No matter how much you originally like someone, it's amazing how sometimes you can go off them in five seconds flat.

A friend once waited for weeks to meet up with a man she'd met at a party and really liked the look of, but on their first dinner date she rapidly began to doubt whether he had the right credentials.

As the wine flowed, the banter came thick and fast, but the booze had clearly loosened him up so much that he thought the following sentence was acceptable: 'I remember this one time in a Spanish whorehouse...'

My friend, a very open-minded young lady at the best of times, looked at him aghast.

'You do know you're on a date?' she laughed nervously.

'It's OK, I didn't go through with it!' he chortled. Well, that's OK then!

But my friend let it go. Keen for the date to work out, she chose to forget that particular conversational gem and tactfully changed the subject. But after dinner, her date was back on the charm offensive with another shock comment.

'I don't know about you, but it's never too early for a line,' he announced, grinning, before heading off to hoover up a narcotic digestif. Rock 'n' roll! Er, no.

So their very first date had been dominated by talk of brothels and drug-taking – and this was him trying to make a good impression?

'Call me old-fashioned, but would a bit of decorum really have gone amiss?' my friend asked.

She didn't see him again, and who can blame her? She was too worried that date two might involve prostitutes and chasing the dragon. Was it too much to ask for a man to just be normal and chivalrous?

Sometimes, however, you can go off someone through very little fault of their own. My initial attraction has been in the past instantly floored by a terrible accent, the sight of a stray bogey lurking in their nostrils or if they've accidentally spat in my face.

When I emailed my friends and asked them what puts them off, the suggestions came back thick and fast: 'Men who talk about how much money they earn', 'Guys who talk to your cleavage', 'Men who kiss you like they're rodding a drain or do weird stuff like lick your face'.

My mum even ventured to say that she once chucked a man for throwing a crisp packet out the car window (I'm so glad she held out for my lovely dad instead).

Bad dress sense was up there too. One girl lusted after a chap at work who looked undeniably hot in his uniform, but then when he turned up for a date wearing tight leather trousers she was mortified. Another image-conscious lady had a holiday romance with a really fit guy, but when she met him again back in the UK and he was wearing hideous shoes – brown dad-brogues – and jeans with creases in it all went so wrong.

'I couldn't focus on anything else,' she admitted. 'I made my excuses and left after about two minutes. How shallow is that?'

A vegetarian friend once spotted a handsome man on the dancefloor of a nightclub. They started dancing together and then he offered to buy her a drink at the bar. He had an alluring French accent – so far, so good. Then she asked him what he did for a living and it all went pear-shaped – he worked in an abattoir.

'As a vegetarian, I was instantly repulsed,' she recalled. 'I kept it polite, but swiftly finished my drink and left.'

A gorgeous friend, Rosie, was on her second 'official' date with a chap she'd met in the pub a couple of weeks earlier when she began to wonder about his idea of humour.

During the first date, they'd really hit it off, and had continued to have lots of phone chats and text conversations afterwards. Their second date had gone well too, and it was only when they were back at hers that she started to worry. Her date kept making really inappropriate jokes that immediately began to put her off him.

'We were watching a comedy show and there was a joke about someone being a prostitute, and one of the characters said, "Nah, I'd never pay for that, she's awful . . ." And my bloke just went, "Yeah, that's sort of why I came round here, but to be honest I wouldn't pay for it with you!"

'I was just a bit sort of stunned. I gave a nervous laugh and carried on watching. Then, a few minutes later, I leant on the remote and changed the channel by accident, and he started tutting and said, "God, I'd definitely ask for my money back now!"

'I think he was trying to be funny, but to be honest it was all a bit weird. I'm not really sure I like being called a hooker – whether it's a joke or not.'

Another young lady was left very excited when a handsome and successful lawyer spotted her walking into a recruitment agency and tracked her down. But on the date she began to have serious doubts when he started to boast about how his 90 per cent success rate for getting defendants off had meant he now got to defend some of the country's most well-known murder cases. The final straw wasn't even when he proudly announced he'd got a Christmas card from one of the most notorious child killers.

No, he finally sealed his fate in Dumpsville with the immortal line: 'If you wanted to bump your other half off, I can tell you how to do it and get off.'

Sometimes you are just dying to fancy someone, but if they're not on the same wavelength it can be extremely off-putting.

A male friend recalled how he bagged a date with a complete stunner, but struggled to converse with her. All she did was giggle and nod at everything he said and he began to wonder whether she possessed much up top. Desperate to find some common ground with her, he suggested they go to the cinema and see a movie of her choice.

'No,' she said, tittering and shaking her head. 'I don't get films.'

Likewise, a himbo may be pretty to look at, but if they're thick as two short planks the attraction can fade in a twinkling.

Another friend, Sarah, always used to go for the stereotypical sporty, hunky rugby man. This was fine when she was at uni and all she wanted was sex with hot, huge-muscled men, but not, she realised, when she had started working and wanted to settle down.

She started seeing a semi-pro rugby player when she was 24 and in her first proper job.

'He was GORGEOUS and amazing in bed,' she said. However, he literally bored her to tears with all his talk about rugby. Apparently, her hunk would give her detailed rundowns on his performance each week on the pitch, and then give her updates after every training session (five times a week) about how he was getting on. Their first proper date was to (yes, you've guessed it) a rugby match, and from then on it only got worse.

His pillow talk even consisted of it.

'It got to the point where I was literally clamping my hand over his mouth in bed and climbing on top of him to shag him quiet,' she exclaims. 'In the end, the great sex just wasn't worth putting up with all the rugby talk and I got rid of him.'

People who have bad manners are a pet hate of mine. When a man shoulder-barges me on the train, sending me flying in order to secure himself that one seat, it takes every ounce of my self-control not to snatch his phone off him and call his mum to tell her loudly what a letdown to society she has raised.

With the overcrowding on the Underground in London, lack of chivalry is rife. I've seen young, healthy men lurching in front of old ladies and pregnant women to sit down. They then whip out a newspaper or iPod and obstinately ignore their surroundings.

It may be futile, but if I'm standing myself and unable to give up a seat, I make it my personal mission that when they look up, there I am glaring at them with all the venom of Anne Robinson eyeballing the perpetrator of an idiotic answer on *The Weakest Link*.

I nod at the poor more deserving person they have selfishly done out of a seat and then move my disapproving glare back to them. My silent death stares have had grown men scuttling out of their seats in a jiffy.

My militant stance on manners is all the more prevalent when it comes to suitors. Holding open doors and being polite to other people are essential.

From day one, when it comes to manners, The Beau was proving to be worth his weight in gold. If I gave even the slightest sign of a shiver, he'd offer me his coat or jumper, and he never failed to carry my bag for me, no matter how pink and flowery it was.

All these small touches had the desired response – they made me ridiculously swoony. It made me think back to how I'd been instantly appalled by a man who I'd once gone to meet in a crowded pub who stayed glued to his seat (as did his friends) while I stood around looking like a plank. They'd carried on talking while I stood awkwardly, looking around for a chair.

The Beau would have been the first out of his seat like a shot, running round finding chairs for me or any of my friends. That's because he's a gentleman.

In fact, as the months passed, The Beau's chivalry was having a funny effect on me. Every time he acted gallantly, I got a little bit more hooked on him. Whenever we went anywhere by public transport, I'd get giddy at the sight of him jumping up to offer his seat to damsels in distress and helping old ladies and mums with their luggage and prams.

I'd stand there silently, with a silly half-grin on my face, gazing at him adoringly.

'That's my new boyfriend,' I'd think proudly. 'Wow.'

The only problem was that my chivalrous suitor was a bit of a yo-yo boy. One minute he seemed keen, the next he was telling me things were going too fast. It was exasperating.

He'd spend the entire weekend at mine, acting like my boyfriend, then leave, telling me he wanted to cool it a bit. I'd curl up on the sofa on a Sunday night feeling miserable, insecure and rejected and then I'd receive a nice text message as if nothing had happened.

I'd literally be tearing my hair out in frustration. After avoiding the cads, I was convinced I'd finally netted a good one, but where was it all going? And had I left all those hideous man-spotting venues behind for good?

Chapter Three

Status: In A Relationship

When my romance with Adam ended, I hadn't expected to fall for someone else so quickly. I'd expected at least a year to pass before I even thought about getting involved in another serious relationship.

I'd planned to enjoy time with my friends and concentrate on my career. Adam had meant so much to me that I needed time to mourn. Finding a new boyfriend was very much on the back-burner.

So when I found myself speedily falling for The Beau in half that time, it made me feel slightly disloyal.

Ironically, it seemed that, just like buses, another one had come along straight away. It was unexpected, but I figured I had to go with it – if I let this one slip through my fingers, who knew how long I'd have to wait around. And, as we've already established, I felt that time was not on my side.

I'll never forget the day after the night before, following my first date with The Beau.

In that strange way that romance works, it had gone so well that the next day was utter hell. I had the sweats (granted that could have been the alcohol), my mind was racing and my stomach was churning. I had full-blown Infatuation Fever and there was absolutely nothing I could do about it.

When Infatuation Fever has taken hold, you are acutely, infuriatingly aware that you didn't even know this person a few weeks ago, but suddenly in your mind they are elevated to The. Number. One. Most. Important. Thing. EVER.

'For God's sake woman, get a grip,' you tell yourself. 'What would Angelina Jolie do?'

But it's no good. The minute you meet a nice bloke who could, just could, be Potential Boyfriend Material, it's like he's crawled inside your mind and pitched a tent.

I realise that at this point feminists often get a bit angry about girls like me, playing into the hands of stereotypes about the weaker sex etc, but what's the point of being anything but honest?

I know and you know that this is what happens. Infatuation Fever is often, unfortunately, unavoidable.

If you are one of those rare women who thinks rationally, switches off and goes back to living life as if you hadn't just had THE MOST AMAZING DATE, then good for you, please give the rest of us just a little bit of what you've got. Anything would be better than that all-encompassing feeling of being completely out-of-control of your emotions just because you've met someone who seems nice.

So anyway, pre-Infatuation Fever, the evening before, The Beau had agreed to meet me from work. As soon as the clock struck six, I raced into the toilets to touch up my make-up and hair and dashed outside to find him waiting for me.

We exchanged awkward kisses on each cheek and wandered down the road. I was chattering like a maniac, something I always do when I'm nervous, and he was being incredibly polite.

We walked to a nearby bar and quickly ordered two potent cocktails. We did all the usual first date stuff: we talked about work, friends, interests; he checked out the music on my iPod and tactfully claimed he liked it.

As the alcohol flowed, we got on brilliantly and I relaxed, although I was still talking nineteen to the dozen. We had another margarita, then a daiquiri, then a bellini.

When The Beau admitted he'd forfeited a night watching his favourite team, Sheffield United, play; so keen was I to impress that I suggested finding a pub that was screening the match.

We traipsed across Leicester Square, stopping to pucker up on the way, then found ourselves in a small Irish pub called The Toucan. The match was playing on a tiny screen in the corner, there were only 15 minutes left and his team were losing.

Gallantly, The Beau tried to keep his eyes on me as we supped pints of Guinness. But after catching him making several furtive glances over my head, I told him to go ahead and watch it. Secretly hoping this show of generosity would earn me brownie points.

When the football ended we finished our drinks and left. I'd not eaten anything since lunch and as I stepped out into the fresh air, I realised the ill-advised Guinness on top of a potent mix of cocktails – and no food – had left me blind drunk.

The Beau walked me to the tube and after another kiss,

I swayed onto the Northern Line, waving goodbye to him and grinning inanely.

'Call me when you get off the other end,' he instructed. I nodded goofily.

The 30-minute journey to my home in Golders Green did little to sober me up. Getting off the other end, I stumbled down the road and into Carmellis, an amazing 24-hour Jewish bakery.

I'd just picked out a rather tasty-looking morsel when my phone rang. It was The Beau.

'Did you get home OK?' he enquired.

'Yesh,' I slurred drunkenly. 'I'm in the bakwery.'

'What are you doing?' he asked.

'Buying spinach quewch,' I giggled, trying desperately to formulate my words. 'It's amaaazing.'

Sweetly, The Beau insisted on talking to me until I was safely through my front door, but in doing so endured another ten minutes of drunken gabble and unattractive chewing noises in his lughole.

Once inside, I bade him farewell, stumbled into my bedroom, flung my clothes on the floor and collapsed onto my bed without removing my make-up.

The next morning, from the moment I woke, puffy-eyed and with a furry tongue that tasted like cardboard, the fear began to set in.

'Why on earth didn't I eat something before I went out drinking?' I cringed to myself. 'Why did I get that drunk?' My head felt like it had been forced through a mangle. In short, truly hideous.

At work, I sat at my computer, desperately trying to do my job, but instead I'd break off every ten minutes to feverishly think about The Beau. I checked for text messages; no, nothing. I read ones he'd sent days before, Googled his name, tried to find him on MySpace and Friends Reunited and stared into space.

As my hangover kicked in with a vengeance, I veered from self-loathing and energy-less angst to silly, giddy highs, where I'd giggle almost hysterically at a colleague's joke, feeling strangely drunk once more.

Never the coolest of girls, by 11 a.m. I couldn't resist texting. So I composed a message saying I'd had fun the night before. After getting at least three friends to vet each word, I pressed send and placed my mobile phone in front of me, willing him to reply promptly.

But an hour later there was no response. I slumped miserably at my desk. Another hour passed, then two, three and four . . . but nothing. Every time my phone bleeped and I discovered it was a stupid, selfish friend sending me a text, I cursed out loud and refused to reply. How dare they give me false hope?

As five o'clock approached, I sat at my computer with my head in my hands.

'Are you lovesick?' a friendly colleague teased, rubbing my arm.

'Yes,' I whined, pulling a pained face. 'I think I've blown it.'

Just then my phone bleeped. It was a message from The Beau. Woooohoooooo!!! It took all my willpower not to jump out of my chair and run a circuit of the office whooping like a madwoman.

He apologised for not texting earlier, but said he'd been out playing golf with his brother all day. Apparently he'd enjoyed the date too and was looking forward to seeing me again soon. Yay!

Panic over, the perma-grin returned. Everything was rosy.

So, so naive! Why didn't I realise I was destined to go through this rollercoaster of emotions, oh, about six hundred times?

Incidentally, the other day, I questioned The Beau at length about what he went through the day after our first date.

Infuriatingly, it went a bit like this:

> Woke up, brief thought about the night before, phoned brother, arranged golf, played golf, read message on phone from the bird from last night – that's nice – fingers too cold to reply, back to golf, six hours pass, oh, better text back.

So, in short, while meeting a man you like can be a thoroughly torturous experience for womankind, men have a useful ability to file thoughts of budding romances somewhere in the brain behind footie, food, beer and golf. Strangely, going completely loopy over someone you've just met and letting them possess your every waking moment (and sometimes your dreams too) is not really seen as a sensible option. If only I had the same amazing clarity on things.

If I thought I'd embarrassed myself on my first date, my drunken slurring was small fry compared to the antics of another young lady I know.

In a cautionary tale, the young strumpet had arranged

to go out to dinner with a fella she worked with, but they got sidetracked by booze in the bar beforehand and never made their restaurant reservation.

Instead, they continued on to another bar and carried on drinking. It was there that she bumped into some friends and confided in them that she was on a date.

'I lurrrve hiim!' she slurred loudly, even though he was right next to her as she swayed against the bar.

If he heard, it didn't put him off. Indeed, as the night progressed, she managed to wangle herself an invitation back to his. But from there on in things went even more downhill. For some reason, she decided to strip (more due to drunkenness than sexiness) and collapsed on his bed. At this stage, thankfully, her date was already out for the count.

But later she woke up feeling disorientated and sick, so started stumbling around the flat in the buff looking for the toilet – to this day she has no idea if his flatmates saw her or not.

When she eventually reached the bathroom, she grabbed hold of a handrail a bit too roughly and ripped it off the wall. Then she fell over, knocking her head on the loo as she went down. After yelping in pain and nursing her sore head tearfully, she fell asleep on the bathroom floor.

She was awoken from a deep slumber the next morning by the sound of her worried date kicking open the bathroom door. He found her sprawled on the floor, hair like a bird's nest, with huge panda eyes where her make-up had run and wearing nothing more than her birthday suit.

Funnily enough, that was pretty much the beginning of the end of the romance and, MORTIFYINGLY, from then on in she had to endure the embarrassment of seeing him EVERY DAY at work.

I, on the other hand, had stopped at drunken ramblings and spitting spinach quewch all over the mouthpiece of my mobile. Thankfully, The Beau hadn't seen the true ugly face of binge-drinking, he'd only heard it over the phone. I was safe and I'd secured date two!

INFATUATION FEVER: THE WARNING SIGNS

- You grab every newspaper and magazine you can get your hands on to feverishly study your stars – and his. Any that appear negative you simply discard, grabbing more and more, possibly searching the internet too, until Venus is deemed in your favour. Phew!

- Maybe, just maybe, somewhere deep inside your head, a little brain cell is secretly processing what his surname sounds like with your first name and hunting around in the attic of your grey matter to rediscover the box entitled 'favourite baby names'. Ssshh. It's only a private thought, no one else needs to know.

- You've found his page on Facebook. Frantically you search every message and photo for evidence of other girls, and of course his friends' descriptions to see if they've 'hooked up'. Who the hell is that willowy blonde who keeps messaging him? She looks like a complete slut. It's his sister? Oh. I feel terrible now.

- You: 'Did I tell you his mum's called Jane and that's my Granny's name?! And we've both been to see the Bonzo Dog Doo-dah Band! Honestly, we're so alike!' Cue bored, pained look from long-suffering friend. Her: 'Yes, you did tell me. Six times already.'

INFATUATION INSANITY: DO NOT GO THERE. EVER.

- Oi you, a word please. I have a sneaking suspicion you're so wrapped up in this one that you're taking dangerous risks. You're not really that bothered about contraception, are you? In the height of passion you just don't care. It's wild and exciting and so, so incredible. How amazing would it be to have a love child?! Hellooooo? How amazing would it be to get a STD? Get to the chemist right this minute, missy.

Forgive me for being smug, but I was so caught up with the excitement of my first successful date with The Beau that I assumed I was home and dry.

This one was a keeper – I could just tell. I was on cloud nine. I'd gone gaga. I didn't envisage any game-playing or tomfoolery. Infatuation Fever had infected my brain and all my defences were down.

In fact, I was pretty much stood in the middle of No Man's Land doing a little jig with pom-poms and shouting, 'Coo-eeeee!' like a hapless idiot just waiting to be shot down.

I should have been a bit more cautious. After all, I had no idea what was around the corner . . .

The problem with a new romance is it's incredibly easy to lose your head. Like new parents do about their baby, you can easily fall into the trap of thinking that what you are going through is so special and unique that you must inform everyone about it every second of every day.

When I was sorting through some old paperwork recently, I discovered a print-out of an email I'd actually sent to a friend where I'd transcribed the first four text messages back and forth between The Beau and I.

He'd scored points for sounding intelligent and funny and using all the correct grammar and spelling without any mind-numbing text speak. I'd tried to match this with my own 'witty' retorts. But did I really need to inflict this on my poor friend? Maybe not, yet women often seemed compelled to analyse every single little detail of the early stages of a romance with their friends.

My single friend Rebecca routinely brightens up my day by forwarding me the email interactions between her and the chaps she meets. These are often accompanied with notes: 'Do you think he likes me?' 'Do I sound stand-offish?' 'Do I sound too keen?' 'Can you believe he took two hours to reply? I know he got it before then as there was a reader receipt. Do you think he's playing hard to get?'

Then I get to be Agony Aunt for a few minutes, offering my pearls of wisdom and analysing the poor unsuspecting man's texts and emails. But trying to second-guess like this can be a dangerous game. No one really knows what the inference of a text really is, apart from the person who sent it.

Men just don't seem to put the same amount of emphasis on texts and phone calls. As one chap explained: 'Life is too short to constantly prattle on all the time. I never understand speaking when there is nothing to say.'

Another revealed that men are acutely aware that calling too soon can sound the death knell of over-keenness.

'Every movie we've ever seen tells us that it's bad to text or call straight away as you'll look too keen and desperate,' he ranted. 'The truth is that ALL blokes, if they like a bird, will want to call her the moment they've closed the door and begun walking away.'

A while ago, I was enjoying a meal with a group of girls when one poor lass who had just met a man asked advice on how to reply to a text message from her new suitor. It was complete bedlam as six drunken ladies attempted to shout over each other as to what they thought was the perfect reply.

We were all in our late twenties, but yet we were acting like hysterical teenagers. It was farcical. By the end, the poor girl was more confused than when she started, but finally typed in the message she'd originally wanted to send.

What a load of hot air over nothing – yet it is a ritual that is repeated throughout the country, day in day out.

It's almost like choosing what to wear to a party. You over-analyse, chop and change and then go back to the original. If only you'd cut out all the faffing and fannying about. But then that's half the fun, isn't it?

Before I went on date two with The Beau I spent A WEEK preparing my outfit – right down to my make-up and jewellery. I could hardly sleep the night before and turned up to the music industry party he'd invited me to ridiculously excited.

When I got there I was met with a warm smile and affectionate kiss on the cheek – so far, so good. But then The Beau introduced me to some of his friends and went off to mingle.

'Fair enough,' I thought. 'I can hold my own.'

But then a lot of time passed and he didn't come back. His friends were asking how I knew him and seemed oblivious that I was his date. I was too embarrassed to spell it out. Feeling tense, I started necking more and more booze.

I took myself off to the toilet for a little pep talk.

'Why is he treating you like this?' I asked my blurry-eyed reflection. 'It's rude to invite someone to a party and then abandon them. You should leave.'

As I walked back across the bar, my mood darkened. There was The Beau, chatting very closely to an attractive blonde who was clearly moving in on him. She was twisting her hair round her finger playfully and batting her eyelashes. He was smiling as he told a story and she was laughing at everything he said. He didn't seem to mind much either. Watching, I suddenly felt very foolish. I realised that in his eyes we weren't on a date at all.

I kept staring, unable to avert my gaze, and then The Beau looked up. The smile fell from his face and he turned back to the girl and whispered for a few minutes more.

Winded, I headed back to his friend and tried to make small talk, all the time glancing over to where he stood with the love rival.

Suddenly The Beau appeared next to me and led me to the bar.

'Look,' he told me sheepishly. 'I've been seeing that girl and I invited her as well as you. I didn't think you'd both come and if you did I thought one of you might meet someone else you liked . . .'

I looked at him, half fuming, half amazed by his stupidity.

'What do you want me to do? Slip into my bikini and mud wrestle over you?' I snapped sarcastically.

Then I grabbed my coat, turned on my heels and left, my eyes prickling with tears as I headed through the door.

The Beau ran after me into the cold; I noticed he didn't have his coat.

'I'll walk with you to the taxi rank,' he said. 'I'm sorry I've upset you. I told that girl I like you.'

'Am I supposed to be flattered?' I hissed back.

At just that moment, the illuminated sign at the bus stop caught my eye. It said 16 minutes until a night bus would take me to Golders Green.

I looked at The Beau, shivering in a flimsy short-sleeved shirt. 'This'll be the test,' I thought to myself.

'I've changed my mind, I think I'll get the bus,' I announced sharply. The Beau's face fell as he saw the sign.

'If you leave me here now, you'll never see me again,' I seethed angrily in my head.

The Beau didn't leave. He sat with me, freezing, looking like he was about to pass out from hypothermia, for 16 whole minutes.

As I clambered on to the bus, I refused to smile and didn't thank him as I left him waving me off in the cold.

But I'd set him a test that he'd passed so, begrudgingly, I granted him date three, on the proviso that Blondie had been kicked well and truly to the kerb.

Irritatingly, once I'd got over my fury at being double-booked, it made me all the more keen. Now I knew that I had competition, I was pulling out the big guns.

Strangely, on date three The Beau offered to accompany me to a posh spa in Chelsea for a free fake tan I'd been given.

Beforehand, pale and interesting, The Beau and I went for lunch. We were enjoying ourselves so much that I turned up for my appointment half an hour late and slightly drunk.

When I emerged an hour later, looking like an oompa loompa, there was a text on my phone from The Beau saying that he hadn't gone home but was in fact in a smoky old boozer round the corner waiting to laugh at me.

Snigger at me indeed he did, then we drank a whole lot more and he kissed me until people started tutting.

The next morning I awoke with a streaky face and absolutely disgusted with myself for succumbing to the most heinous of side-effects of Infatuation Fever – the PDA (Public Display of Affection) – one of my pet hates.

I am ashamed to report this wasn't to be the last time The Beau and I had a regrettable PDA mishap.

Some time later, when my mother was holding a jewellery sale at her friend's house, The Beau and I went along to offer our support.

Sadly, after about half an hour, he had to leave to go and see The Charlatans. I escorted him to the door and we had a sneaky snog.

Suddenly there was a knock on the window. We both jumped. I opened the door and couldn't help giggling like an embarrassed teenager. The prim-looking lady who'd arrived for the sale looked unamused and dashed past us.

When I walked into the other room, I noticed she was showing off a very bling gold necklace to the other ladies.

It suddenly dawned on me: we'd been caught necking by the esteemed town mayor.

A couple of years ago, Sofie and I decided to take our aunt and uncle from Australia on a tour of London. This included a ride on the London Eye.

We squeezed into the capsule with about 20 other people and gazed in wonder as we were transported higher and higher, taking in a panoramic view of the London skyline.

But no matter how hard I concentrated on the Gherkin building or the Houses of Parliament, there was always something distracting in the corner of my eye. A young couple eating each other's faces.

They'd paid to go on the London Eye, yet the only thing they were taking in was each other's saliva. Surely the money they wasted could have paid for a more private ambience in the local Travelodge?

The only time they seemed to pay attention was when our half-hour journey was coming to an end and they positioned themselves at the front of the capsule to slobber away for the group picture.

So, rather childishly, I crept up behind them and pulled a face like I was going to be sick as the flash went off.

I may be an old prude, but it seems that other people positively get off on being caught out.

Recently, at barely past 9 on a Saturday morning, I found myself squirming with discomfort on a train to Stratford-upon-Avon.

Sitting opposite me, a couple were indulging in a far too amorous display. There was no alcohol to blame, it wasn't dark, and they weren't even being subtle. The girl was practically licking his face. Then, despite the fact that I was clearly in her line of vision, she shoved her hands down his trousers, all the while grinning filthily.

Call me old–fashioned, but what happened to a bit of decorum? They could at least have saved it for the bogs.

It reminded me of a brilliant sketch by comedian Harry Enfield from my teens. It featured a couple on a train, sat opposite each other and repeatedly kissing and counting: 'One kiss, two kisses, three kisses . . .' After reaching about 604, they turn to the poor long-suffering passengers next to them and declare in nausea-inducing baby voices, 'We love each other,' before smiling soppily and returning to their lip-smacking marathon.

I actually met the real-life version of this couple last summer, when a pair of equally beautiful lovebirds kindly offered me a lift home from a party.

I say 'kindly', but the journey turned out to be on a par

with Chinese water torture as I sat in the back of their car in the full grip of gooseberry hell.

'You choose the music, babe,' Mr Handsome said at the start of the jaunt, smiling adoringly at his lady.

'OK, Pooh Bear,' she cooed back.

Then they had a brief giggly, kissy play-fight while I sat awkwardly in the back feeling like a bit of a voyeur.

Thankfully, Mr Handsome seemed to realise he had to concentrate on driving and got on with the job, although he still managed to rest one hand on her perfectly toned thigh.

To my alarm, Miss Gorgeous then turned her attention to me.

'Are you in love?' she asked sweetly.

'Um, yes,' I replied, caught off guard.

'Good,' she smiled. 'We're so in love. We're so happy.'

I looked at her, speechless, wondering if she was on drugs.

She then paused for a minute and her pretty face crumpled. 'I just want everyone to feel the way we do,' she said, her bottom lip quivering.

'Ahh, you're so sweet, babe,' Mr Handsome replied, turning to gaze at her. I prayed he'd keep his eyes on the road.

'How long have you been together?' I enquired.

'Six weeks and four days,' she grinned back. 'I've never felt like this before!'

Hearing her answer, I suppressed a knowing smile.

'Hmm, interesting. Well, we'll see,' I thought to myself.

I find any couple who are that sugary-sweet all the time unnerving to the core. Call me a cynic, but honeymoon-period behaviour of that magnitude has to have a shelf life. One of them surely has to lose patience with all that 'Pooh Bear' and 'Princess' bollocks.

By now I bet they're fighting like cat and dog – either that or they're a couple of sickos in the bedroom.

THE EARLY DAYS AND HOW TO MAKE 'EM RUN FOR THE HILLS

Perhaps I am a miserable old trout, but I find it odd that a newly together couple should be completely head over heels without one of them being a f**kwit, standoffish or playing games. I just don't buy it.

Don't get me wrong, during those early days, The Beau and I were indeed getting on well. But we were also having our fair share of trials and tribulations.

In fact, The Beau was busy yo-yoing his way through the first six months of our relationship:

'I really like you . . . I need some space.'

'Come meet my friends . . . It freaked me out that you've met my friends.'

'I don't have time to see you this week . . . I want to see you, do you want to come round?'

Things were looking pretty precarious as I got more and more irritated with what I viewed as some seriously flaky behaviour. So when he asked for less pressure, I obstinately applied more. After three months, I finally voiced my objections that the girlfriend word was still banned in favour of 'You're my lady friend.'

'I'm becoming weary and indifferent to all this and that is a bad sign,' I warned him.

Then my sadistic compulsion to push the boundaries as far as I could kicked in.

I asked The Beau to attend a wedding. He refused, saying it was too early to be that couple-y.

When I arrived at the wedding, my mood only worsened when I discovered I was the only single on a table full of couples. I sent The Beau a shitty text message then I switched my phone off.

The next morning I awoke to find half a dozen texts and concerned voicemails stretching from 7.15 p.m. through to 2.45 a.m. I felt very mean, but that didn't stop me throwing my toys out the pram on many more occasions.

Next The Beau cried off from a friend's birthday meal. I desperately didn't want to go on my own as I knew it was all couples – and, even worse, one girl who'd be there, in a complete misunderstanding, had seemed to think I'd been making a play for her bloke on a previous occasion. That is the worst thing about being single: the assumption that you are after every man you meet, whether they are attached or not.

I'd woken up that day feeling timid and unconfident. I felt sick at the thought of having to face everyone on my own. I needed support.

I begged and begged The Beau to come, but he refused, claiming he had to work. So, with a heavy heart, I went along solo. It wasn't actually as bad as I thought. In fact it was lovely: no one made a big deal that I was on my own, and I even made up with the girl I had been terrified of seeing.

But when I next saw The Beau and began asking about work and how it was going, he admitted he'd lied.

'I actually spent the day in the park playing football,' he confessed. 'I'm sorry.'

'Whaaaaaat?' I shrieked. 'How could you do that to me? You know how I felt about going on my own.'

Tears were pouring down my cheeks and I started howling. Suddenly I didn't care if I lost him or not. I needed solid commitment.

'I can't do this,' I wailed. 'I can't be with someone who is flaky all the time. I've been here, done all this before, and I don't have any more time to waste.'

My body shook and my voice rose. The Beau's eyes were wide with alarm as I practically screamed the next sentence: 'I've had ENOUGH. I'm looking for a HUSBAND. I want to get MARRIED. I want to have BABIES. If you're not on the same level, then I'm just not interested in WASTING ANY MORE TIME.'

Bingo. I'd finally launched into *How to Lose a Guy in Ten Days* territory.

HTLAGITD, starring Kate Hudson, is actually one of my favourite films. It may just be a movie, but blimey, art imitates life.

If you haven't seen it, you should, if only to gain some clarity on how deranged ladyfolk can get when they meet a chap they like.

In the film, Kate's character is challenged to push a gorgeous advertising executive, played by Matthew McConaughey, further and further with her clingy, needy and deranged behaviour.

Along the way, she commits the worst man-repelling

crimes she can think of, veering between split personalities quicker than you can say schizophrenia. It's brilliantly, and at times painfully, funny.

I won't spoil it by revealing any more, go and rent it out, empathise totally with the plot – and have a good long laugh at yourself.

I actually have it on video, and at one point forced The Beau to watch it. Throughout the film, he alternated between staring in disbelief at the screen and looking at me, mystified, as I sat there giggling.

'Has this given you inspiration?' he commented, trying to suppress a knowing smile.

'No, it makes me feel normal,' I grinned.

But, rewinding back to the time of my incredible outburst, I was feeling nowhere near normal. In fact, I was feeling – and with a red, snotty face most probably looking – pretty deranged.

'This is what I f***ing hate about relationships,' I thought to myself, as I tried to regulate my breathing and examined The Beau's shocked face.

'I've probably scared him off now, so that means that one day I'll have to go through all this shit again. Oh joy . . .'

As I suggested earlier, there is something about Infatuation Fever – and, even worse, the initial feelings of love – which makes even the most rational ladies lose their minds.

And if you're not particularly rational in the first place, it's no wonder you could potentially be labelled a complete mentalist after a handful of dates.

THE PSYCHO CHRONICLES

Over the years, there are a couple of names that I cannot erase from my head. They are not particularly significant in my dating history and they were certainly not loves of my life, yet I will always recall them. The reason being that even now, years later, I still look back at my odd behaviour around these certain individuals and feel mortified.

I can't stand the thought that I acted like a complete weirdo and, even worse, they probably told their friends (and their friends' friends) all about it.

Occasionally, late at night, I torture myself by imagining conversations between them and their pals: 'Remember that barmy bird you met at The Academy, whatshername? She was a bunny boiler, wasn't she? Proper cuckoo that one.'

It is probably utterly ridiculous and self-centred that I even contemplate such conversations existed. A more likely scenario is that I have been forgotten about, which would be a very good thing. But in my mind, my crimes will fester on. For ETERNITY.

I can hardly bring myself to speak of my shame. However, for the greater good, I'm prepared to share.

Crime 1

Once, when I was young and foolish, I was bored at work and had access to the electoral roll. I was going on a date with a young man and decided it would be *hilarious* to wind him up by looking up his address and parents' names. Just in case you ever think of partaking in such a jolly prank, please don't.

He actually thought I'd be sitting outside his house with binoculars. He cancelled our date and I NEVER SAW HIM AGAIN.

Crime 2

When a fellow dumped me after a couple of months, I took it very badly. I wrote him a long-winded, highly emotional and frankly cringeworthy letter explaining how I felt about being ditched and why I liked him so much. Then I begged him to have a 'casual relationship' with me. When he refused, gently but firmly, I called him back half an hour later. And then did so again. Repeatedly. Until he answered. Then I cried and told him I was worried he'd tell all his friends I was a freak. OF COURSE HE DID.

Crime 3

Oh God, it gets worse. About three weeks after the same bloke canned me, I read in the paper that a middle-aged woman had been mugged on his road, so I phoned him, out of the blue, just to check it wasn't his mum. As I dialled his home number, I knew what I was doing was so, so wrong, yet I could not stop my fingers from punching in the numbers.

'He'll think it's thoughtful,' I lied to myself.

'No, it wasn't my mum,' he told me in a terse voice. In one 30-second phone call I lost all dignity. FOREVER.

Looking back, it makes me blush. What have I learnt from the above incidents? Should I really feel so bad?

Granted, Crime 1 was ridiculous and extremely ill-advised, but, if he had any common sense, he should have realised it was a joke. What sort of shit stalker actually admits to their snooping before they've even stolen a few personal effects to create a sick shrine with? No, if I'd been an actual stalker I would have kept up my espionage for some time. Well, at least until I'd managed to rummage through his bins for more information and photographed him in his underpants through the window.

Crime 2? Well, it was silly, and maybe, in hindsight, the whole sorry affair could have ended with me skipping off into the sunset with my self-respect still intact. But the truth is I was bloody upset! I was having a shit time at work, I'd been through a whole series of crap dates with unsuitable men and then I met the first man in ages that I felt had real potential and I felt happy.

He'd quickly introduced me to his friends and his mum and seemed to really like me, so I dropped my guard. When he dumped me, I was genuinely gutted.

So what if I acted a little bit OTT? I had a right to tell him how upset I was and if he were any kind of gentleman, he would have had the decency not to laugh at my expense with his friends. You never know, perhaps he did save me from my blushes, so why do I insist on torturing myself?

Now, Crime 3 – it's a hard one to justify. What can I say? Temporary insanity? Clearly it was never going to achieve anything apart from him giving himself a hearty pat on the back to acknowledge his lucky escape.

Maybe deep down I needed to push myself to that level of humiliation in order to gain closure on the situation? I had to take myself to the point of no return so that I could never contact him again.

As it happens I didn't. So it obviously worked.

However, I do think this is a great example of how, during a period of heartache, you should always stop and think.

If only I'd just paused for five minutes, taken a deep breath and listened to the inner voice of reason crying out. If I'd just admitted to a friend what I was planning, he/she would have kindly told me it was complete madness. The call would never have been made and I'd not still be obsessing about it now.

After the incident, I did put into place a safety measure in the hope of avoiding future humiliations.

I vowed to entrust all phone numbers to a third party in times of relationship crises. That way if I wanted to get in touch with the man in question I would have to go to my friend and justify why I needed the number. It does work, as long as you don't cheat and keep a spare copy of his number somewhere, which, during periods of insanity, is sorely tempting.

I have also enforced this measure on equally weak-willed friends in the hope of saving them from the same mistakes.

But there is hope. It doesn't always end badly. You'll be amazed at the staying power of a man who genuinely likes his girl.

A friend, Lorna, spent several months of a new relationship getting blotto, accusing her bloke of not really liking her and firing off mentalist text messages.

She just couldn't seem to help herself and each time she reacted badly, the self-loathing would get worse. We begged her not to do it and a male friend even made the analogy that her poor devoted man was hanging off a cliff, trying desperately to claw his way up to her, only for her to constantly prise away his fingers to prevent him.

It was only when he whisked her away for a romantic trip to Paris for her birthday that she finally believed the level of his devotion and now everything is fine.

When I blasted The Beau for failing me in my time of need and screamed at him that I was looking for a husband, we'd been going out for about six months.

After my outburst, I sat there staring at him with a crazed look in my eye, challenging him to scarper.

But remarkably he didn't.

Instead he put his arms round me and gave me a big hug.

'I'm sorry,' he told me. 'I'm not messing you around. I want the same things too.'

I could hardly believe my ears. I'd pushed and pushed but he wasn't running away. He was staying put.

After that the flakiness appeared to end. I began to relax (slightly).

I'd love to say that knowing I was in a loving and rewarding relationship with The Beau made me more stable when it came to my behaviour. Well, it did to an extent, but now and then, ever so occasionally, I'd fall off the wagon and insanity would set in once more.

They say the devil makes work for idle hands and that's the only excuse I can feasibly give for why, one day, while bored at work, something strange came over me.

It all began as I innocently contemplated how well I really knew The Beau. Kind of like my own Mr and Mrs quiz:

What colour is his toothbrush? Blue.

Where was he born? Hertfordshire.

What's his favourite book? Oh Christ, I don't know. *Noddy Goes to Toytown*?

But did I actually know how his mind worked? Psychologically?

What happened next was always going to be a bad idea. But like a child who can't resist playing with fire, I carried on anyway.

Foolishly, I decided to see if I knew my boyfriend well enough to guess his hotmail password.

With the benefit of hindsight, this could obviously be misconstrued as wanting to pry into my boyfriend's private correspondence, but I genuinely saw it as bit of a sudoku-style challenge. *If I guess the password, I am clearly a genius.*

I tried different variations. Titles of songs he liked, my name, his mum's name, his ex-girlfriend's (I'm not sure what I would have done if that one had actually worked). But, alas, nothing. I was just cursing The Beau's superior brain, when to my horror a message popped up announcing that the login had been suspended. Because of 'security' issues.

'Shit!' I thought. 'I've broken his email!'

Panicked, I confessed my crime to my workmate Isabel.

'You tit!' she laughed, shaking her head.

Then I called The Beau and owned up.

My admission was met with a deathly silence.

'Why were you trying to hack into my email, Charlotte?' he asked.

I noticed he'd used my full Christian name instead of 'Charls' or 'my little mentalist', which indicated I was in big trouble.

'I don't knoooow, I was booooored' I whined churlishly.

The Beau sighed and then uttered the following mortifying sentence: 'I'm really disappointed in you.' Bugger.

As it happened, my futile amusement had another alarming consequence.

That day I'd been wearing a 24-hour monitor which took my blood pressure every half an hour. The doctor had insisted on it, as my BP is routinely high for my age and he wanted to see what it averaged during a day.

Typically, it went off, whirling and squeezing my arm, in the middle of the attempted-hacking drama. When I inspected the reading after my grovelling phone call to The Beau, my blood pressure had gone through the roof.

I could have died of a heart attack. I blame the devil.

When I ask The Beau why he tolerates my behaviour, he normally just smiles.

'It's just you,' he tells me. 'I kind of find the madness a bit endearing.'

But not everyone is as lenient as The Beau. When I grilled my male friends at length, I discovered that unless they really, really like a girl, they often have a zero tolerance rule when it comes to mad foibles and freaky behaviour.

One chap, Stan, was a young single lad when he met an intense girl called Lindsay.

She worked in the local grocery store and used to turn up at his house with 'presents' of random boxes of out-of-date confectionery, or nibbles like Wotsits and Pickled Onion Monster Munch.

He claims that the point at which he knew for sure she was a little crazy was when they went to see *King Kong* at the pictures.

'At the end of the film, the lights came up and she was actually WEEPING real tears,' he gulps.

'Nothing I said would stem the heavy sobs and people were walking past us giving me dirty looks as if I were to blame!

'Eventually, I managed to get her to her feet and help her to the car.'

Not that weird, you could argue, but apparently the poor girl was crying over the film for days. *King Kong* is moving, but, really, days?

After just a few months, Stan decided to end it all, but the King Kong experience told him it could all be very messy.

So instead of telling Lindsay face-to-face, he took the coward's way out by sending her a postcard breaking the news whilst on a lads' holiday thousands of miles away in Greece. He never spoke to her again.

Another man says he felt very out of his depth when he met a sex-mad divorcee.

'She was a little older than me, divorced with a kid, and quite a looker,' he recalls.

'I copped off with her in a nightclub and she invited me back to her house. When she told me she had a child and had been married, it didn't worry me at all – until we got back to hers in the wee small hours.

'There, waiting, was her babysitter – her ex-husband! Then she announced he would be sleeping on the settee while we went to bed!

'As our night of passion got underway, I was horrified to find she was a real screamer!

'I kept imagining her infuriated ex becoming more and more angry, reaching for the sharp knives and heading up the stairs to do me in. It really put me off my performance.'

After a restless night's sleep, he legged it out the house at the crack of dawn. It was all a bit too much to cope with.

No wonder girls have trouble, when there are so many mixed messages out there. If you read any lads' mag, you'd think we should all be embracing our inner ho – with dirty talk, wanton behaviour and X-rated demands. But when it comes to making it a reality, it seems the chaps aren't always so keen.

'I once met a mad girl who started talking dirty to me in the pub,' reveals one friend.

'Against my better judgement, I took her home, even though she looked like the man-faced one off *Sex and the City*.' (Sacrilege!)

'She insisted on sticking on one of my blue movies, then started getting off to it – very loudly. I was glad to finally bundle her out of my flat.

'We didn't exchange numbers, but a week later she

turned up on my doorstep unexpectedly. I live in a flat on the first floor, so she waited outside until someone left, then let herself in to get to my front door.

'Anyway, to cut a long story short, she'd come back to get my number. I gave it to her, but after I persuaded her to leave, I texted her and said I'd met someone else.

'But whenever I was out in town after this, she would mysteriously turn up at the pub and start whispering in my ear about letting me do something very intimate and all sorts of porno chat in front of my new lady.

'In the end I had to just tell her to f*** off, and yes, I did feel like a bit of a git afterwards.'

While most of us have walked the halls of shame when it comes to being bonkers with boys, it's good to occasionally stop and take stock.

There's the kind of mental antics where you can laugh, red-faced, at yourself over a glass of vin rouge, and then there's the kind of behaviour that's just not funny.

While, regrettably, you may at some stage have been branded a psycho, please feel assured that you are not actually that unbalanced. Unless, of course, you have actually indulged in the terrifying way I am about to reveal.

This tale of woe comes from a male friend, now happily married, but still watching his back after the frankly unhinged behaviour of his ex.

While the girl in question had a fiery temper, it was only after my friend broke up with her that she went into full-on bunny boiler mode.

From the minute he ended the relationship, she lost the plot, chasing him out of the house and climbing on to the bonnet of his car. After manic sobbing failed to reverse the situation, she slid back off the bonnet, taking his windscreen wipers with her. She flung them on the ground and then started punching and kicking his car until he drove off.

He hoped that would be the end of it, but over the following months she continued to hound him. She phoned him incessantly, shouting abuse or breathing silently, until he discovered she was parking outside the phone box down the road.

When he saw her in a nightclub and asked for his CDs back, she threw a punch. He dodged it and she lamped his mate.

His car was mysteriously vandalised and the word 'Wanker' scratched on the roof, then the RSPCA turned up to say they'd had an anonymous complaint that he was cruel to his dog.

Next, he was housesitting for a friend, only to return from the pub to discover that none of the lights worked because all the fuses had been removed from the external fuse box.

After he told the story, his sister asked him what we'd all been thinking: 'Did you cheat on her?'

Surely infidelity had to be at the root of such an unrelenting campaign of venom?

'No,' he replied earnestly. 'I think she actually had big problems.'

As if she hadn't done enough already, the same girl then spread vicious rumours around the area for years, insinuating that he'd even beaten her up.

'I was terrified she'd turn up on my wedding day,' he admitted. 'I just wouldn't have put it past her.'

Suddenly I felt so much better about my email-hacking episode.

A ROUGH GUIDE TO BONKERS BIRDS

The following scaleometer was composed by a brilliant friend of mine. For fear of reprisals, he sadly wishes to remain anonymous. Thankfully, he has assured me that I could just about wing my way in at 'nicely a bit bonkers', which is very kind. He's never been out with me though, so has clearly escaped the worst of my behaviour.

1. Nicely a bit bonkers: puts on silly accents; trips; falls; burns toast; talks to strangers in public parks; has a variously dry and wicked sense of humour; does innocently daft things from time to time, such as when you call her from the pub and ask for your spare key because you're locked out and she comes round and puts the key through your letter box. *But you can't be mad at her because you think she is adorable.*

2. A bit bonkers: brings home people she meets in the park so they can have a warm cup of tea; is always late; does nicely bonkers things, but on an annoyingly regular basis, like forgetting where she parked the car. *Still endearing, but getting borderline. You start getting annoyed, but it's not a really big deal. Honest.*

3. Bonkers: wears ear plugs in bed; wants you to meet her parents for Sunday lunch after the first week; when you look at her differently she says, 'You want

to dump me, don't you?' *You can't relax and you're already thinking of looking for a reason to break up, but you think things might calm down if you can help her through her rampant insecurities.*

4. Violently bonkers: tries to claw your eyes out and throws all your stuff out the hotel window after a petty disagreement; throws a loud, screaming tantrum in the restaurant when you don't sit beside her. *She's very, very attractive and incredibly intelligent, and you're dangerously besotted. The relationship is going to end in weeks rather than months. There is no hope. You leave a big tip for the rather attractive waitress who served you all night.*

5. Bunny-boiler bonkers: leaves 45 messages on your answering machine after you don't return one call. *The relationship is always one row away from over.*

While The Beau is very patient when it comes to my idiosyncrasies and even laughs at my little episodes, I'm not a complete moron. Of course I held back a bit before I unleashed the full bonkers onslaught. I wanted to hook him first.

Indeed, in the first few weeks, I attempted to reel him in with a persona of laidback coolness. Although it seemed silly to construct a kind of fantasy woman persona, I still did it.

And although I didn't do anything weird – like pretending I had a famous half-sister called Cat Deeley – I may have exaggerated some of my interests and hobbies, all for the greater good, of course.

As a new relationship flourishes, I think all girls (and

perhaps some boys) are guilty of taking on certain interests and characteristics they think a new love interest may like.

When The Beau first stayed over at mine, I can recall rearranging certain things in my shared flat in the hope that they would give a suitable impression. I shoved some of my favourite CDs – *Dirty Dancing*, a *Pop Idol* album and *The Phantom of the Opera* soundtrack – in a drawer and carefully formed the perfect stack of retro gems from The Who, The Clash and The Kinks. Then I removed all fluffy girls' books from beside my bed and replaced them with more thought-provoking reads like *In Cold Blood* (a genuine favourite), *The Bookseller of Kabul* and a massive doorstep of a book called *A Suitable Boy* which my brother bought me for Christmas at least six years ago and I still haven't read. ('Take time for this book, it'll stay with you for the rest of your life,' the review on the back read. How intimidating!)

When The Beau came round, he sat on the bed and bent down to pick up something by his foot.

'What's this?' he asked, producing a shiny album. 'Girls Aloud?'

I was just about to splutter an excuse when his face broke into a smile.

'Girls Aloud are rockers,' he said.

'I know, that's one of my favourite albums!' I bleated pathetically.

That night I cooked him a posh monkfish dinner and produced ice-cold beers from the fridge. Then I pretended I'd quite like to watch football.

If Carling did girlfriends, then they'd be just like me.

However, at that stage I wasn't his girlfriend. I was just someone he was seeing who was trying desperately to fit the mould.

I'm not the only one who resorts to such tactics. I once rang up my friend Rebecca before she went on an evening out with her new high-flying love interest and caught her listening to Tchaikovsky rather than the greatest hits of the 80s on Heart FM.

'Are you listening to that so you can talk about your intellectual taste in music on your date?' I enquired.

'Nooo!' she protested a bit too much.

'I bet you've got a pile of the Sunday broadsheets in front of you as well, haven't you?' I joked.

'Stop it!' she laughed. 'You know me too well!'

Another lass confessed to becoming an avid runner as soon as she started going out with a man who loved sprinting marathons.

Then there was the young lady whose boyfriend loved motor racing. As a dutiful girlfriend, she was so convincing as a sports-car fanatic that he actually bought her a driving day from Red Letter for Christmas.

On a different note, how many girls practically starve themselves for two days before a date so they look thinner?

Or why is it that when you first meet a chap, you may well have been your usual outgoing self – the thing that attracted him to you in the first place – only for you to become a shy little mouse on the first few dates, afraid to speak in case you put him off you?

Why do we constantly try to be things we're not – and assume that everybody wants the same thing: a woman with the body of Kelly Brook, the wit of Claudia Winkleman and the intellectual capacity (and looks, goddammit) of Dr Linda Papadopoulos?

Surely there's someone out there for everyone, no matter how clever or funny they are or what they look like? Indeed, there are whole songs championing the charms of girls with big butts, so what are we worrying about?

My cousin first caught the eye of his wife when he cleared the dancefloor as he Riverdanced to a Barry White remix in a club in Swindon. She was instantly mesmerised.

In my case, at first The Beau was getting the hard sell, the glossy finish, but as soon as I bagged the position of 'girlfriend', I morphed back into my usual uncool persona. Out came the *Best Chickflick Soundtrack in the World* and Jade Goody's autobiography.

The Beau noticed that my intellectual books were covered in dust and that I'd Sky-Plused *The X Factor* rather than *Panorama*. And while I did cook on special occasions, once I'd officially bagged him, he was lucky if I microwaved a Somerfield fish pie.

Chapter Four

Serious Stuff

Once the honeymoon period has worn off and you have stopped trying to fake interests and hobbies, it's time for the serious stuff.

Is this man a keeper? Could he even be 'The One'?

By now your love interest may be morphing into one of two categories: a cocky alpha male or a more sensitive beta.

Personally, after coming across one too many alphas in the past, I had no desire to date one again. I didn't want someone who selfishly thought he was always right and who made me feel nervous when I was around him.

Back at the beginning, when The Beau double-booked me at the party, I began to wonder if this lovely, polite man, who took time to listen and seemed extremely in tune with people, was in fact an alpha wolf in beta clothing.

It may sound cheesy (and slightly psycho at that early stage), but what I was hoping to find in The Beau was someone who had the criteria to be a good father and husband.

Before The Beau, there had been several long-term relationships which had followed pretty much the same pattern. When each one had ended, I was optimistic I'd meet someone else to have fun with. But now I wasn't just hoping to find a boyfriend for a few years, as had been the aim when I was younger; I was looking for a life partner.

I wanted the real deal. Someone who made me weak at the knees, was kind and loyal and made me feel like I was the only girl in the room. I didn't want to be a stop-gap to his future wife or just one of a collection of dolly birds on the scene.

If The Beau still had aspirations of sowing his wild oats, then he was too alpha for me. I wasn't looking for a pushover, but I was bored with game-playing.

I wasn't the only one. Hordes of my friends were making similar statements. We'd had enough of covering the same well-trodden ground over and over – it was time to move on.

A gorgeous friend, Raquel, who should have had her pick of decent blokes, summed it up with the following statement: 'I'm sick of having bad taste in men – I'm fine-tuning my wanker radar.'

And why not? We'd encountered stalkers, commitment-phobes, the emotionally repressed, the ridiculously immature and the men we'd simply shaped up for someone else. All we now wanted was a half-decent gentleman who was respectful and attentive and still had an air of mystery without being a bastard.

'But that all sounds a bit too beta to me,' another friend observed.

'You say you're sick of game playing, but pursuing an alpha male is much more challenging and exciting.

They are the uncompromising ones, the leaders who want things their way, the hardest men to ultimately crack.'

But I wasn't convinced. I was sick to the back teeth of alphas. I saw them as cavemen types. They might keep you swooning with unpredictability and their constant fight to be top dog might seem manly and strong, but they'd hardly evolved.

Would an alpha man be selfless enough to jump out of bed in the middle of the night to get you a hot water bottle if you had period pains? I doubted it.

But my friend was sticking to her guns; she thought having a constant power struggle with her man was sexy and exciting. She was a braver woman than I. At times the alpha male she was dating made her feel deeply insecure, but she almost got off on the misery. In fact, the way he kept her on her toes was almost like a drug.

'I can't help it,' she added. 'I'm convinced he has a softer side that I want to delve in to, not have it thrown in my face like a wet flannel. I don't want to be courted by a man who could double up as my female best friend.'

Her words certainly gave me some food for thought. I'd gone through a power struggle with most of my previous boyfriends. I'd fought to wear the trousers, but once they'd succumbed to what I wanted – probably to ensure an easy life – some of the mystique had gone.

Worryingly, I was already getting very bossy with The Beau. Maybe it was because he'd kept me on my toes so much at the beginning, perhaps I was just naturally bossy – either way, I was certainly trying to throw my weight around.

My pet hate was the way he refused to plan anything

until the last minute and I felt his memory for our arrangements was appalling. So I'd bought him a diary.

I was already chastising him about drinking too much as well (despite clearly needing to take a dose of my own medicine on the binge drinking front). Was I trying to force my way into the same destructive relationship pattern with The Beau? Would I boss him about, mother him and then inadvertently send him off into the welcoming arms of his future Miss Right?

When I'd first met Adam, at work when we were both 23, the fact that he seemed a little rough around the edges appealed to me. He was a bit of a geezer, a joker, one of the lads. He had a history of finishing with girls in appalling ways, and, before we got together, had kept me horrified for hours on end with his roguish tales.

'To be honest, babe, it wasn't one of my finest moments,' he'd tell me apologetically in his gravelly sarf London accent, but failing badly to hide the amused twinkle in his eye.

Adam had the dishevelled air of someone who didn't own an iron. His wardrobe largely consisted of items his mum had found in charity shops, and he proclaimed proudly that he'd not bought an item of clothing in three years. His favourite 'loafing' outfit was a dirty yellow hoodie and baggy jeans.

While he was funny, charismatic and extremely bright, Adam's lifestyle infuriated me. He could rarely afford to do the nice things we talked about, but frittered away what little cash he had at the casino, bookies and lap-dancing clubs.

When we moved in together, we both worked shifts as

newspaper reporters and on Adam's days off I'd come home to find him sitting in front of the telly, drunk and rowdy after an all-day drinking session.

But while all these things were disagreeable, my gut instinct told me my wayward boyfriend would eventually give up the laddish behaviour.

At face value, Adam was far from ideal boyfriend material – as proved by the stories he recounted, like the time he ended a six-month affair by simply never returning the unfortunate girl's phone calls. But he was infectious, with a warmth of character that made everyone he met instantly fall in love with him.

For all his outrageous antics, we got on fantastically. He could make me laugh until I hyperventilated with mirth. He showed me vulnerability that no one else was party to, and his kindness shone through.

Perhaps because of an underlying desire to feel needed, I was keen to encourage him to make the best of himself.

Thankfully, my efforts weren't in vain. With a little TLC, Adam's visits to the bookies and strip joints began to peter out and instead of constantly going out on the lash, he'd take me to the cinema or out for a meal. We'd talk and laugh for hours on end and I even persuaded him to come shopping with me to find things for him.

Up until then, Adam clearly hadn't thought about improving his image. But when I started to take an interest and encourage him to smarten up, he began to change.

Originally, just trying to get him through the door of 'poncy shops' like Topman was a challenge in itself, but the first time he admired his reflection in a new shirt I saw something click in his mind as the realisation dawned on him that he looked really good.

Adam was undergoing a New Man Makeover and loving every minute.

THE TRUTH ABOUT MAN MAKEOVERS

- 'Much as men complain, I think the majority of us like to be mothered and trained in some way, providing we are not made to feel too bad about it – and given *some* say in how a room should be organised.'
- 'My dress sense before I met my wife wasn't the best. I had my own "unique" style, shall we say? I had an awful pair of bowling shoes I used to love. She soon changed all that.'
- 'Henpecking is incredibly annoying and often seen as a control thing and an effort to break us down and destroy our confidence before re-building us. I believe the SAS use similar methods – but with less shopping!'
- 'I don't think girls intentionally do it, it just slowly and gradually happens in the course of living in each other's pockets. Most guys really don't mind and actually quite like it.'
- 'I had an ex who took it upon herself to dictate all my hair cuts, demanding it be longer at the back to get my curls going. I went along with it, as I believed if she thought it looked hot, other women would think so too. They didn't. I had a mullet.'

- 'Most things women teach us are beneficial: use nice bed-linen, change your sheets, tidy up, do something with your hair, get nicer furniture, wear nicer clothes. But most of these things only make us more attractive to the next girl after we dump the mad one who keeps trying to change us.'

And the other side of the story . . .
'I once dated a very sweet guy who was really sexually inexperienced. I spent a great deal of time and effort to teach him what girls like and a few tricks to blow a woman's mind (i.e. MINE). He then dumped me, and I have subsequently heard from several people that he is great in bed. Uh, YEAH.'

Soon Adam was going off shopping on his own and then that progressed to ordering himself fancy Paul Smith suits.

I once went to a designer store with him only to be amazed as the staff fawned over him and rushed to show him matching cufflinks for his suit. I couldn't believe it. It was such a stark change from the Adam I'd first known.

But something weird began to happen. The more Adam shaped up, the more I began to question whether we were destined to be together in the long run.

The roguishness had clearly been much of his appeal in the first place. I'd made a lot of effort to help him change, but was my handiwork now putting me off him?

It had been much the same with my exes Jack and Tom. I'd even helped Tom with his university dissertation when he'd cracked under the pressure, claiming he couldn't do it. And I'd painstakingly written letters for him when he first applied for jobs.

But out in the real world, when we were both holding down our first full-time jobs, we'd drifted apart.

What was wrong with me? Did I have some weird urge to mother these men, then lose interest as soon as they went off and stood on their own two feet? Either way, I wondered whether one day I'd take my constant henpecking a step too far.

'I call them "Mr Almost Right" girls,' revealed a scathing male friend. 'They find a nice-ish guy and then go about turning him into the perfect guy, normally based on someone who dumped them in the past. Clothes, aftershave, hobbies and friends will all be moulded to fit in with the ideal.'

I was acutely aware that men hate to be emasculated. One easygoing man I knew had even admitted that being pushed around so much by his girlfriend had led him to have an affair.

'She'd ask me to make a decision on something and if I didn't instantly give her an answer, she'd look at me like I was completely stupid and decide for me,' he explained.

'I'm not making excuses for my behaviour, but I resented the way she spoke to me and wanted to feel like a man. In a warped way, cheating with another girl achieved that.'

It made me uncomfortable, but clearly dating a really nice guy could sometimes bring out a bullying urge to belittle them. The fact that they were so amenable too was almost perceived as a weakness.

Another friend recalls how she behaved atrociously with an agreeable beta type because he was so well-behaved and did everything by the book.

'He was a strait-laced policeman, so for some reason I turned into this crazy wild-child with a penchant for criminal behaviour,' she recalls.

'I'd get so drunk in pubs, we would get thrown out, just so I could see the look on his face.

'Then once I got so hammered that we had a blazing row and I locked myself out of his house at 3 a.m, in little more than my underwear, with my car keys in my hand.

'I thought, "I know what will really piss him off," and jumped in my car and drove it to the end of his cul-de-sac.

'I was so drunk that I had forgotten where I was, so I got out of the car and wandered up the road and, well, handed myself in to my policeman boyfriend.

'He didn't arrest me, but I was dumped soon after.'

Clearly she was pushing her boyfriend to bring out some alpha tendencies. It was destructive, but she obviously didn't want to date what she viewed as a complete pushover.

While The Beau wasn't a pushover, he was certainly a beta.

As our relationship progressed from dating to full-fledged love, he proved to have an almost saint-like tolerance for my neuroses. At times I exhausted even myself with my mood swings and often PMT-induced episodes but he remained infuriatingly patient – and even bought me some Evening Primrose Oil.

Yet he seemed to instinctively know when I needed a bit of alpha firepower too.

When we ventured on our first holiday to Brittany, I found myself hiding timidly behind him as he boldly wowed the locals in a bar with his pidgin French, even cracking jokes. They responded warmly, even buying us drinks. It made me gaze at him in awe, feeling really quite swoony.

Likewise, when he was round at my flat, he took control whenever I (arguably the most accident-prone woman in the world – I even had my behind X-rayed once after I sat on a needle) attempted to undertake a dangerous chore.

'Be careful with that knife,' he'd frown as I nearly lanced myself preparing vegetables. If he caught me tottering precariously on a wobbly stool, attempting to get something into my loft, he'd bark at me to get down and would finish the job for me, making my heart flutter.

But it was the chivalry that really made my tummy churn.

Walking down the street, he never failed to hold my hand and firmly steer me to the inside of the pavement. As The Beau, 6ft 1 to my 5ft 7, towered over me protectively, he made me feel little, looked after and loved.

Yet occasionally, when I was in a bad mood, I'd still try to push him around.

Like a petulant child, if I was feeling hormonal, I'd deliberately do things to annoy him. I'd snap at him for nothing or pathetically turn the music up as soon as he'd turned it down.

But, ironically, his never-failing patience and reluctance to wade into the argument I was angling for wound me up even more. I wanted to torment him, get a rise out of him. I wanted to push him, see some venom.

But the less he would react, the more irritated I'd get – until finally The Beau would lose his patience, telling me calmly that there was no reasoning with me. Then he'd pick up his coat and head out the door.

It always had the desired effect. Suddenly his disapproval of my behaviour would leave me dashing after him, panicked.

I'd wail for forgiveness and attempt to cling on to him like a koala bear. Exasperated by me, his body would remain rigid as he rebuffed my attempts at affection.

'I'm sooooorrrry,' I'd find myself whining, until finally he'd relent and then I'd spend the rest of the morning/afternoon/evening attempting gingerly to make it up to him.

To be honest, I have no idea why I feel the need to go through this whole f***ed up process time and again (I still do it now). Perhaps it is just that I need to know that I can't get away with it?

When I overstep the mark, I need to see that The Beau will calmly put me back in my place. That way I know he's not a walkover. I'm sure a psychologist (the sort you see on *Big Brother*, analysing the housemates) would say my behaviour is on par with that of a three-year-old.

In my defence, such incidents don't happen that often. I am, more often that not, very nice to The Beau, hence why after a temper tantrum he generally sighs and gives his wretched wench a hug.

'Birds,' he says. 'You're all mental.'

While to an untrained eye I may appear to be the overpowering force, both The Beau and I secretly know that it is actually he who wears the trousers. Despite my nagging, he has always controlled the speed and pace of our love affair.

Indeed, for a fair while into our relationship, the commitment gripes I had with The Beau continued. As well as it taking him forever to call me his girlfriend and it was an age until I met his friends, his parents had no idea I existed. It irritated me. A LOT. (Perhaps it would be fair to point out that we're talking months here – not years, like some poor lasses have to wait for a sign of commitment – but I've never been very patient.)

'I'd like to meet your family,' I'd tell him, only to be met by silence and an unfathomable smile.

So, as per usual, I tried to force the situation. One evening, when he was over at their home, I told him I was driving past (admittedly, I may have taken a small detour) and could I pop in to use the loo? He saw right through my pushy plan.

'You'll have to use the outdoor toilet,' he said. 'It's not convenient to introduce you now.'

'The outdoor one?' I repeated. 'Does it have a light?'

'No,' he replied, unflinching. Clearly outsmarted, I crossed my legs and drove home huffily.

'Why won't you tell them about me?' I whined the next time I saw him.

'All in good time, Charls,' he deflected good-naturedly.

It was only after I'd stopped the nagging for a few weeks that I finally got the long-awaited call.

'My folks are having a barbeque today, would you like to come over?' he asked casually.

'OK!' I replied, trying not to sound too excited. By the time I put the phone down, I was actually shit-scared. Now it was crunch time. It was a make-or-break situation.

I'd stayed at a friend's house the night before, so had to

go in what I was already wearing – a denim mini-skirt and T-shirt top.

'I don't look slutty, do I?' I asked apprehensively.

'Yep, they'll hate you,' she replied.

On my way to their house, I stopped off for a bottle of wine and procrastinated for ages about whether to buy his mum flowers or not. It would be meant as a polite gesture in return for her hospitality, but what if she thought I was sucking up and viewed me suspiciously from there on in? I decided to go for it anyway; it's always nice to get flowers, after all.

When I arrived at the house, The Beau met me outside the door and I made a fearful face, my stomach churning with butterflies. But any nerves I had were soon alleviated when I was met by an instantly recognisable, grown-up, 6ft 4, Daddy version of The Beau wielding barbeque tongs. He was wearing a huge smile and a full-frontal Michelangelo's David apron.

'Lovely to meet you, darling,' he proclaimed, with what seemed like genuine delight.

The Beau's mother was just as welcoming, and to my glee appeared thrilled with the flowers.

'Cornflowers! My favourite!' she exclaimed.

I loved them both instantly. And as we all chatted easily, I could see The Beau visibly relaxing.

I was also relieved. I knew that getting on with The Beau's parents was essential and if they hadn't liked me then it could have been the beginning of the end.

Like the initial encounter with the parents, the first meeting of the friends can be a minefield too. Again, if you don't hit it off then you are in deep trouble.

Male friends aren't usually too bad – as long as they're not pissed off that you took away their pulling partner.

But ultimately, as things get serious, one of the hardest friend-pools to crack is The Harem – his circle of intimidating female friends who you are forced to compete with.

While I hate to criticise my own kind, women can be ridiculously territorial when it comes to meeting the new love interest of a male friend. There is nothing more intimidating (even the gut-wrenching ordeal of meeting the parents) than being eyed suspiciously by a gaggle of girls who make no bones about the fact you have a LOT to live up to if you're going to make the grade with their man.

They drop in casual digs about how they and your beloved 'go back years' and, horror of horrors, may even mention how they are still the best of mates with his ex.

'She's not as pretty as you,' you imagine them reporting back bitchily. 'She seems a bit possessive as well…'

The most infuriating thing is that your bloke is likely to be completely oblivious to the frosty reception you are getting from his gal pals. Just because they are smiling, he thinks all is well. What a fool! What he's actually missing is that, on closer inspection, their cold eyes have all the friendliness of those of a circling vulture.

In fact, they're boring into you with a death stare that says in no uncertain terms: 'I'm watching you, missy. He may think you're the best thing since sliced bread, but take one wrong step and I'll eat you for breakfast.'

Then there's the female friend clearly struck down by a bad dose of unrequited love. Strangely, again he appears to have no idea.

But you've noticed. All the warning signs are there.

When your man talks, she gazes at him adoringly, her head tilted to one side. When he cracks a distinctly mediocre joke, she laughs hysterically and touches his arm. Suddenly YOU feel like the gooseberry.

'Excuse me, sweetheart,' you want to interrupt, narrowing your eyes. 'Only I get to laugh like that at his crap jokes, OK?'

But instead you find yourself trying to outdo her with stupid guffaws. You let out a horse-like snort. WHAT ON EARTH ARE YOU DOING?

While discussing this subject, a friend revealed how there'd been a constant strain on her relationship with her ex-boyfriend because of his harem of girlie hangers-on, many of whom clearly had crushes.

'I used to feel threatened all the time, only to be told, "What? We're just friends,"' she explained.

'He always claimed he was totally oblivious to the fact that they fancied him. But how could he not know?!

'One used to regularly get drunk and cry about how she had no confidence and was rubbish at everything. Several tried to snog him. No, they didn't fancy him at all!

'After a while, I came to the difficult realisation that they were all quite young and naive and that in a weird way he was getting off on the attention.

'It may have been subconscious on his part and from my position of worldly experience I knew nothing would happen, but still I had to take their smug looks without saying anything. If I had, I would have looked like I cared and really thought there was something in it.'

The worst thing about a situation like this is that many men are unlikely to look a gift horse in the mouth.

Whether he admits it or not, if a girl pal is secretly in love with him, then she's probably pulled him – maybe not while you were on the scene, but before, on one or more drunken occasions.

When I polled some chaps about their real intentions when it came to female friends, a few were adamant that relationships with mates of the opposite sex were purely platonic – apart from the odd sneaky look at their boobs. But, tellingly, the majority admitted they *would* consider crossing the line with their female chums.

One revealed: 'I think that all guys do, or once did, fancy their female friends, at least a little bit. But what allows the guys to be friends with the girl is that they've never acted on their urges.'

Another added: 'Yes, the large majority of my friends are girls and I have been with most of them at some stage over the years. It normally happened while drunk, although now we are a little older it rarely happens.'

A third man I asked even sheepishly confessed to deliberately taking advantage of a girl mate – only for it to backfire dreadfully.

'I had a friend who I knew liked me, but I wasn't really interested,' he admitted. 'One night I was drunk and a little in need of lovin' and moved in on her. Next day, I made my excuses and left and then didn't call. It was a crap thing to do, but in my defence I was embarrassed about having done it. I wanted to avoid the "chat" where I would have to admit I was a prick, but by doing that I acted like a bigger prick.'

At least he owned up to his crime.

A long-term boyfriend of mine had a female friend who

clearly had a bad dose of unrequited love. While she was always on the charm offensive when I was around, from the moment I met her I knew they had a history. The way she looked at him made it obvious, but of course he denied it.

Regardless, I decided it would be a good idea to keep my enemies close, so attempted to befriend her. But when we met up one-on-one, she seemed vacant and uninterested, so I figured she really wasn't worth the effort.

My suspicions were finally confirmed when my man and I were in a watering hole and I was ordering drinks at the bar. The girl in question, who was randomly in the same establishment, had clearly failed to spot me, giving me a ringside view of how she behaved with my boy when she thought I wasn't around.

You know in old war films when the brave hero is returning to his devoted darling after many years fighting for king and country? It was a bit like that.

As she spotted him, her face instantly lit up with a look of delight. Then she was off, rushing towards him, her hair flowing in her wake (I could almost hear the dramatic film score). She took a flying leap, straddled him and started licking his face. Well, maybe those last couple of things didn't happen – but she did jump gleefully for joy, hugging and kissing him like a long-lost love.

If I needed any proof, it was the expression on her face when she finally spotted me watching. In a split-second there was an unmistakable look of shock and disappointment at my presence. Then quickly she forced a weak smile, gave a little wave and mouthed, 'Hi!'

I couldn't help myself.

'Hi!' I returned, with an obviously sarcastic smile, and

turned back to the bar. I grilled him at length later, after
I'd loosened him up with truth serum (beer).

'Yes,' he finally admitted. 'We have pulled a few times
and I think at one stage she thought we might get
together.'

'Ha!' I shouted triumphantly. 'I knew it!'

Then I added menacingly, 'Don't ever try to pull the wool
over my eyes. I'll ALWAYS know. I'll instinctively know.'

It's my woman's intuition you see. (Sometimes, when
I've had a few too many vinos, I claim I can talk to the
animals too.)

Thankfully, I found that The Beau had very nice
friends, including, to my great relief, some friendly – and
not at all territorial – girl pals.

When it came to introducing my friends to him, I was
nervous too. If they didn't like him then I'd be gutted.

Just before I'd met The Beau, I'd dispatched a man I'd
previously been quite keen on because he behaved so
abysmally in front of my friends and sister. I don't know if
it was nerves, but when I invited him to meet my friends
down the pub, for every round of drinks we had, he
ordered himself an extra shot. Unsurprisingly, he was
well-oiled and decidedly lairy by the time the bell rang out
for last orders.

But it was as we congregated outside, trying to
make up our minds about what to do next, that the rot set
in.

'For f***'s sake, this is ridiculous,' he snapped, folding
his arms moodily. Out the corner of my eye, I noticed my
friends and Sofie giving each other knowing looks as I
tried to pacify him.

I gave him the benefit of the doubt for that one, but when he nastily branded me boring because I wanted to go home rather than queue for a club, I finally snapped. Giving him a filthy look and turning on my heels, I stormed off. He didn't come after me.

Maybe I should have put it down to the alcohol and given him another chance, but the fact that Sofie and my friends already disliked him made it a no-brainer.

I also figured that if he'd behaved like that after just a few dates, when he was supposed to be making a good impression, lord only knew what he'd be like in the long term.

As it happens, a week later I met The Beau.

When it came to introducing him to my friends, he breezed into the pub, offering to buy everyone a drink and chatting animatedly to each of them. I was thrilled when, at the end of the night, he got a unanimous thumbs-up.

So fast-forward through a few flaky teething problems (and unwelcome love rivals) and all was good with The Beau. We'd proclaimed our love, he'd introduced me to his parents, his pals were great and my friends adored him – my wish list had a lot of boxes ticked.

Now all I needed to do was persuade him to move in with me. Yeah, fat chance.

As it stands, The Beau and I are yet to cohabitate, although he as good as lives at my flat. He'll move in one day, he's loosely agreed, but when that day will come is anyone's guess. And will I own my own teeth?

I like to think I am quite nice to live with. I bring cups of tea to bed, run nice bubble baths with candles and I don't take up that much of the duvet. What's not to love?

There were a whole host of reasons why I was getting keen on co-habitation.

For one, the military planning that went into preparing for a stay at The Beau's abode week after week was exhausting. While all a man needs is a pair of clean underpants, a toothbrush and possibly a fresh shirt, spending the night is an altogether more complicated and arduous affair for a lady.

As well as packing a toothbrush and clean underwear, we need a fresh outfit for the next day (including shoes), something to wear in bed, numerous potions and lotions, make-up, a hair-dryer, hair-straighteners and a whole host of other essentials.

But men just don't get that. The Beau had on various occasions suggested I make an unexpected stopover at his. While I'd got to the stage where I'd been allocated space in his bathroom cupboards for cleansers and cosmetics some time previously, this foolish suggestion was naturally met with the contempt it deserved.

'Go into work tomorrow wearing the same clothes I wore today? Are you insane?' I spat. 'That would be social suicide. The knowing looks, the bitchy suggestions that I'm a dirty stop-out . . .'

'Well, borrow something of mine,' came the good-natured response.

'Like what?' I asked scornfully.

Horrific images of me strolling into work wearing baggy rolled-up trousers (with high heels – ugh!) and an oversized jumper raced through my mind. My vanity would never allow it.

Of course, in the past I have donned The Beau's

belongings to counter the cold or when in need of comfort, prompting soppy looks of love from him and inducing nice feelings of being small and fragile for me. However, out in public it is a whole different scenario. I have no desire for anyone else to see me looking – in unbiased reality – like a bag lady.

So cohabitation was clearly the answer to all these problems, I'd decided. You get continuous access to your man with no worries of forgotten toothbrushes, pyjamas or packets of contraceptive pills. Perfect.

However, for all the advantages of never having to lug a heavy bag of my belongings back and forth again, I was aware there were many pitfalls too.

Taking the plunge with your man can have all sorts of hidden perils (which is what I naturally reminded myself after The Beau turned down my offer to move in). In your head you'll have ideals of building the perfect home together. But no matter how much you dream of domestic bliss on a par with a glorious At Home shoot in *Hello!* magazine – lavish but tasteful furnishings, you and your man gazing into each other's eyes by the spa (that's the Remington foot spa he got you from Argos for Christmas) – there will always be grotesque items he inflicts on the home, causing you to turn up your nose and flounce out of the house, flicking your hair like Lawrence Llewelyn-Bowen.

When you have taken tender loving care to put together a living environment that gives your visitors a sense of class and charm, it can drive you to a near coronary if said sophisticated space is polluted with kitsch artefacts courtesy of him indoors.

As living partners went, Adam was pretty easy to reside with. He didn't have too much stuff and did the washing up on request. We both liked to watch *Wife Swap* and he didn't hog the bathroom.

But my biggest bugbear was a ridiculous Russian doll set that Adam had drunkenly purchased on a holiday to Prague. Weirdly, it featured the heads of great Real Madrid players of the time such as Zidane, Ronaldo and Beckham. He insisted on placing it next to the television, where it constantly angered my eyes as I attempted to watch *EastEnders*.

As time wore on and this 'artefact' became coated in a thick layer of dust, he didn't appear to notice. So naturally it was my pleasure every couple of weeks to spring-clean a piece of tat I detested.

Other items to leave me seething with hatred during periods of cohabitation with blokes, whether in a relationship or not, have included a plaster of Paris model crafted when the chap in question was ten, the ONLY creative thing he claimed to have ever made – and not actually that creative. Then there was James Bond-themed soap and aftershave (sorry mate, but 007 does not dance comically in the kitchen to 'Sex Bomb' after a night on the sauce).

Adam's pride and joy was a giant poster of a naked, writhing Carmen Electra on the inside of his wardrobe. Each morning he'd get up, open the door and chirp, 'Morning, Carmen'. I'd then strop past and kick it shut. But could I remove it? No way.

The thing is, no matter how much you want to sweep through the flat like Rentokil, exterminating any tasteless tat you find cowering in the corner, you just can't.

Even I, a pernickety hen-pecker, knew that militant attempts to bamboozle an unwilling chap into radical change could be viewed with a lot of suspicion – and even put him off you.

One married friend revealed that in recent years there have been many changes in his home life, although, notably, he was unsure if they'd been sparked by his wife, his job or his age.

'The art of being a great girlfriend or wife is to make those changes via stealth means,' he reckoned. 'My wife hates all my clutter, so once she put things in bags hidden away and left them for a year. It proved that I never touched or looked at them so we needed to chuck them away.

'If she tries to just dump something, I go bonkers and grab hold of it like it's my child.'

Another married chap agreed.

'If you are trying to hook a man, can I offer this advice? DON'T TRY TO CHANGE US!' he warned. 'It is possibly one of the most likely things to put men off. We don't want to be bullied into change.

'I'm sure my wife has changed a fair bit about me, but she's done it subtly enough for me to think it was my own idea.'

It was good advice, but I was finding it hard to follow.

I instinctively wanted to meddle and instil The Knowledge in my poor unsuspecting man.

MAN MAKEOVERS: THE KNOWLEDGE

1. Odd socks, whether clean or dirty, but either way strewn around the abode, can drive a woman DEMENTED. Particularly when they appear to be multiplying by the day and the poor wench actually has to lower herself to the sniff test to see what category of cleanliness they fall into. *Grim*.

   For one boyfriend, I devised a foolproof system, which included his very own laundry basket for the dirty ones and a 'sock pot' (a flower pot at the bottom of his wardrobe) containing all his clean odd socks. His glee whenever he deposited lovely clean items in the sock pot and was given praise was almost unnerving. Who said men weren't simple creatures?

2. It is never, EVER acceptable to use your girlfriend's credit card in a strip club.

   The culprit was given the card for emergencies. Sadly, his idea of a crisis was running out of cash to insert into strippers' thongs on a night out with the boys.

   Up until this point, my attitude to lap-dancing clubs was fairly liberal. Knowing full well that the fella in question had quite the penchant for pole-dancers, I saw no point in banning all access (he'd blatantly go anyway) so instead I suggested a one-dance rule. That way he would spend £20 on a striptease rather than £220 and thus the next day I could be rewarded for my lenient stance with a slap-up meal and flowers. He'd get the best of both worlds and still save money. Everyone's a winner.

However, the one-dance rule was suspended when my credit card statement came through with a hefty transaction made at Spearmint Rhino.

Perversely, as I fronted him up, waving the evidence at him, I was strangely amused by the whole sorry incident. How on earth did he think he'd ever get away with it? He'd taken stupidity to a whole new level.

3. When asked to hang out the washing, is it really necessary to handle the damp clothes as if you'll catch leprosy? They are clean. You won't.

   Instead of depositing them in crumpled lumps on the radiator, why don't you actually try shaking the creases out? You do remember how much my Rigby and Peller smalls cost, don't you? When my best panties look like they're made from crushed velvet, it disappoints me.

   If this is a sneaky attempt to make me realise that washing is in fact woman's work, I am not going to bow down to your sly manipulation. Instead, I am going to tell you where you are going wrong for next time. You're not listening? *Oh, you will*.

   As time will tell, I will not be offering you any guidance once you notice that the same crushed-velvet look has infected your work shirts on the day of an important meeting.

   Yes, you do look like you've been dragged through a hedge backwards. No, looking like that will not earn you a promotion.

   What can you do? Well, there's an object called 'the

iron' in the kitchen cupboard. Why don't you try that?

4. If you are not contactable for hours by text or phone after stepping out the door for 'a couple of beers', there will be severe consequences.

If you arrive home at 4 a.m., looking bleary-eyed and stinking of stale ale, you will be met at the door by a raving, red-eyed hag. And it's a situation of entirely your own making.

Excuses like 'I didn't want to wake you', 'I got lost' or 'My phone battery died' will not wash.

Expect to sleep on the sofa and you will be holidaying in Coventry for the next 48 hours. Presents may help.

Be it fair or not, I felt that all final decisions about decorating, furnishings and fittings should be made by me – and not Adam. After all, it was me who made the bed and decided the bathroom needed cleaning, while he appeared to be conveniently oblivious.

Yet I tried to remember it was his home too.

I found it in my heart to tolerate his tat and football memorabilia – well, just for a while, until one day all traces of Liverpool FC were subtly relegated to the loft. As I suspected, he didn't even notice. Ha!

As well as collecting naff crap, Adam was obsessed with writing notes on scrappy bits of paper. But instead of using these notes effectively and then throwing them away, they were quickly forgotten about and discarded around the house. This was something that nearly drove me to distraction.

Adam's piles of paper appeared everywhere: by the bed, by the phone, down the side of the sofa, by the cooker, by the telly, next to the sodding Ronaldo Russian doll. Hundreds of cryptic notes, scrawled in illegible spider's writing on note paper, pizza pamphlets and old envelopes.

'Do you really need this?' I'd ask, time and again, pointing to a list that read: '1 x margarita, 1 x chicken dippers, 2 x chips, 1 x coke.'

'Um, not sure,' he'd reply, without even looking, shoving the scrappy bits in his pockets, only to deposit them later by the bed.

'What the hell are these doing here?' I'd say, waving the offending wad of paper at him. 'For God's sake, please, please, please just throw them away. I feel like Stig of the Dump.'

Living with Adam revealed just how much he liked a tipple too. To my misfortune, a night on the booze and too many fags was often accompanied by some monumental snoring. As an extremely light sleeper, I get very upset, bordering on deranged, if I don't get my rest, so living with a prolific snorer did little for my peace of mind.

I always knew when I was in for a night of insomnia. I'd lie in bed feeling anxious, well aware that my partner had already fallen into a deep slumber. I'd try desperately to drop off before the noise started, but then I'd hear the first warning sign – heavy breathing with each exhale.

Next would come a slightly nasal rumbling noise, then another, and another, each increasing in volume, until the final crescendo came in a thundering snort so loud it would even cause him to wake up. While the noise had nearly blasted me out of bed, he'd stir slightly and then fall back to sleep. The same maddening pattern was then repeated over and over.

Annoyingly, if I dared wake the warthog and ask him to sleep on his side, he'd become the grumpiest man on earth, muttering obscenities and falling straight back into his stupor. The snoring would resume ten minutes later. Consequently, I'd kick him as hard as I could in the shin, then jump out of bed before I lowered myself to more GBH. I spent many a frustrated night on the sofabed, too livid to sleep and fantasising about the bollocking I was going to give him in the morning.

In the end, I took matters into my own hands and purchased a snoring remedy. From then on in, when Adam staggered in from the pub I'd be waiting for him.

'Open wide,' I'd order, collaring him. He'd begrudgingly obey me and he'd screw up his face and make gagging noises as I sprayed his gob with the foul-tasting liquid. Amazingly, it did work.

While I thought I had it bad, pity the poor friend whose boyfriend took sleepwalking to a whole new level with his late-night loo stops.

On the first occasion the Phantom Pisser struck, she found him contentedly urinating all over her clothes and her frantic attempts to stop him proved fruitless. The next day he was suitably mortified and, feeling sorry for him, she even cleaned up the mess.

But a few months later the Phantom Pisser made another visit during the witching hour. This time he opened the cupboard containing his own clothes and started hosing down his work shirts. Once again she tried to stop him, but was met by flailing arms and angry cries of 'Get off! I just want a piss.'

Looking down at the puddle rapidly appearing all over a pile of his shoes and socks, she felt smugly satisfied.

'You carry on then,' she said and headed back to bed.

The look of disgust on his hungover face when, the following day, armed with a bin liner, he miserably scooped up his soggy belongings was priceless.

After all this relentless man-bashing, I should acknowledge that it can work the other way as well.

One male friend admits he is so anal over the cleaning and what he views as his wife's inability to complete chores up to his clinical standards that they've hired a cleaner to avoid escalation into a full-scale war.

Adam also hated many of my habits: the way my attempts at cooking had a scatter-gun effect on the cupboards in the kitchen, my laziness with the washing up, the speed with which I greedily polished off the orange juice ('It is there to be drunk!') and, cheekily, the fact I left the toilet seat DOWN.

I may not live with The Beau, but he is well aware of what he'll be letting himself in for if he does throw caution to the wind and we move in together.

He has already addressed the annoyance factor of my six loo stops a night before I actually even try to go to sleep. My relentless obsessive compulsive checking of whether the door is locked, the gas is off and my alarm is set also drives him to distraction.

I'm ashamed to say that I've even forced my OCD on him when we're not together. Last thing at night, I make him text or call to reassure me he has checked everything

in his own home is switched off. He also has to confirm
that the key is in the door so he has an escape route in case
of a fire.

'You promise you're not just humouring me, you really
have done it?' I ask him repeatedly, well aware of how
nuts I'm sounding.

'Yes,' he normally sighs, sleepily. 'It's all done.'

'I honestly think that is the most ridiculous thing
you've ever told me about yourself, and I've heard a lot,'
my friend Clare laughed, when I admitted this bizarre
routine recently.

'He must *really* love you to put up with that!'

'I know,' I replied. 'It is the worse kind of nagging, but
if I don't go through the same routine night after night
then I lie awake worrying he's burning in his bed.'

While my actions were a tad extreme, when I
questioned my female friends many of them admitted they
had the urge to protect, mother or coach their chaps too.
It was a natural rite of passage.

In fact, it seemed bossy birds everywhere were trying
to change or house-train their beloveds from the moment
they met them.

But it could often be a good thing, as one friend
commented: 'I was with my ex for years. During that time,
I encouraged him to develop an interest in literature,
refined his wardrobe (i.e. binned the velvet turquoise
shirt), helped him to quit smoking . . .

'One of my biggest challenges though was that his belly
had grown considerably since we started going out. It
wasn't something I begrudged (it's not like I wasn't bigger
than when we first got together), but I gently suggested

that he might want to start going to the gym or eating a bit more healthily.

'After months of nagging, he finally bought a bike and started going to the gym three times a week. We broke up soon after. About six months after our split I met up with him. He had lost loads of weight, was seeing someone else and said things like, "You taught me that I should be more romantic, so with my new girlfriend I now send her cards and leave her little messages and I'm better at listening to her."

'To be honest, in my experience, I don't think it's possible to change a man (he has to do that himself), but I'm quietly proud of my work.'

In another Man Makeover success story, a canny young lady proudly recounted how she'd trained her man to like vegetables.

'When we first met, he refused to eat any sort of greenery and couldn't even cope with tomatoes in his spaghetti bolognese,' she revealed.

'I used to have to flavour it with gravy, but, bit by bit, I began to add more tomatoes and mushrooms. He'd eat mashed potato so I added cabbage to it. Now he'll eat most vegetables.'

She admitted she was adopting the same slow, methodical approach to his morning cuppa. 'At the moment he likes his tea milky with loads of sugar, but I'm slowly fazing out the sugar and cutting down the milk.

'He still puts salt on his food without even trying it first though. That's really annoying.'

So why do women feel the need to interfere with everything, ranging from eating habits to life skills?

'I think some girls try to change their boyfriends not out of any malicious intent to be the powerful or dominant partner in the relationship, but often out of being insecure and wanting to take every step to shore up the validity and longevity of their relationship,' one man ventured.

'By making their partner the mirror image of themselves, it becomes harder for the pair to separate, as there are too many shared life viewpoints, habits and experiences to overcome in the event of one of them wanting to move on. Also, I think girls naturally want to have empathy in every aspect of their lives, whereas blokes are happier just to bumble along in their own bubble.

'For instance, birds share bonding moments on a more emotional level than blokes [as well as on a superficial level too, I might add] and maybe they just want the fella to be in tune on that basis, so they can feel a closeness to them which will give them a heightened sense of love and commitment.'

He also thought that the need to change their men was perhaps engrained in women's DNA.

'Women are essentially programmed to look for a mate to have their offspring,' he suggested. 'Maybe by changing the facets of the fella which she doesn't like, she is listening to some kind of genetic calling urging her to ready this particular ship for landing?

'Once all the creases have been ironed out, he will then get permission to land.'

Interestingly, a female chum came up with a very similar theory.

'Men, as the traditional hunters, won't do anything unless they feel they really need to or want to do it,' she reasoned. 'Basically, they're programmed to shag around.

'Women, on the other hand, are creative and more in touch with their emotions. They have an urge to build a home and kick-start family life.

'In most cases, men need a fair bit of coaxing to convince them that they should stick with one girlfriend, get married, help with the chores and have children – but eventually they realise it's a better life with loads of benefits!'

It was interesting that she viewed women as having a natural urge to nest. I was glad to hear her philosophy. When The Fear first set in – because it had seemingly all begun with some comments about my age and relationship status – I'd wondered if I was just being predictably malleable.

Why did I so badly long for a husband, a home and kids? Was I succumbing to an age-old stereotype that this was a woman's worth? Was it because so many of my friends were doing it? Had I been conditioned not to be fully content with my lot unless I was keeping up with everyone else?

No, I decided. While I was deeply conscious of the fact that half my Facebook friends were married with children, my own feelings were instinctive. I had friends who admitted they felt nothing when they saw a baby. I, on the other hand, was itching to mother any cute child I spotted. It was a deep-rooted longing.

Even one of my most fiercely independent friends admitted she felt the same way.

'Every time it's my time of the month, I feel resentful that I'm flushing my eggs down the Swannee,' she confided. 'My periods are getting later and later every month. I'm convinced my body is trying desperately to hold on just in case I can get pregnant. Do I sound insane?'

Not to me she didn't. At work recently I'd complained of feeling sick in the morning and a colleague had quipped that maybe I was pregnant.

A few years previously that sort of comment would have turned me white with fear. But instead I couldn't help grinning. Now it didn't scare me at all – in stark contrast, I'd be delighted.

Chapter Five

Marry Me or It's Over

*R*ecently *I have* been dreaming about marriage a lot.
One such night, my subconscious came up with a disturbing little story.

I was about to wed The Beau when the church suddenly filled with gatecrashers. Weirdly, in a disjointed way, I was looking down on myself wearing a strapless wedding dress and bright-red lippy, about a stone lighter (nice), with my hair tied back.

The me that was not me and my betrothed were up in a pulpit with the priest. The cleric was trying desperately to conduct the ceremony, but no one was listening and the three of us were crammed into a very uncomfortable space.

Suddenly the church had turned into a hall or abbey covered in festive decorations. There was a thumping dance tune on and everyone was jumping up and down in a fiesta mood – the kind of party you'd see on *Ibiza Uncovered*.

'Hey!' I shouted, to no avail. 'Heeeeey! What about my wedding?'

A few nights later I had another wedding-themed dream.

This time I was in Gretna Green – only I've never been, so how did I know?

My Gretna Green was lovely. There were green rolling hills and a strange church that looked like an old farmhouse with a conservatory. The church was located between the hills and led down to a pebbly coastal bay. There was also a huge tor towering magnificently into the sky.

The Beau and I were wandering around the beach before the ceremony with a brood of children that had just appeared. I think they were ours. As we paddled, the sky suddenly darkened and an eerie mist descended, obscuring the hills and the tor.

The waves became angry and strong and the tide began to pull at our feet. The water wasn't even up to our knees, but the current had such force that it took every effort to retreat. But I did so, scooping up one of our magic offspring.

Dumping the child on safe ground, I rushed back into the water, where The Beau and at least one other child were still struggling. I was terrified I wouldn't be able to get to them. Thankfully, at that point my alarm went off, waking me from my fitful dream. I clambered over The Beau, who was sleeping peacefully next to me, to turn it off. My nightclothes were drenched from a cold sweat.

My third marriage dream in as many weeks saw me panicking because it was time to go to the church and I didn't have a wedding dress. The only thing to hand was a too-tight, white, sequined mini-dress and trashy heels. I ended up tottering and tripping down the aisle looking like a dodgy Tina Turner.

I didn't tell The Beau I'd had another marriage dream – I was worried he'd think I was cuckoo. So instead I Googled 'weddings' and 'dream interpretation' and came across a website called www.paranormality.com.

It told me: 'To dream of any unfortunate occurrence in connection with a marriage foretells distress, sickness, or death in your family. For a young woman to dream that she is a bride and unhappy or indifferent foretells disappointments in love, and probably her own sickness. She should be careful of her conduct, as enemies are near her.'

Well, that's good news then.

Why do we believe this cosmic claptrap anyway?

A long-suffering lass I once knew had a frankly awful boyfriend that she stayed with through thick and thin. He cheated on her repeatedly and while she thought about breaking up with him, a visit to a psychic changed her mind.

'Stick with this one,' she was told. 'He'll put you through hell, but he'll come good in the end.'

So she did, through frequent, painful infidelities, until, finally, he dumped her and married someone else within six months. Somebody shoot that psychic.

Not surprisingly, given stories like this, The Beau worries that I delve into the mystical world, as he, quite sensibly, thinks I should look for answers in real life and not rely on tarot cards.

But while I draw the line at ouija boards, I have a sadistic compulsion to keep getting my future read, no matter how much it seems like hocus pocus.

The first time I visited a medium, when I was 17, she

told me I'd marry an American. For years afterwards, every time I met a chap from the USA I'd look at him curiously wondering, if he was 'The One' – even if he was ugly, short and boss-eyed.

The only time I've come close to pulling an American was a comedian I met at a bar in Milwaukee. I was extremely inebriated and decided to try to wow him with my English wit.

'What kind of bees make milk?' I asked. He looked at me blankly until I delivered the punchline: 'Boobies! Get it?'

As I chortled to myself, he seemed fairly amused and rewarded me with his email address. Indeed, when I got back to the UK we exchanged a few messages, but that was as far as it went. So nope, he wasn't the husband.

I decided to write off that prediction.

The next psychic, continuing the American theme, told me I'd get engaged in New York in the New Year. However, that was two years ago and it certainly ain't happened. In fact, nothing she said made any sense at all.

The third psychic (stick with me) was a gypsy at the Isle of Wight Festival. I stumbled into his caravan with a fuzzy head after a heavy night watching the Foo Fighters.

'He's a nice man,' he told me, presumably about The Beau. 'I can see you marrying him and having two children.' HURRAH! I grinned at the news. But he hadn't finished.

'He's not the one for you though,' he added. 'You won't find your true love until quite a bit later in life.'

As my heart sank to the pit of my stomach, he continued that this 'true love' was supposed to be Mediterranean and some kind of flash property magnate. Sounded like a bit of a greaser to me.

Editing real life stories at work had left me very suspicious about being wooed by Latino lovers or Turkish toyboys abroad. Of course I'm not suggesting all Mediterranean men are that way, there are merely a few that give the rest a bad name. But you would not believe the amount of rational middle-aged women who head off to Turkey for fun in the sun only to find themselves being wooed by a 21-year-old stud from the local hotel or bar.

'I find girls my own age immature,' they always croon. 'Young women have nothing to say.' Then they invite you for a romantic walk on the beach and later bid you a teary goodbye at the airport. Textbook.

Then, lo and behold, Jean from Crawley and Denise from Devizes are being lured away from the daily grind, selling up the homes they've worked so hard for over the last 20 years, to pursue promises of marriage and happy ever after with a man half their age.

They head off to Turkey with high hopes of giddy romance, but no sooner have they wandered down the aisle than lover boy needs to borrow some money for the family.

Although at first he wants to live in Turkey, he kindly suggests they could go back to England if his wife wants to. Then – who'd have thought it? – he does a runner.

Some women's magazines even dispatch reporters to holiday resorts in Greece and Turkey over the summer just to find stories about local love-rats preying on naive British women.

Of course this isn't always the case – it's only fair to say that some Shirley Valentine-style romances do work out – but, equally, I've heard about far too many that end in heartache and deception.

Back at the Festival, I wobbled out of the caravan and called The Beau. 'A psychic said we're going to divorce,' I howled. 'It's just not fair. I want to stay with you and the kids forever.'

To his credit, as he attempted to pacify me, he tactfully didn't bring up the fact that we had no plans to marry – let alone divorce – and didn't have any kids. Eventually, I managed to stifle my sobs and listened to The Beau's protests that it was all a load of bollocks anyway.

But yet, as the weeks passed, the terrible prophecy stuck with me.

Bizarrely, the gypsy man had not boasted of former celebrity clients such as Nicole Richie and Julie Andrews. No, of all the weird and wonderful people to traipse through his caravan, the one he remembered the most fondly was Piers Morgan.

'He was just starting his career and I told him one day he'd be very famous,' he told me proudly. 'Look at him now!'

As luck would have it, a few months after I'd seen the psychic, I actually saw Piers Morgan at a National Television Awards party. I approached him nervously and tapped him on the arm. He was busy talking, so I tapped him again . . . and again. Finally, he turned and eyed me suspiciously.

'Hello, Piers. This is going to sound a bit odd, but I just wanted to ask, I hope you don't mind, but have you ever been to see a psychic?' I stammered, idiotically.

He looked at me with a withering air of disdain that I'm sure he picked up from Simon Cowell.

'Probably when I was very drunk,' he answered, moving as if to turn his back on me again, his attention wavering by the second.

Flustered, I tried to explain my dilemma, rambling on: 'So I wondered if you'd met this one I'd met, because he said you had, and if anything he told you came true, because he told me horrible things...'

'Look,' Piers interrupted, this time not unkindly. 'I can't remember it, so it can't have been that insightful. It's all a load of rubbish anyway.'

'Thanks,' I grinned, relieved, and skipped off, deciding to take his word for it.

I'd like to say that after that I quit while I was ahead and no longer sought out advice via mystical means, but sadly I didn't.

Like some kind of sadist, I was back shuffling the tarot cards again recently. This time to a softly spoken medium called Monica.

As well as telling me that I had a 200-year-old Spirit Guide called Jamie who'd been attracted to my quirkiness – I liked the sound of that – she mentioned The Beau.

'I think you're going to live together very soon,' she said.

She then paused. 'You want to marry this guy, don't you?'

My throat tightened with emotion. 'Yes,' I gulped.

'You want to know if he wants to marry you too,' she continued. 'Charlotte, I think you already know the answer.'

At which point I let out an embarrassing sob and fumbled in my bag for a hanky.

I really need to get a grip – but at least the marriage vibes are looking good.

I've often wondered what it is about some girls that seems to prompt every man they meet to suddenly produce a rock? Do they instinctively pick a certain type of man or are they wifey types who just radiate 'marry me' vibes?

While some girls I know have racked up two or three proposals, others are still eyeing up bridal shops to no avail.

Is there some secret formula which is guaranteed to see your man racing off to ask Dad for your hand and then finally do the deed?

I asked my male friends to explain the credentials a wife needs:

WHAT MAKES A GIRL MARRYING MATERIAL?

- 'It has to be someone you can imagine having sex with for years to come and, equally, someone who can make you laugh and challenge you. The relationships I have found hardest to get over have been with girls who are funny and kind.'
- 'Someone who has not had too many sexual partners and doesn't put out on the first date. Someone reason-

ably smart, not a fussy, dippy "I can't do anything for myself" person. Someone who is faithful and who you can actually go out drinking with and laugh together at the same things. That last point is a massive one for me personally.'

- 'Obviously it starts with sexual attraction, then having common interests, and all the usual stuff. I guess the main thing is that the girl has to bring out the best in you, and let you bring out the best in her, while being strong enough to retain the characteristics that drew you to her in the first place. It's a tough balance, but there's no point in just turning into clones of each other.'

- 'Someone who just fits into your life – your best friend, a good shag, family-friendly – whatever your priorities are.'

- 'Ah, the six million dollar question. It really depends on the guy. Obviously someone you can live with and who won't do your head in. For me, it would be someone who's a bit of fun and wants the same things (kids, career and so on).'

- 'A girl who makes you want to be a better bloke and who you can't imagine being without.'

So, in short, the perfect wife should be someone who can bring out the best in a bloke, is great at sex but still virginal, is funny, kind, smart, not dippy, family-friendly, career-minded, likes a drink and can make him laugh, all without losing their own identity. Yikes.

There have been two occasions when I wondered if The Beau was contemplating marriage and allowed myself to get totally carried away with the idea that he was about to get down on one knee.

The first was when he took me on a date to Zippo's Circus.

The Big Top was less than half full and the acts distinctively unpolished. The whole thing had an air of desperation about it. We sat uncomfortably in our seats, watching as a rather crap clown performed mediocre tricks.

In the interval, we stood by a burger van reading newspaper cuttings about the circus, which had been laminated and put on display. Bizarrely, one article featured a quote from the ringmaster claiming the before-mentioned clown was 'one of the most naturally talented clowns' he had ever come across. As we were chortling at the absurdity of this statement, The Beau paused and his voice became serious.

'Charlotte,' he said, looking at me intently. My stomach lurched.

'Would you like some popcorn?' he continued.

I started laughing hysterically. 'Oh my God, I thought you were going to propose!' I shrieked, fanning my flushed face with my programme.

'What?' he frowned. 'At Zippo's Circus? Give me some credit. Why on earth would I propose here?' I didn't really have a rational answer and he continued to look at me as if I resided on Mars.

The second non-proposal occurred after The Beau and I had spent the evening at a friend's engagement party.

Both decidedly the worse for wear, we were at a bus stop on Kilburn High Road, waiting for the 189. I was greedily devouring a chicken kebab and The Beau was talking to a tramp.

The vagrant seemed to be bending my boyfriend's ear about conspiracy theories and The Beau was drunkenly indulging him.

'I know, man,' I heard him say. 'It's not good.'

Then suddenly the tramp turned his attention to me.

'Who's this young lady?' he asked. 'Is she your wife?'

When The Beau stated I was his girlfriend, the tramp's eyes boggled with outrage.

'What's wrong with you?' he barked. 'Ask her to marry you!'

The Beau looked at me with a twinkle in his eye.

'Charlotte?' he asked, just as the 189 pulled up.

I shot him a look that said 'DON'T. YOU. DARE.'

Then I jumped on the bus and stomped upstairs to the top deck, The Beau in hot pursuit. As he sat down next to me, I glared at him.

'You actually thought about proposing to me because a TRAMP TOLD YOU TO?' I raged.

The Beau doubled up with laughter, tears streaming down his face, as my fury only fuelled his hysteria.

'I was only joking,' he said, putting his arm around me, trying to keep a straight face.

The next morning I awoke to a text message from my sister. It announced that my cousin, who is the same age as me, had just got engaged to her boyfriend. Thoughts of the tramp-inspired proposal immediately came flooding back.

I crossly thrust my phone in front of The Beau's sleepy face, and then leapt out of bed to sulk on the sofa in front of *Hollyoaks*.

I didn't speak to him all morning.

'I'm sorry,' he said later, kissing me affectionately on the forehead.

'You shouldn't joke about things like that,' I mumbled grumpily.

It may not be a joking matter, but for some reason complete strangers – like the tramp and on another occasion a random nutter in Ladbroke Grove ('Marry her, man! Once in a lifetime bruv, once in a lifetime ...') – often encourage The Beau to play at popping the question. Sometimes my life feels like a fictional film entitled *Carry On Dating*.

Even recently, as we stood at the checkout in Marks & Spencer at Paddington Station, the subject was raised.

'Anything for my lady,' The Beau joked, as he kindly contributed 74p towards a snack for my train journey.

For a minute the sales assistant studied us intently.

'For life?' he asked, rather bizarrely.

With a wicked grin, The Beau nodded, as he once again made as if to propose. I rolled my eyes at this comedy and headed for the train platform.

I wonder if I will take him seriously if he ever asks for real? One thing is for sure, if he even thinks about proposing to me in a supermarket or outside a kebab shop, I'll lamp him.

But stranger things have happened. A male friend, who will remain nameless, recounted with glee how he proposed to his future wife at her father's wake.

'I was on the gambler when her brother said, "Why don't you propose?"' he revealed. 'I turned to her and said, "Do you want to get married?" She said "Yes," then I said, "Great! Can you lend me a pound for the slot machine?"'

Being, as he claimed, 'completely tight', he managed to blag his future mother-in-law's engagement ring to do the job, so didn't even have to splash out for a rock. Unsurprisingly, the marriage didn't last.

But for a girl, even the perfect proposal can be, to quote a female chum, 'the most horrible moment of your life'.

The lady had been with her boyfriend for years; she knew marriage was on the cards and she really wanted it. However, when they went on a romantic walk, she suddenly had a terrible feeling of foreboding.

There was no one around, the setting was achingly romantic – cometh the hour. As he said her name, she considered turning on her heels and legging it, but instead found herself paralysed with fear as he smiled at her lovingly and fumbled in his pocket to produce the ring.

As he uttered the million-dollar question and she dutifully muttered, 'Yes,' nausea washed over her. Thankfully, her happy fiancé was blissfully unaware of her troubled mind, and off he whisked her to celebrate.

It's not that she didn't want to get married, she explained later, it was just the enormity of the verbal contract she had just agreed to.

Women may have drawn the short straw when it comes to smear tests, period pains and childbirth, but at least the trauma of asking is generally left to the men. Unless we decide to bite the bullet on 29 February, we are, thankfully, spared the stress of planning the perfect proposal.

I have heard so many stories about how poor lovestruck folk have tried desperately to pop the question, only to have their romantic intentions thwarted at every turn by their unwitting brides-to-be.

There was the chap who wanted to take his girlfriend out for the evening and ask for her hand, only she was 'too tired'. Plan B was abandoned too when she vetoed the romantic stroll he had planned for the following day. So in the end, not wishing to drag it out any longer, he proposed at home, when they were snuggled up on the sofa.

Then there was the poor man who spent a whole night in Paris travelling to and fro with his girlfriend in tow, trying desperately to find the right location to do the deed. To his horror, the restaurant he'd painstakingly picked had double-booked, the next eatery was not a suitable spot and the Eiffel Tower at night was far too spooky.

So, finally and wearily, he took the plunge back at the hotel, where, I am delighted to report, she said, 'Yes'.

But by far my favourite tale is from a workmate whose future husband took her for a lovely meal, then suggested they take a romantic walk back home over Waterloo Bridge. It was a thoughtful idea – the panoramic views of the River Thames and stunning lights of the London skyline at night would have offered the perfect setting for the perfect proposal.

Only my friend complained she was cold, so took it upon herself to hail a taxi and jump in. Her man dashed in after her and as the cab whizzed over Waterloo Bridge he decided to stick with the original plan and blurted out the question as quickly as possible while she sat next to him gawping.

But as much as I have sympathy for the stress men go through popping the question, I've never understood the ones who propose on TV or in front of hundreds of people at a football match or even in front of the family.

To me there's something very suspicious about such a public proposal. The woman can hardly say no, can she? But perhaps that's the idea behind it?

Agreeing to marry someone is a huge, mind-blowing decision, but you're pretty much expected to put the poor man out of his misery there and then, giving yourself up to a lifetime of commitment, patience and tolerance.

Although I have one friend who actually made her husband-to-be wait TWO WEEKS before accepting.

'I just wanted to be sure and wanted to think it through,' she reasoned. It might have been the longest fortnight of her poor fiancé's life, but you have to admire the girl.

Another bride refused to say 'I do' until her intended signed a pre-nup agreeing to bring her a cup of tea and two digestives in bed every morning without fail.

But no matter how long it takes you to decide and under whatever terms – if you even accept at all – it's still nice to be asked.

So why is it that so many women want to get married so badly?

Is it all down to the delight of being able to mark your man with a wedding band? Is it the thought of referring smugly to 'my husband' at every opportunity? Or is it just a great way to get rid of a crap surname?

'I don't really see the point of marriage,' a male friend announced the other day. 'All that money spent on one day and wanting to be the centre of attention, what's that all about?'

'But it's nice,' I insisted.

'Why do you want to get married?' he asked.

I had to stop and think for a second. Was it because everyone else around me was getting hitched and I felt a bit left out? Maybe, but it was also so much more than just a competitive need to keep up with the Joneses.

'Because it's a lifelong commitment to the person you love, an age-old tradition and everyone loves a good party,' I eventually said. 'Bloody expensive though.'

What I didn't admit to him was that while weddings are lovely, happy occasions for most people, they also provoke severe reactions in young ladies yet to make it down the aisle.

Envy is never nice, but it is definitely out there, simmering beneath the fancy frocks and perma-grins as the church bells ring out, along with frustration, disappointment and jealousy.

If a fraught bride-to-be can be branded a Bridezilla, then it is only right to reveal that her unmarried friends can be prone to becoming monsters (albeit green-eyed) as well.

If you are permanently single or still hankering after that long-awaited rock, then there is nothing like a friend's nuptials to set you off swaying dangerously close to funny-farm territory.

Although I've enjoyed many of my friends' weddings, I've also had a heightened feeling of pent-up emotion – not just induced by too much booze and tear-jerking speeches.

At a wedding I attended with Adam, I felt desperately sad, as I knew deep down we'd never experience the same thing. Our love just wasn't on a par with that of the couple getting hitched. In fact, it made me wonder if I'd ever experience feelings of that magnitude, or was I destined to feel like I'd almost got there, but not quite, for the rest of my days?

But there are lots of other things going on at weddings that make the unmarrieds feel distinctly maudlin.

If you're a victim of the minefield of table planning, then you can end up feeling very inadequate. If you're single, you'll be routinely placed on a table with all couples, or, possibly even worse, all couples and one other unattached person that your thoughtful friends think you'll 'get on brilliantly with'. However, you can guarantee that the match in question actually has all the appeal of a date with Darth Vader.

He's usually an extremely obnoxious or weird man, probably shorter than you, with a very good reason for being single. *Perhaps that's what they think of you too?*

Often, if a bloke is single at a wedding, he is viewed as some kind of novelty, the 'charming' bachelor who evidently can't be tamed. It's nearly noble! No one ever mentions that he might have serious personal issues or irreversibly grim halitosis.

Indeed, the best man, hoping that his special role will ensure a shag as a reward for duty done, shamelessly revels in his appeal during the speeches. At which point people nudge you and you wish the earth would open up and swallow you.

But, humiliatingly, even your ageing aunt thinks you should have a crack. That's how desperate you've become, in everyone else's eyes. Your face burns as you realise you're being pointed out across the room.

If you are seeing someone but they haven't accompanied you, you face whispers that it's not working out or, even worse, that you made your man up.

If you sit next to a couple, often the romance of the occasion will inspire them to regale you with stories of how they met and how parenthood changes your life, for ever. Yawn.

As everyone gets drunker, it can only get worse. When you hit the dancefloor, it seems that you are fair game. Suddenly it's a free-for-all for disgusting, sweaty men to target you. Before you know it, they're strutting towards you, gyrating their pelvises in a way that emphasises their beer bellies so beautifully. Often they are so drunk they've forgotten their wives are sitting nearby, who, incidentally, have decided to give you, as the token 'single slut', daggers. *Thank you so much for involving me in your domestic.*

At least during the service you can centre all your attention on the bride and groom. But during the speeches you become acutely aware of all the couples looking lovingly at each other or squeezing each other's hands as they (vom) remember their own special day.

After a few glasses of wine, the man next to you feels the need to vocalise loudly his concerns for your lack of suitors. 'What's wrong with you then?' he slurs.

'If I knew that then I wouldn't be single!' you bark back.

THE PERFECT PATRONISING COMMENTS FOR THE SINGLE WEDDING GUEST

'Are you married? No? Never mind, you'll get there eventually.'

'I've put you next to John. He's not met a nice girl since he was diagnosed as bi-polar.'

'Have you been single for long? You have? Oh dear . . .' (Make way for the tumbleweed.)

'Why are you single? Good-looking girl like you. Are you frigid?'

'Do you think you'll *ever* find a man?'

'You can have one dance with my husband if you like. Just so you don't feel totally left out.'

There's nothing like a good wedding to make you acutely aware of your relationship shortcomings.

Even if you are there with a partner, it can be equally awkward. You could cut the tension with a knife as courting couples flinch in their seats, a spotlight seemingly radiating down on their unmarried status. Often the man uncomfortably avoids eye contact and the woman stares accusingly.

And if the couple getting wed had the audacity to meet after you and your man, there is nothing to stem the inner rage.

'What's wrong with you, you sodding, miserable commitment-phobe? This should have been MY big day,' you silently seethe.

Four glasses of champagne in and you're grinding your teeth aggressively, trying with all your might to avoid blasting out your contempt at your stupid, lily-livered, non-fiancé.

'What's the matter with you?' he asks, as you fix him with a stony stare that would give Medusa a run for her money, 'You're acting like a psycho.'

'I'm entitled to be a psycho,' you hiss. 'We've been together five years. I WANT TO GET MARRIED. WHEN. ARE. YOU. GOING. TO. MARRY. ME?'

Before you know it, you're standing in the middle of the dancefloor, stamping your feet, face streaming with tears and screaming like a banshee at your hopeless, marriage-shirking boyfriend. Suddenly the music has stopped (right at the crucial moment, just like in *EastEnders*) and everyone is looking, whilst pretending not to. From now on, you'll always be known as the deranged cow who ruined the wedding.

'I hope you're happy,' you seethe at your man on your way out. 'You've ruined everything.'

But don't expect him to understand where you're coming from. Men just don't get it.

When I asked some single male friends how they felt about going solo at weddings, they seemed to revel in it and – it gets worse – even admitted to taking advantage of emotionally charged females.

'Weddings are great places for random scores because girls go slightly barmy,' one revealed.

Lord help us.

But it's not all bad. You could turn up at a wedding to find yourself being wooed by a very eligible man –

even if he is slightly taking advantage of your singleton neurosis.

A delightful young lady I know happily bagged herself the dapper best man at a wedding six months ago. They've been head over heels ever since.

Although thus far I have managed to avoid a scene at a wedding, I am guilty of trying to brainwash The Beau with badgering about betrothals. I like to chat animatedly to newly engaged couples in front of him, asking all about the proposal and even cheekily asking to try on the ring.

Then I'll make a comment like 'Yes, it's beautiful, very classic and understated. I think I'd have to choose one a bit like this,' hoping that someone, somewhere is taking note. Ahem.

Of course I can dream all I like, but I can't get away from the miserable reality that one in three marriages end in divorce. But, for those who've never been asked, this can be an immensely satisfying statistic.

And, if you do actually stop and think about it, for all the well-meaning vows in the world, marriage is a scary commitment.

You've just signed up for life and, whether you've been together six months or six years, realistically you will have no idea how you'll feel about that person in 30 years' time.

Will you still fancy them when their beer gut hangs over their belt? Will that cute habit of laughing at his own jokes annoy the crap out of you when you're 55?

But the long and short of it is you have to stop being selfish and only thinking of number one. Now there are two people to think about and the whole world no longer centres around YOU. Are you ready to be selfless?

Are you sure?

Consider this:

Now you'll have to admit you actually spend more than half your monthly wage on shoes, cosmetics and chardonnay. And, even worse, you'll probably have to get a joint bank account.

Imagine the scrutiny you'll face when he notices a hefty transaction at H&M.

'Well, the new Roberto Cavalli range is out,' you'll whine, sticking out your bottom lip and realising how pathetic that sounds considering you've just been caught frivolously spending the cash allocated for the new carpet.

'I'm really disappointed in you,' he'll frown, looking disapprovingly at your new, fabulous frock, which you blatantly look really hot in. He should want to ravish not reprimand you.

'Is that really worth £60?' he'll scold, eyeing you with the sort of disgust normally reserved for someone who has stolen from their dying grandmother. 'Maybe you should think about returning it?'

Point taken, you'll dash into the bedroom and crossly wrestle with the zip, letting the dress slip off into a crumpled heap on the floor. Then you'll put on the most disgusting jogging bottoms and top you can find. This outfit is normally reserved for decorating and hair-dying, but drastic times call for drastic measures. If he's going to be tight, then he better jolly well get used to seeing you looking like a complete minger.

It's funny how the prospect of being always the bridesmaid and never the bride can really get the imagination going.

But men, all this bitterness about wedlock, they're just not buying it.

'Why, in this day and age, does any woman ever feel in any sense odd being at the wedding on her own?' demanded one man.

He questioned why both sexes felt the need for the socially acceptable routine of a white wedding in the first place.

He gave the example of a friend who wanted to get married in black, but didn't in the end because of the protocol surrounding it ('It would have pissed her family off something chronic').

He also challenged the many religious-shirking couples who choose to exchange vows in a church.

'Why?' he ranted. 'Tell me what the first reading meant to you, then? Oh yeah, sure, you'll start going to church now you've got babies on the way.

'The only novel thing about church weddings is seeing your best mate has "God help me" Tippexed on the sole of his brogues when he's kneeling down.' Charming.

Another marriage-shirking male was equally scathing:

'I can sort of understand a girl wanting to go down the aisle, as it sounds fun and they get to be the woman in white.

'Undoubtedly it will be a magnificent day – there will be nice flowers and a great party. But it's the inevitability of it all in the grand scheme of life that I find not off putting, but, I don't know, somehow just uniformly inevitable.

'Once people get married they can have their own rowdy kids who go through life making the same mistakes as we all did, hoping for the best but getting the worst. They'll realise it's the survival of the fittest and everything they've ever been told was a big lie, because all they're doing is passing on their genes until eventually they're pushing up the daisies.

'Why not cut out the middle man and not bother? At least then you can save twenty grand of your mum and dad's pension.'

But what's wrong with hankering after the inevitable? Do you want life to be a constant adrenaline rush, flying by the seat of your pants and refusing to conform? Or could you actually be very happy surrounded by the love that nuturing your own family unit can bring?

'While I know that sometimes my married mates think, "This is my lot, the rest of my life is this and that's it, no surprises, my future is mapped out already," I envy the fact that they have met "The One",' one female friend in her 30s admitted earnestly.

'I know it happens at different times for everyone, but I feel left behind. I'm jealous of married friends with children. My two best friends and sister already have husbands and babies.

'By the time I make it down the aisle and have my kids, their children will all be so much older. I make jokes about it all the time – that my godchildren won't be pageboys, they'll be ushers and so on. But I do feel like I'll have an "older" wedding now.

'My dad is worried about me because my parents are not getting any younger and my sister is married with a baby, but I'm all alone. He's worried that they'll die and I'll have no one. I end up feeling guilty that they are worried about me, but can't just meet someone to please them.'

Here's the rub. When you're in your early 20s, you

barely register as many of your friends get boyfriends. But as the late 20s set in, there are engagement parties and weddings and you start to sit up and take notice.

Then, as the 30s arrive, there are crying babies everywhere. Over the years you morph from being in the majority to the minority and, social conditioning or not, you do think about it.

Unfortunately this is heightened by the fact that every time you go home your mother has yet another loud chat to herself about wanting to be young enough to 'enjoy' her grandchildren. What she doesn't know is that the chance to give her some would be a fine thing!

'I've always wanted to have children,' says one maternal friend. 'Why? Natural instinct. It's the norm. I'm the same as my married friends: I want to commit to a man I love, to leave something behind when I die, perhaps have someone to look after me in my old age.

'I've just turned 30 and often think that if I got pregnant by accident I'd have to keep it in case it's my only chance. I think women are more likely to keep an unwanted baby in their 30s than in their 20s.

'I have two godchildren and have said that if I'm not lucky enough to have children myself, I'm blessed to have children in my life. I can see that at the moment it's great to be able to have fun without all the sleepless nights. So there are benefits.

'I guess it's all down to the individual. One of my friends recently started talking about having her eggs frozen at 30 because she's so worried about not being able to have children.'

By the time your mid-30s are underway, it's highly

feasible that all your best friends are married with kids and a mortgage. In contrast, you could be the only one left painting the town red, still searching for 'The One'.

'Is there actually something wrong with me?' you might begin to wonder, summing up your options, seemingly fewer by the day. 'Is it time for drastic action?'

If you take a stroll around the self-help section of any bookshop (trying desperately not to be noticed), you'll find the shelves brimming with books promising you a quick-fix solution to the problem of finding a man.

Well, unfortunately, the grim reality is that it isn't that easy. It's an uphill slog, it's a battle, and it's a curse.

THE CURSE OF THE SMUG MANUALS

When head-over-heels in love, it is easy to get a little carried away, particularly once you have the security of a wedding band on your finger. However, don't, whatever you do, preach about your own foolproof method of bagging a bloke or how to achieve marital bliss (especially in the bedroom).

Kim Cattrall and Heather Mills McCartney both penned smug books about having the perfect life, only to separate from their husbands soon after.

So remember: SMUG = EGG ON FACE.

(Although I'm not being smug, I'm quite fearful I have just penned a self-fulfilling prophecy and will get dumped just before this book is printed. Oh, the irony . . .)

Attached friends, contentedly mopping baby sick off their shoulders, may look at you sorrowfully and announce: 'Don't worry, you'll meet someone nice soon.' But what do they know? You could really do without their patronising comments.

People who are already married, attached or shacked up think it's so easy to meet someone nice – just because *they* found the right person.

As a single friend acknowledges, 'One of the worst things about being terminally single is that people ask constantly why I haven't got a boyfriend. Just as bad are the ones who know me really well, who have actually stopped asking, "How's the love life?" because the answer's always the same.

'Then bloody married friends try to tell me I'm being picky just because I haven't found someone, which is really irritating. Okay, so I'll stick with the next person I meet then, even if I find him irritating or unattractive or wrong or a psycho, shall I?'

The ugly truth is that it's a nightmare trying to meet someone even remotely nice.

Unfairly, there are bitches-from-hell who've effortlessly got their claws into wonderful boyfriends and husbands, yet some of my most gorgeous, clever and lovely girl pals wonder if they'll ever meet someone even half decent.

Some girls flit from one perfect guy to another, others continually get shat on from a great height. Contrary to the popular saying, nothing is fair in love and war.

Then, if you have found a man you want to stick with, getting him to make an honest woman of you can be an uphill struggle.

A young lady recounted the sad tale of how she spent five years trying to convince her commitment-phobe boyfriend to propose.

'All I ever did was try to prove myself worthy enough to be his wife,' she revealed.

'I told him a million times that if I had to leave him to make him propose, it just wouldn't work. I wanted him to love me and want to marry me. So one day I decided I'd had enough and I finished it. I told him that I wasn't prepared to waste my time on a relationship that was going nowhere. He left and returned a month later with a ring and got down on one knee.'

She got caught up in the moment and said yes, but a week later the engagement was off.

'I realised that it didn't feel right,' she says. 'For five years I'd been working so hard to make him want to marry me that I hadn't stopped to think about whether he was actually good enough for me.

'Once I did, I found that he came up short. Why? Because the man I end up with will not need five years and me threatening to leave before he sees that I should be his wife.'

When you're with someone you know you're ultimately not going to end up with, it can be a hard fact to face up to. I call it Blinker Syndrome.

So many girls I know have tried desperately to carry on regardless, blinding themselves to the truth that the man they are seeing is just not 'The One'.

We often do the same thing with clothes. It looked great on the model pictured in the window, but now the same garment is making you look like a sumo wrestler in a catsuit. But yet you battle with your rational mind in the changing room: 'If I lose a few pounds it will fit', 'This changing room has really bad lighting' or 'I'm sure it'll look better with heels'.

You buy it and every Saturday for the next three months you put it on and parade around your flat, seeing what it looks like in several different mirrors before huffily shoving it back in your wardrobe. What a waste of £90.

But this crime against your bank balance is nothing compared to the time and energy you could waste trying to convince yourself and all your concerned friends that a man is right when he so clearly isn't.

It is all too easy to hang on, in denial, with someone for much longer than you should, deliberately dispelling all negative thoughts of why it isn't working from your mind. If you're not thinking about it, it isn't happening.

But at random uncontrollable times, these thoughts may seep through to the forefront of your consciousness. (While watching emotive dramas on ITV was always a killer for me, I would find myself in floods of tears when the plot was a bit too close to home.)

You may even break down and confide in friends, only to later dismiss everything you said as drunken pre-menstrual guff and be wracked with guilt for admitting it in the first place.

But whether you are already plotting an escape route or simply decide to do it on the spur of the moment, actually having the balls to take the plunge is easier said than done. Once those words have tripped off your tongue, there's no going back, the emotional floodgates have opened and you have to deal with all the fallout.

Before Adam and I had 'The Chat' which sealed our fate, I'd lie awake at night listening to his breathing and feeling sick with anxiety over our fading relationship. If, in those dark, twilight hours, I could have taken a happy pill to fix all my niggling doubts, I would have downed it in a second.

If you're not fighting with the person, then it is almost worse. There is something so shattering about loving and admiring someone deeply, but yet knowing that things just can't be salvaged.

A friend describes how she spent two whole years going out with an ex she didn't really want to be with because it was easier than going through a break-up.

'He was my boyfriend all the way through the first year at uni, and then, as we were about to start our second year, he dumped me,' she recalls. 'It was the first proper break-up I'd had, and I was a complete mess. I didn't eat for four days and I could barely speak to anyone.

'The problem was that we had the same group of friends, so when I did feel brave enough to go out, he would be there. He seemed a bit upset too, but his way of dealing with it was by getting pissed with his mates, being really loud and chatting up women. It was awful to watch and I felt sick every time I saw him.'

After three months, she picked herself up and started to enjoy herself again, and it was just as she began to feel happy that her former boyfriend began to take interest again.

'I'd lost loads of weight, met other blokes and things were really good, but when my ex told me he still had feelings for me, I thought all my Christmases had come at once,' she says.

'However, as I sat there on my own the night after we had officially got back together, I thought to myself, "I don't think I really want this at all." But when I weighed my options up, I thought that I really could not handle seeing him with a different woman each week, not when we were in the same group of friends. I wouldn't be able to just shake him off – he'd be a fixture of my university life, whether I liked it or not.

'I did love him, and we did have some fun times. But when we left uni and he went back home, I knew that was it. I split up with him over the phone, and he was a right mess.

'I cried for one night and then moved on. I honestly don't regret leaving it so long to break up with him. I know the other option would have been much, much worse.'

Another, now married, lady reveals how she was with her ex-boyfriend for years but regrets how long and drawn-out their break-up was.

'Before I met my husband, I'd been going out with a sexy boyfriend I'd met as a student. He was my first love, but the last couple of years of our relationship were hell for both of us.

'I fantasised about other men, snogged a few and had a passionate affair with a beautiful Matt Dillon lookalike who had a high-flying job. It was all very cloak-and-dagger. But we started taking more and more risks. One morning I left a cheeky love letter in his flat for him to find when he got back from work. I didn't anticipate that his girlfriend would get there first!

'Another time, I accidentally locked him in my house when I went to work and had to send a courier round on a bike with my keys to break him out before anyone found him.

'The guilt was awful. Being together was too complicated so we decided to end it. But when I did turn my attention back to my boyfriend, I found he'd been having an affair with the secretary at the ad agency where he worked. Her calling card was orange fake tan, all over my crisp white bed linen.

'Even though I'd been unfaithful too, I was so hurt. We just weren't meant to be together, and had been struggling along for far too long. He wasn't "The One" after all, and it was time to end it for both our sakes.'

Many of us would struggle to admit it, but it is often the fear of being on your own that can leave you bailing at the last minute as you gear up to break up with someone. But often the sense of relief you feel once you do finally set the wheels in motion will tell you everything you need to know.

I even read recently that researchers in the US have discovered that splitting up with someone is a lot easier than you envisage it to be. Apparently, a group of volunteers were asked to imagine how they'd feel if they broke up with their partners.

When, at a later date, some participants did part company with their loved ones, they found they weren't nearly as devastated as they'd expected. Often the fear about the action you are considering is much worse than doing the deed itself.

Although the first few weeks after any break-up were

hellish, after a little while I'd always find myself feeling optimistic. It had been the same rite of passage with Jack, Tom and Adam.

With Jack, I was desperately sad, but eventually missed him less and less as I weaned myself off him. I also had the advantage of being away at university with different surroundings to keep my mind distracted.

In Tom's case, he and I spoke on the phone and I missed him badly, but I kept myself occupied meeting up with friends and even going on a few dates. Although we wanted to be friends, we agreed not to see each other for a while to enable us both to make progress. And as each day without Tom passed, I knew for certain we'd made the right decision. I wasn't lost without him. I really could cope on my own. For the first time in ages, I felt fantastically independent.

It was the same with Adam. Granted I'd spent an enormous amount of time and effort encouraging and helping him to pursue his dreams, but he'd helped me too. I realised that, rather than it all being a massive waste of time, I'd gained a wonderful friend.

In each case, I'd finally taken off the blinkers.

Amazingly, accepting that I hadn't been destined to marry each ex wasn't nearly as painful as I'd foreseen. My main priority was to continue to do my own thing and enjoy time to myself. Beyond that, when I felt ready, I also had the opportunity to seek out a man I thought I might end up with. It was exciting.

Chapter Six

Game Over

Around the time I split from Adam, I heard of numerous friends who had also broken up with long-term boyfriends. It was almost an epidemic.

Rightly or wrongly, the late 20s appeared to be provoking a 'grass is always greener' crisis for womankind.

While some of the break-ups had been as predictable as when day turns to night, others came like a bolt out of the blue. Even girls who had perfectly nice boyfriends were jumping ship.

These were ladies who'd been happy with their boyfriends, but were suddenly craving a last-minute gamble. As the approaching pinnacle of their 30th birthdays loomed down on them, they'd suddenly decided to go for broke, angling a selfish shot in the dark to see if they could net someone even better.

Unexpectedly, their unwitting boyfriends were sent packing and they were off hedging their bets on someone new. Previously, they'd waxed lyrical about how they believed their other halves to be 'The One', but now they were going solo in the hope that an even more One-like prize was out there, just waiting to be claimed.

The stakes were dangerously high, but feverishly they'd roll the dice, convinced that as time slipped through their fingers this was their last chance to hit the jackpot.

'I don't have any more time to waste!' they declared. 'I'm not prepared to invest all my time in someone who I'm not one hundred per cent convinced is "The One".'

So were my newly single friends suddenly throwing off their blinkers at last and chucking the chaps they'd been miserably putting up with for ages? Or were hasty decisions being made out of an age-related panic to snare an all-singing, all-dancing Stepford husband?

One confused girl couldn't even give a valid reason why she'd just finished with her boyfriend of eight years.

'I really don't know why,' she admitted. 'I just woke up one morning and thought I might find someone even better.'

The grass might have seemed greener. But were the risks really worth it?

If we are to believe romcoms featuring Jennifer Lopez and the soppy plots of many chick-lit books, there is arguably no need for girls to carry on coasting along with their dependable boyfriends. Instead they can snare an AMAZING man who has it ALL.

Spurred on by articles about biological clocks, you could almost hear the diva switch flicking on in their heads.

'Yes, Mr Average is very nice to me, but he snores, picks his toenails in bed and breaks wind,' they reasoned. 'He hogs the telly with his mind-numbing sport and scoffs at my dreams of learning Reiki. No, I won't take it, I'm unleashing my inner J-Lo. I won't compromise on my standards.'

So, feeling empowered, the soundtrack to *Maid in*

Manhattan or *The Wedding Planner* playing in their minds, they were ditching their boyfriends.

Then off they'd skip, in the risky belief that a chisel-jawed man who was loaded, witty, kind to little animals and had a body to die for and all the sincere compliments in the world tripping off his tongue was just around the corner.

Many women seemed to have a list of qualities that made their perfect man – but were they really examining the small print?

Unless you yourself are completely flawless, your body is perfection personified and you also happen to be the most thoughtful and amazing person in the world, then just how likely is it that this beautiful being will gravitate to you?

Years ago, I went on a date with a man who I believed ticked all of the right boxes. He was funny, handsome, family-orientated and was training to be a pediatrician (he wants to help sick children get better! SWOON!) but so intimidated was I by his perfection that I might as well have had 'DESPERATE' tattooed on my head. Inevitably, I felt so inferior in his presence that I could hardly speak.

That – and the slightly crazed look in my eye that may as well have flashed 'FUTURE HUSBAND ALERT! FUTURE HUSBAND ALERT!' – meant our brief courtship was always doomed to fail. He cancelled date two, so I never got to discover whether or not he deserved the ridiculous pedestal I'd propelled him onto. (You see, there's always a yin to the yang and in reality his number one hobby was probably taxidermy or something grim like that.)

I was interested to read a survey recently which suggested the man of a girl's dreams has the following credentials: he is tall, dark and handsome with blue eyes, drives a silver Mercedes, has a posh pad, a degree, hates football, is clean shaven, well-educated, has never been married, has no children and likes to eat out regularly.

However, hilariously, a similar survey listing what the average boyfriend in his mid-20s is actually like revealed that he never brings his girlfriend flowers, takes her out to dinner just once a month and buys his pants at Marks & Spencer.

Welcome to the real world, ladies.

Could it possibly be that our expectations are a tad unfair? One frustrated male complained to me that men are sick of being constantly told they don't live up to what women want.

'Girls want a tough, sensitive, funny, serious, playful, mature guy who will sweep them off their feet with spontaneous and romantic gestures but is also stable and responsible,' he listed, exasperated. 'So a guy has to prove he has this endless list of contradictory characteristics in two minutes in a crowded club? You expect the impossible!'

Another man suggested that perhaps the more pernickety ladyfolk should remember that the stark difference between the fantasy and the reality leads to disappointment the other way round too. The ideal lady is often a far cry from your bog-standard bird.

'In an ideal world, I want a girlfriend with the body of a glamour model, who's an amazing cook, a complete nympho, smart and fun to be with, who does my washing and keeps our home spotless,' he revealed.

'However, in reality my girlfriend is incredibly untidy, announces she's too tired for any action on school nights and forgets to shave her legs. But she's also loving, kind, funny and pretty, so she does have many of the qualities I've been looking for. In fact, she is pretty much perfect. I can overlook the rest.

'Perhaps women should cut us some slack and not expect the world. It's completely unrealistic.'

He had a point. Even when friends did meet seemingly perfect men within weeks of breaking up with their exes, nine times out of ten it wasn't long before the cracks began to show.

One friend admitted the biggest mistake of her life was canning her dependable boyfriend after becoming fixated with a work colleague.

She soon realised that everyone went through spells in relationships where things seemed a bit staid and unexciting, but rather than running away at the first sign of problems, it didn't hurt to try to solve things first.

The object of her lust was undeniably gorgeous and had a body to die for, but beyond these skin-deep attributes he had little to offer, as it soon transpired.

She began to go off him rapidly. She realised they had very little in common, and it especially annoyed her that he had absolutely no interest in current affairs. She also realised how two-faced he was with people – constantly being charming one minute and slagging them off behind their backs the next. She found herself missing her ex more and more.

Finally, she made the decision to break up with the himbo and reconcile with the boyfriend she'd given up so easily. But she was in for a shock. Her once faithful and devoted ex wasn't interested. He'd found himself a new girlfriend and had moved on. She'd had 'The One' all those years and now she'd lost him forever.

I watched a programme recently about a woman in her 40s who had yet to find Mr Right. She had a long tick list of traits her perfect man should have. He needed to be well travelled, a good dancer, have a full head of hair and not want children, to name just a few of her inflexible demands. She'd been looking for this suitable chap for 20 years, but still no one had made the grade. The problem was that the older she got, the fewer men there were to choose from.

Her family and friends went on the hunt for suitable suitors, but they were few and far between – it seemed all the best ones had already been snapped up. Finding an eligible bachelor to meet her needs was like finding a diamond in the rough.

I've heard this phenomenon dubbed 'Plenty More Fish in the Sea Fever' or 'Won't Settle Syndrome' and there's definitely something in it.

Do we girls, who are taught to aim high in our lives, careers and relationships, expect too much and cast off a man who ticks some of the boxes so we can resume an unlikely hunt for someone who ticks all?

There does seem to be a real danger with sticking rigidly to a list of what a potential partner should be like. Everyone has their flaws and if you instantly dismiss someone because he doesn't earn enough or has the wrong colour hair, who knows what you could be throwing away? There could be a whole host of glorious things about this man you are missing if you reject him straight away simply because he doesn't obviously meet your immediate requirements.

Equally, if you finish one relationship in pursuit of an impossible dream, then it is quite possible that you could end up alone.

An avuncular figure once gave me a great piece of advice. Talking about the wisdom he had acquired after many years of marriage, he said, 'There were always going to be offers, there would be temptations, there would be ups and downs, but you reach a point where you know this person in your life is someone uniquely special and you realise they can share with you the kind of companionship and love that no one else can come near to.'

But what happens when a boyfriend has seemed right for so long and then suddenly he isn't? Do you put it down to going through a bad patch, or is it time to blow the whistle? Only you can make that difficult decision and go with your gut instinct.

This was something I pondered when Adam and I first parted company. In so many ways he'd been perfect: we got on, we thought the world of each other and everyone always said what a nice couple we were.

But my gut feeling told me it had to end. I couldn't be swayed by fears that I'd never meet another nice man.

A friend reinforced my belief that sometimes, no matter how much you want a relationship to work, you have to give in in the face of unbridgeable differences and circumstances sooner or later.

'When I was eighteen, the girl I'd been dating for just

under a year and to whom I lost my virginity went off to uni, as did I,' he recalled.

'Despite being hundreds of miles apart, we were head-over-heels and continued the relationship for two years. There was a lot of train travel and a lot of lovely, lusty weekends followed by tearful, traumatic goodbyes. We both thought at the time that what we were doing was for the best and that we'd be together forever.

'Truth be told, the likelihood is that we were holding each other back socially and romantically, and I began to suspect this was the case. When she went to America for a gap year, I ended things because I thought it was time to move on.

'Absence certainly made the heart grow fonder while we were doing the long-distance thing. And when I went out to see her while she was in America, I was severely tempted to try for a reconciliation.'

A female friend revealed that she'd decided firmly that she could no longer be with her boyfriend because he'd been a bit too happy to sponge off her.

'I'd been supporting him for a long time and no longer respected him,' she says. He was studying for exams, so I paid for the rent and groceries for months and months and months, but the longer it went on, the more I started to dislike everything about him.

'I resented him for making me struggle. I couldn't buy new clothes and I couldn't go out for drinks with my work colleagues. Supporting him as well as myself meant there was no money for luxuries.

'I found I didn't fancy him any more. In fact, I almost pitied him. When you take on the role of "man of the house", you lose respect for the actual man of the house. Never mind all the equal rights crap, a woman wants to be looked after.'

Although there is always room for compromise and working at things, deep down you need to feel happy in a relationship – and sometimes taking the risk of starting again is the only way forward.

After my break-up with Adam, my resolve was boosted by a friend who recalled how she met 'The One' in the most unlikely of scenarios after splitting from a long-term love.

She was convinced she'd never find love again. Bereft, she spent many a night driving home from her job in Brighton, tears streaming down her face, listening to the saddest Portishead and Smiths tracks she could find.

Desperate for a distraction, she started seeing a man to whom she made it clear she was only interested in him for sex. But then one day he introduced her to his flatmate.

'It was love at first sight,' she said. 'Fireworks literally went off. I was gobsmacked. The first thing I thought was "Why am I not with you? You're perfect for me!"'

In a tactical move, she carried on seeing her Mr No-strings, purely so she could spend time with his flatmate.

'We got to know each other as friends and whenever I left their house, I couldn't wait to see him again,' she revealed. 'I finally realised he was too nice to ever make a move on me while I was dating his flatmate, and that my destiny was in my own hands. So I did something I'd never done before: propositioned a guy.

'We were sitting on his guitar amp at a house party when I turned to him and said, "I've got something to tell you, have you any idea what it is?"

'He said, "Yes, I think so," and that night we had a little kiss on the doorstep.'

She quickly ditched her Mr No-strings and got together with his flatmate. Ten years on, they are happily married.

'Like all couples, we've had our ups and downs, but basically we're meant to be together, so things have only got better between us,' she says.

'It proves that someone can come along when you least expect them to and hit you like a bolt of lightning. The spark between you can be instant and last a lifetime.'

Sometimes, of course, a break-up comes out the blue, with no third person to blame, no rhyme nor reason for it, leaving you completely winded. Unbeknown to you, you've been dating a closet commitment-phobe. Inexplicably it's all over, and it hurts like hell.

It's always a similar scenario with a runaway rogue.

You meet, swap numbers, you call/they call, you go out, you have fun and you start seeing each other. They compliment you, you go out dancing, you stay at theirs, they come round to yours, it's electric between the sheets, they lie in bed cuddling you in the morning, make you cups of tea, whisper sweet nothings in your ear and send you nice texts in between dates.

This scenario has been going on for a good three, four, five or even six months. Everything in your eyes is just perfect, you're excited, happy and smitten. When you meet up with your friends, you're grinning from ear to ear. They berate you for being nausea-inducing, but kindly agree he does sound perfect.

But then something terrible happens. One day, while

lying happily in his arms (you're nuzzling into his chest, he's stroking your hair), you utter one or more of the following sentences:

'Am I your girlfriend?'

'I really, really like you.'

'I think I'm falling in love with you.'

'Shall we go on a mini-break somewhere?'

'I'd really like to meet your family.'

Everything changes in a second. You feel his body bristle, you notice there's a tense tone in his voice and wonder why he's suddenly not staying the night after all. In the back of your mind there's a little voice telling you: 'Yikes, he doesn't like me any more.'

But common sense has to prevail. There's no reason for him to go cold. The last few months have been amazing. His mood must be down to tiredness.

Yet when he leaves, he's elusive about when your next date will be. A few hours pass and your tummy begins to churn. Where is the sweet text message he usually sends saying how much he enjoyed seeing you?

A day or two passes, but nothing. You're fraught, anxious and can't stop playing over the last date in your mind, wondering what went wrong. When you do finally see him, receive a text or speak to him on the phone, it's as if he's had a lobotomy. His voice is cold, zombie-like and, if you have met in person, he can't look you in the eye. He utters one of these sentences:

'I think you want more than I do.'

'I'm not ready to settle down.'

'I can't give you what you want.'

'I just need a few weeks to get my head together.'

'Hello?!' you want to shriek. 'One minute everything was fine, you were really into me, and now I've said one tiny little thing and you've had a freak-out? How does that work? What on earth is wrong with you?'

But instead you nod dejectedly, a silent tear rolling down your face as you realise that, to this man, you will never be 'girlfriend material'.

A friend of mine once dated a guy, and for three months he seemed smitten. He cooked for her, doted on her and even drunk-dialled her for half an hour during a boys' holiday to Thailand, telling her how much he liked her and missed her.

She mistakenly took this to mean he was really into her, so when he returned from his break she dropped her guard and declared her feelings for him. He dumped her a week later.

Another heartbroken lady revealed how her male friend was only too happy to sleep with her, but just could not fathom making the transition to boyfriend and girlfriend.

'I was sleeping with him for about nine months on a fairly regular basis,' she explained. 'We were best friends, got on really well, and every week or two we would get drunk and end up having great sex together.

'I absolutely adored him, but was a bit scared about broaching the topic of whether we could actually be together rather than just friends-who-shag. I suppose I just assumed he would ask me out if he wanted to, and as he hadn't, I kept quiet. Besides, it was better to have him in my bed on a regular basis than nothing at all.

'Finally, I cracked and, in a very drunken moment,

blurted out that I didn't see why we couldn't be together. I'll never forget the look of absolute astonishment on his face as he said, "What? You mean you fancy me?"

'He said he'd never realised that I had feelings for him and just thought I was happy with our arrangement. Clearly he had no understanding of the female brain at all.

'What I don't understand is how you can have a great friendship with a bloke, find each other physically attractive and have great sex and yet they don't want to go out with you. I mean, why not?'

Ask any man if he has been guilty of such behaviour and the majority will sadly admit that they have. One fellow I grilled admitted to dumping smitten girls the minute they asked for any kind of commitment.

Interestingly, he said that on most occasions the rot had set in long before they pushed for commitment. The commitment issue just happened to be the final nail in the coffin. The girls were actually dumped for a series of unknown crimes leading up to their demands to speed things up a notch.

Men, it seems, are happy to cruise along in a relationship that is going nowhere for a number of reasons, including an easy life, getting their rocks off and fear of being alone. What a bunch of yellow-bellied rotters.

Bizarrely, the crimes boys detailed that got girls canned were as trivial as laughing at their love interest's pyjamas, telling crap jokes incessantly, and – slightly weird this one – staring at their man while he slept.

A bad lad revealed that one unfortunate girl reminded him of his pet dog. 'Every time I throw a stick for my dog, she runs after it and brings it back, tail wagging, gazing up at me adoringly. The girl was the same. Where's the challenge in that?'

Another man told me he knew he was going to dump a girl the moment she leaned over in bed and puked into a pint glass. 'She was really ill,' he admitted. 'But I just couldn't move on from it.'

Oh Lord, help us all.

I know I claimed I wouldn't come over all judgmental, but here are a couple of things I do truly believe.

Firstly, no matter how much you like a man, don't be a sap. If a guy is giving you the runaround, don't put up with it. He'll lose respect for you and you will lose respect for yourself. It's easy to doubt yourself, but you mustn't. Not everyone in this world is compatible, so there's no point flogging a dead horse. Secondly, when a guy dumps you soon after you make your feelings clear, it is easy to regret 'putting them off' by wanting to move to the next level.

'If only I'd kept my stupid mouth shut,' you reason.

'Let's keep it casual. I can handle it!' you might beg.

No. No. NO.

When Ed (the chap I completely humiliated myself with – he of the tragic letter and phoning his mum) dumped me, I downed neat vodka and finally fell asleep in my housemate's bed after sobbing uncontrollably until the wee small hours.

The next day I cried all day at work and then when I got home that evening not even getting in the shower could stem the tears. I clambered out, still crying, and lay on the bathroom carpet, a snotty, shivering wreck, convinced I was having a breakdown.

But I did, eventually, get over it.

Once I'd got to my lowest point, the only way was up. It was horrific, but ultimately I'm glad I found out that his feelings weren't in sync with my own, because it meant I could cut my losses and move on.

In this situation you have to be strong and think, 'Thank God I did bring it up!' Can you imagine if you'd spent another six months with a man who had no intention of committing to you? So much better to find out now, don't you think?

If a guy did bite the bullet and end it, admitting it didn't feel right, in theory you'd respect him. But perhaps not if he went from devoted to uninterested seemingly over-night, as happened with one friend, Helen.

She had been with her man for a while and in her eyes everything was going very well – indeed, he'd fallen out of her bed with a big smile on his face just two days earlier.

So despite having great difficulty getting into central London, she eagerly rushed to see him when he suggested a date in Leicester Square. But when she'd battled through the crowds to meet him, his face was serious.

'I'm not in love with you after six months,' he told her coldly. 'I want to break up.'

'Actually, it was five months,' ranted my friend. 'He wouldn't even hug me afterwards. He drank water and I drank a large glass of red and headed home.

I was so mad because he chose that location, knowing I didn't drive and the two tube lines to my home were down. So it cost me £25 in cab fares to get to the neutral destination to meet him – all for the privilege of being dumped. He also knew I'd been working at an event until 3 a.m. the night before, so I was completely exhausted. His timing was utterly charming.'

But when one door closes, another one opens.

The following week at a party, Helen got talking to a dashing man who she has been dating ever since. 'As far as I am aware, the ex is still lonely and single,' she asserts with a smug smile.

So why do men woo, bed and then dump perfectly nice girls?

Thankfully, it is a complete myth that only the inadequate get dumped. Unless you are really deranged and scary, it's actually often more down to timing. It really is them, not you.

When I quizzed a number of men, the answer was almost unanimously the same: right girl, wrong time.

I sort of have a theory that the majority of women are open to finding love at any point, but the majority of men have a small window of time when they can be persuaded. You could be the most perfect potential partner in the world, but if he's not in the zone, then there is nothing you can do.

At a party recently, I got talking to an inebriated man, aged about 30, who was waxing lyrical about a girl he'd dated in his early 20s. 'She was perfect,' he said. 'She was clever, gorgeous and completely lovely, but I broke up with her.'

'Why?' I asked.

'Right girl, wrong time!' he confirmed. 'She'd already had a couple of serious relationships and she was ready to settle. It was my first serious relationship and I wasn't ready to commit. I wanted to experience life a bit more before putting all my eggs in one basket.'

As it happened, Ed claimed he dumped me because he had a very demanding job and routinely worked 12-hour days. 'I just don't have time for a girlfriend,' he'd said, even though I was prepared to fit round his work.

A month or so later, I heard that his work contract had ended and, rather pathetically, this news made me chortle to myself. I felt vindicated because I used to think that this sort of brush-off was a major cop-out, but perhaps men do genuinely think more methodically about timing?

It certainly seemed that way. During my research, the tales of break-ups for practical reasons came in thick and fast from men. Predictably, the need to play the field scored high too.

'When I left my university town, I broke up with a girl who was pretty much perfect,' one revealed. 'Until I met my wife, who is also perfect, my friends would often remind me of her.

'It was the timing thing though. She was a little older and wanted to settle down. I wanted to move to London and live the dream.'

Another said, 'I dumped the perfect girl because I was too immature to handle the fact that I'd met marrying material so soon. I was stupid for doing it, but I would probably have cheated on her in the long run because I hadn't sown my oats.'

One straight-talking husband even admitted that if he'd met his future wife five years earlier, things would have been very different.

'If I'm being brutally honest, it probably has every bit

as much to do with the timing as the girl,' he said candidly. 'We've all had points where we've walked away from a relationship and wondered if it may have gone the full distance had we been a little more patient. But had I met my wife five years earlier, I doubt we'd be together now because we just weren't ready to settle.'

Another common reason for breaking up with a perfectly nice girl is if she was, well, too nice.

'I dumped a girl who was very pretty and lovely and would do anything for me,' was another male confession. 'Why? I think it was because she allowed me to be too dominant. The very definition of that x-factor is someone who keeps you challenged, someone who has a mind of their own and someone who keeps on surprising you and making you laugh.'

WELCOME TO DUMPSVILLE: THE CHARGES

- 'One past girlfriend said that I reminded her of her father. Now that's just weird. Why would you say that? It exudes some sort of Freudian complex that I'm just not comfortable with.'
- 'It can take a while to identify a "clingy girl" and that is what I fear the most. One girl went crazy on me after three months. After a drunken night, she bombarded me with texts and missed calls asking where things were going. I had about twenty at the end of the night.'
- 'One girl I'd only been dating a month or so told me a

lot of terrible stuff about herself and kept me on the phone till 4 a.m. listing her truly harrowing past. It sounded like she'd had a shocking time, but she really wasn't my responsibility and I was better off out of it.'

- 'I went on a blind date with a stunning girl who spent the whole time talking about her parents' huge house and her uncle's yacht. It left me completely cold because she had no real personality of her own. In hindsight, I should have launched a charm offensive to land a free holiday on the yacht.'

- 'There was one girl who took me home when I was drunk and literally raped me. In the morning, she bizarrely took a picture of me as I was opening my eyes. Days later, she sent me a letter saying how head-over-heels she was and how she'd framed my photo and mounted it over her bed! I often wonder if the picture of me half asleep, dribble down my chin and fear in my eyes is still on the wall.'

And then there's the Domino Effect.

I thought I'd heard it all until recently some candid men revealed a whole new phenomenon in male dumping.

During a discussion about a girl they knew who'd been given the heave-ho, they divulged she had become a victim of what they dubbed 'the Domino Effect'.

Apparently it's rife: one man breaks free from the old ball and chain and the others follow in hot pursuit.

Essentially, it's caused by single-pal envy. Who wants a night in with the bird listening to her complaining about her bitchy boss and watching *Friends* re-runs when you can be out sinking beers, discussing footie and talking about weird science facts?

Apparently, like the commitment issue, the seed of doubt might already have been sown long before, but men, often being naturally cowardly, are not going to venture into Singledom unless they're backed up. The swines.

That was another reason I believed Ed fast-tracked me to a town called Heave-ho. On our first date, his best (tellingly single) mate turned up at the bar and although I didn't think it was that weird on that occasion, I did find it odd when he also appeared on our second date and phoned Ed constantly throughout the night of our third (including twice during our candlelit meal). I remember feeling more than a little peeved when Ed finally agreed we'd go and meet him down the pub. There clearly wasn't room for another person in that little love affair.

It seems to go back to my friend's theory from earlier.

Being loved up, getting married and having kids doesn't always come naturally for men and for a long time they believe it's their rite of passage to battle against it.

One girl sighed, 'Men, they fight us all the time. They want companionship, they want someone to look after them, they want security, they want all the things that women want, but what they don't want is for a woman to come along and spoil boys' club.

'They fear we are going to turn into their mothers and start telling them what time to be in and that they mustn't play with that boy because he is a bad influence.

'They don't trust us, so we have had to come up with all

these tricks and games and try to outsmart them, only to find out that in the end very few of them are actually worth the trouble!'

And after all that 'wedding fluffing', there's nothing worse than hearing your ex is engaged to 'The One' six months after you parted company.

A pal, Amelia, reveals how she broke up with an ex who appeared to be devastated for all of about five minutes before proposing to her 19-year-old replacement.

'I wasn't overly bothered about him getting a new girlfriend,' she says. 'But he could've at least made his mourning period a bit longer!

'When I met her, she looked a bit like Red Rum, so that made me feel a bit better. I haven't had a functional relationship since though – I think he cursed me.'

Another lass admits she was left shocked when the former love she'd always assumed she'd get back with got someone else pregnant.

'When I heard he was going to be a dad, I was stunned,' she reveals. 'The news devastated me. I knew that with a baby around we were never going to have the fairytale reunion I was hoping for in years to come.'

Being traded in for the love of your ex's life or discovering he's suddenly embracing fatherhood can really hurt. But there is a method to the madness.

As one man explained, when men come out of long relationships, the novelty of being single can wear thin very quickly. With time marching on, a man may suddenly decide to commit – and it's your sodding bad luck that you just missed the boat.

'Although we don't have the same body clocks as

women, lots of men also panic if they are single and over thirty,' he admitted. 'Playing the field is not as fun as you imagine. In fact, it's a horrible emotional battlefield, so after a few bloody experiences, you grab the nearest life-raft and get the hell out of Dodge.'

Another lad concurred: 'It makes no sense, but maybe a man just reaches a point when he's ready to settle. If he's proposing after six months, then he was probably stringing out the relationship before, even though he knew it was going nowhere.'

Sadly, another factor seemed to be that some men just didn't see their exes as marriage material, even after years of dedicated service.

'Chances are the original girlfriend got dumped because the guy was thinking about marriage and realised that she wasn't the one,' says one candid chap. 'Then he goes looking for a wife rather than a girlfriend, two very different things!'

THE CAD FILES

'When I was eighteen, I shagged two girls – who were close friends – on the same night.

'We were at a house party and the one I was sort of going out with, asked me to walk her home. We stopped en route and had a totally joyless, pointless shag on someone's front lawn. Then I went back to the house party and ended up sleeping with the hostess. It was equally crap, to be honest.

'The next day, the girl I'd been seeing came round to my house and we started having sex in my room. Halfway through she just pushed me off and said, "Do you think I don't know what you did last night?"

'Turns out she had spoken to the other girl, and this was some sort of bizarre revenge. Frankly, I was utterly relieved to be shot of her, as I wanted to get some A level revision done.

'I'm not particularly proud of it now, but I'm not ashamed of it either. Why did I do it? Because I'd spent most of my teenage years trying in vain to persuade various girls to give it up. I wasn't going to look any gift horses in the mouth.'

'I think most men have acted like cads at some point in their lives. Normally out of cowardice. At university, I once waited until a girlfriend had gone home for the summer holidays to break up with her over the phone. I should have done the decent thing and ended it much earlier – face-to-face – but I opted for the easiest way out.'

'My particular low point was penning a letter to my best mate asking whether I should dump my then girlfriend and go out with my housemate. I listed the pros and cons of both, which meant detailing all the current bird's downsides, including being really dull in bed. Then went out with housemate, while girlfriend went elsewhere.

'She came back early, wandered into my room and

found the letter ripping her personality to shreds. I came home hand-in-hand with my housemate to find she had fled in hysterical tears. Basically, I should have just dumped her, but was suffering from rare uncertainty. I eventually did and went off with the housemate.'

Of course, sometimes you find yourself mourning the death of a relationship where the man who finished with you really was a rotten egg.

During the relationship he bullied and belittled you, and even now, after tearing your heart from your chest and stamping on it, he's still baying for your blood. He doesn't want you, but he vindictively still wants you to want him.

I'd experienced this kind of manipulation first hand before, so was saddened to hear it had happened recently to a friend of mine.

She had been seeing a guy until he kindly broke up with her within weeks of saying he loved her. Despite having already done plenty of damage to her self-esteem, he couldn't leave it be.

He bombarded her with emails accusing her of ignoring him, only to accuse her of being stalkerish when she replied. His final pay off was the revelation he could hardly walk after a night of passion with another girl. She was so upset, she had to leave work for the day. This psychological torture continued for some time. As I said to her, she really was best out of it. What sort of happy, contented person behaves like that?

In years to come, she'll be very happy with someone else much more deserving, but he'll still be in the same pattern of warped, destructive behaviour – so let that be his punishment.

In an ideal world, when it's you who's been left broken-hearted, the person responsible should have the respect and compassion to leave you be. Often a clean break is the only way you can get over someone. But if the person who left you disconsolate is still in your face all the time, re-igniting your feelings for them, then it can be near impossible to get over them.

Instead there will always be a part of you hoping you can get back together. Every time you hear they're dating someone new, you'll feel physically sick and every time you see them you'll make an extra special effort with your outfit. In their company, you'll be the life and soul of the party, only to end up in tears at the end of the night, when they haven't pleaded with you to get back with them.

A friend, Kim, revealed: 'I've been pretending to be friends with my ex for four years and during that time I've slept with him probably a couple of times a year, written two full journals of misery about him and cried a river over him.'

About a year ago, Kim bumped into her ex at a black-tie ball. He'd told her he wasn't going, but then, as she was on her way, he texted to say he'd bought a ticket and would see her there.

'My stomach literally lurched and I spent the first half-hour in the toilets with the runs,' she admits. 'Probably because I was so churned up about him.

'I found out he had just finished with his girlfriend, so

of course we flirted all night. Eventually, we ended up shagging in a back alley on the way to another party, with my lovely ball dress hitched up around my waist. Classy.'

Afterwards, when Kim asked him if it was just a rebound, he shrugged and said, 'Probably' and once again she was inconsolable.

On another night, her ex phoned her four times and bombarded her with texts because he'd got it into his head that she was seeing a handsome friend of his and was wildly jealous.

'We had a drunken chat and agreed to meet up the next day,' she recalls. 'We hadn't met up for about six months and the last time we were due to see each other he'd made some crap excuse and bailed.

'The following day, I couldn't think of anything else, convinced this would be it and we would finally get back together. But then he texted to say he couldn't make it because he was really tired and wanted an early night.

'I realised I meant so little to him that he couldn't even make the effort to meet for one coffee. Yet he'd spent the night before worried about me getting together with his friend!'

It's all too easy to find yourself being led down the garden path by a man who chops and changes like the weather. And when you have been misled by mixed messages, sometimes you can find yourself being ditched before it's even begun!

You have to pity the poor lass who had obsessed over a chap for more than a year. After lots of flirty behaviour between them, he at last invited her round to his for a romantic dinner date.

After being promised a fancy home-cooked feast, she went out and bought a whole new outfit, then, after preening herself for hours, arrived on his doorstep grinning from ear-to-ear.

But when she stepped into the house, she was confused when he immediately introduced her to a male friend who was waiting eagerly in the front room. As the doorbell rang again and a very attractive girl waltzed in, followed by a cloud of perfume, the penny finally dropped. She was on a double date – but her date was her crush's friend.

The next few hours were torturous, as she watched her crush make eyes at the other girl and tried desperately to rebuff the advances of his friend. To add insult to injury, the main course contained mushrooms – her all-time worst food.

At the end of an awful evening, she was left alone in the front room with the friend who, to her horror, made a lunge. When she spurned him, he immediately guessed what was wrong.

'He's never going to fancy you,' he snarled. 'You should get over it.'

She still hasn't.

But while unrequited love hurts, nothing is worse than the bare-faced deceit of a man you've trusted.

It's undoubtedly every girl's nightmare to learn that her boyfriend has been secretly living a double life. No matter how happy you felt before, suddenly everything has changed forever and you are left with no choice but to dump him.

In a plot that could have been lifted from a soap opera, one friend, Jenny, discovered all was not what it seemed with the mature student she dated for two years at university.

'He was twenty-eight to my nineteen and I was completely besotted,' she recalls.

'He was from Holland, but although he had to go home regularly, I had no reason to doubt him. Every time his father came to visit him, we'd all go out for dinner and I'd go away for weekends with his dad and his step-mother. One big, happy family.'

But in the middle of term her man had to fly home, saying his mum was sick. He was away on and off for three months.

'We spoke every day,' she remembers. 'Then he came back a bit distracted and knackered. I just assumed it was the stress of his mum being ill.

'Things soon got back to normal, but to cut a long story short, one Sunday, a few months after he came back, I was cooking brunch and he was in the shower. His phone started ringing and it was a foreign number. Worried it might be to do with his mother, I thought I ought to answer it.'

The conversation Jenny then had went a bit like this:

Jenny: 'Hello, John's phone.'

Caller: 'Hi, is John there?'

Jenny: 'He's in the shower, I'm afraid. Can I take a message?'

Caller: 'Yes, sorry to disturb. It's Marianne, just letting him know that Talulla has been allowed out of hospital, is on antibiotics and has a check-up next week. Tell him not to worry, he doesn't need to fly back for it, the doctor says it's just a formality.'

Jenny: 'Gosh, I'm sorry and I don't mean to sound rude, but who is Talulla? I thought it was his mum who was ill?'

Caller: 'Not that I've heard. She lives in America. She gets married again next week, but I can't go, as Talulla can't fly. Talulla is our six-month-old daughter. You probably didn't realise she has a normal name, as John always calls her Bishey. It's sweet, isn't it?'

At that point the bathroom door opened

Jenny: 'Oh, hold on, MARIANNE, he's just out of the shower. I'll pass you over.'

There were then lots of hurried excuses as he terminated the call. Followed by lots of screaming and shouting, as Jenny wreaked revenge with the frying pan that had been conveniently heated up ready to fry the eggs. She then shoved him out the back door dressed in a mere bath towel.

'The next day, he was on the doorstep from 9 a.m. till midday with a huge hamper,' Jenny adds. 'Inside were four bottles of champagne, smoked salmon and caviar. Sorry, were we supposed to be celebrating the immaculate conception of his baby daughter?

'I eventually opened the door, and as he grovelled, offering the hamper, I took out the champagne, bottle by bottle, and very carefully dropped each one on the pavement. Next, I unwrapped the salmon and threw it at him and stamped on the hamper and tried to set fire to it with my bic lighter.

'Then I called the police and told them I was being harassed by my ex-boyfriend and he'd just gone crazy with a hamper. I swore I'd never speak to him again.'

But, to her misfortune, Jenny bumped into him four years later, while on a client lunch with three blokes.

'He actually had the cheek to send over champagne,' she fumes at the memory. 'He came over and started acting all attentive, wittering on about "the good old days".

'I was a bit pissed, so said, "As attractive and generous as you seem to be, I am afraid that I really don't know who you are. I think you have the wrong girl, but thanks for the champers anyway."

'That shut him up. Arse.'

While it's easy to claim the male species are snivelling, spineless wrong 'uns, guilty of the worst of courting crimes, it's never good to get sucked into the 'all men are bastards' mantra. Women can be just as guilty of some heinous misdemeanours.

A while ago, I bumped into an old friend at a party and listened as he happily told me how he'd proposed to his girlfriend and was over-the-moon. He emailed me again the other day to describe how, months before they were due to get married, he was dumped by his fiancée.

'I had just come back from a week away on business and pretty much the first thing she said as I walked through the door was that it was over,' he revealed.

'There was no warning, no arguments, no cooling-off period, so I was in total shock. She said there was no one else, but it wasn't long afterwards, that I discovered (by accident) that she was seeing someone else – a younger guy she met in some smarmy City bar.

'She then went off to Greece for a week and basically told me, on her return, that she'd got off with a bunch of guys. Classy.

'Meanwhile, she told her friends and family that "it just didn't feel right" and they all praised her bravery in not going ahead with it.

'She omitted the small detail that there was another bloke and that she'd gotten over the whole thing by turning into a one-woman snog-fest. I wonder what they'd have thought if they had the full story. Needless to say, I've not spoken to her since. Nice, huh?'

Subsequently, the poor lad had to move out of his lovely flat and embark on a series of disastrous house shares. In the end, he changed his job and went travelling to put it all behind him and is just beginning to rebuild his life.

For all the times men have slighted us, I think if we look deep inside ourselves then we will find many examples of our own offences against them.

One guilty pal recalls how she kissed her boyfriend's best friend on New Year's Eve in front of him as the clock struck midnight. Another reveals how she drunkenly snogged the younger brother of her heartbroken ex, not surprisingly sparking World War III in his household.

Also I do believe that all the weakest excuses, such as 'I'm just not looking for a relationship right now', 'I've got back with my ex' and 'I live too far away', have at some stage tripped off our tongues too.

There have been many times when I've ignored text messages or never called back just because it was, well, so much easier than admitting the truth to the person. But I've always managed to justify my actions by unmercifully picking holes in all the odd/weird/obsessed aspects of their characters, which of course meant they deserved the cold shoulder.

When I wracked my brains, I realised guiltily that I'd really had my moments of being a complete bitch to blokes.

One really sweet guy I dated for a few weeks could not have been nicer to me. I, on the other hand, was a nightmare from start to finish.

For our second date, he arranged to pick me up from my home to go to the cinema, but when some friends invited me to the pub in the afternoon, I texted instructing him to collect me from there instead. By the time he turned up to meet me, I was completely off my trolley.

In mitigation, I had asked a male friend to buy me single gin and tonics. It was only after I'd necked three that the big joker confessed he'd ordered me triple shots with each one – oh dear.

Swaying out the pub, I met my date, grinning like a Cheshire cat and twittering on inanely. But being really good-natured, he simply laughed it off and bought me a super-sized lemonade and popcorn to soak up the alcohol. To this day, I have no idea what film we saw. Indeed, by the time it ended I'd forgotten the start – which I delighted in telling him.

Obviously a glutton for punishment, Mr Nice asked to take me out again. But after another, slightly less drunken, date I decided that although Mr Nice was very pretty to look at, he was too quiet for me.

Then I fell ill with a nasty cold and although he sweetly texted me regularly, I couldn't really be bothered to arrange our next date. Instead, I was non-committal, unkindly leaving him hanging.

As soon as I was better, rather than call him, I went on

a wild night out with some friends. I was introduced to a very loud and charismatic guy who I flirted with all night and swapped numbers with. Yet I still didn't give Mr Nice any indication of whether we were on or off. He was proving to have the patience of a saint.

Of course, in an age-old scenario, as I relentlessly pursued the outrageous, funny and rapidly proving to be unsuitable Mr Charisma, I got given the runaround. There's a moral to this story.

Mr Nice wasn't a mug. After putting up with my flaky behaviour for several weeks, I heard he'd charmed someone else – the flatmate of a friend of mine.

'What?!' I raged.

Meanwhile, Mr Charisma had given me the brush-off.

Annoyed that I'd been left with egg on my face, I sunk to new depths, pathetically sending Mr Nice a sarcastic text wishing him well with his new lady.

Funnily enough, this all happened about four months before Adam and I started going out – and it was he who chastised me the most. Knowing Mr Nice, he sent me his straight-talking verdict on my childish behaviour.

'You're a knob,' he texted. Couldn't have put it better myself.

Chapter Seven

When Love Takes

a Sort of Break

*S*o you've uttered your final farewell, fought your last
battle over the TV remote control and watched as the
life slowly ebbed out of your relationship.

That's it. Dead as a dodo. You're back on Solo Street.
Or are you?

Occasionally, just when you think you've uttered your
final tearful goodbye, along comes a last-minute reprieve.
Suddenly the kiss of life has been administered to your
poor dying relationship. And there's a pulse!

Turns out your big dramatic break-up is actually a
mini-break-up. Now miracles can really happen.

Whatever the original reason for sounding the death
knell – be it non-stop arguing, an infidelity, lack of passion
or the fact that you just don't get to see each other –
sometimes the words 'it's over' can be a temporary thing.

Whether you are the dumpee or the dumper, it's only
natural to miss someone who previously shared so much
of your life. And sometimes the grieving process of a
break-up can be just too much to stomach.

Having the stamina to last the distance can be near impossible and before you know it your break-up has turned into a temporary glitch and you're charging back into your lover's welcoming arms.

When Adam and I had been together for 18 months, we split up for what would turn out to be a three-month mini-break-up. As I soon discovered, calling time on a romance when you still think the other party is your favourite person in the world can be unbearably heart-breaking.

Adam and I decided to part company because everything was feeling a little stale and predictable. We lived together, but were getting irritated with one another. We were basically taking each other for granted.

Adam slept uncomfortably on the sofa for a week, while I got lost in our big double bed that was now so unwelcoming without him.

Unable to cope with the pain and the weirdness of us still cohabiting but not really being together, I quickly arranged to move into the first one-bedroomed flat I could find. It was on the ground floor of an old Victorian house and, having never lived on my own before, I felt lonely and isolated.

As it turned out, the flat was riddled with damp and I had some unexpected lodgers – phantom nocturnal slugs that would crawl out in the middle of the night. In the morning I'd walk into the living room to see their glistening tracks in silvery swirls all over the carpet, but I could never find the slippery culprits.

In the bedroom there was a huge frosted single-glazed window next to my bed and the whole room was really badly insulated. At night it was so cold I would have to go to bed with two duvets, a woolly hat, a hoodie and two pairs of socks.

The chap who lived above me was a musician and loved to burn the midnight oil. I'd often be woken by the thumping sounds of Black Sabbath's 'Paranoid' vibrating through the ceiling.

And that wasn't the only thing disturbing my sleep. One night I awoke to an eerie roar. The mattress was shaking and the light fixture above me was rocking. The only explanation I could think of was that my flat was haunted.

After sitting on the loo trembling for a while, I reluctantly headed back to bed, my heart pounding, and lay there terrified, reciting the prayer 'Now I Lay Me Down to Sleep' over and over feverishly in my head.

It wasn't until the next morning when my mum called to say Birmingham had been hit by an earthquake in the night measuring 4.8 on the Richter scale that the ghostly goings-on fell into place.

Although I was relieved to hear it was a freak natural phenomenon rather than a ghostly apparition that had disturbed me from my slumber, I began to worry about my ability to go it alone.

My lowest point was when I managed to pull a muscle in my chest during an aqua aerobics class (yes, really, that ultra light, low-impact form of exercise). As the strain manifested itself, shooting pains seared through my chest. So naturally I lay in bed crying, convinced I was having a heart attack.

With no Adam to look after me, I eventually called

NHS Direct who, on hearing my symptoms, told me I needed to go to casualty straight away. Recklessly ignoring their advice that someone else should drive me, I clambered into my clapped-out Corsa and headed for the local A & E.

Once there, I was bundled into a curtained-off bay and fitted with apparatus to measure my heartbeat. Admittedly, I wasn't wearing a watch and I was feeling panicked, but it seemed like hours passed before anyone came back.

I lay on the hard bed trying to find something distracting to look at in the clinically white cubicle. As I tried to breathe calmly, inhaling the unsettling smell of antiseptic, I could hear a rowdy drunk being moved on by hospital security guards outside. Every time their raised voices seemed to sway closer to the curtain of my cubicle, I gripped the iron frame of the bed, wishing desperately Adam was with me.

Of course it was all a fuss over nothing. My heart was fine and I was instructed to take ibuprofen for the strain. But the whole episode made me realise how badly I was coping with my break-up.

Determined to forget Adam, I started dating someone else, but it didn't last long. When Adam admitted he was seeing someone too, I felt sick.

Because we had the same friends and still lived in the same area of Birmingham, it was impossible to avoid him. Adam's favourite watering hole was at the bottom of my road and it was impossible to sever all ties, as I kept running into him.

One night I went out to a party and ended up pulling a

friend of a friend I'd met a few times. He came back to mine and, although nothing happened apart from a drunken snog, it was the straw that finally broke the camel's back.

Lying in the bath, hungover and sobbing, I called Adam and told him I wanted to give it another go. He admitted that things had run their course with the girl he was seeing and he missed me too.

We met up the next day and tentatively started seeing each other again. Now with more thought for each other, we slipped back into a rewarding relationship and six months on we moved back in together. In the end we managed another two years before we broke up again. This time for good.

Although we split because of much the same problems, I never regretted our decision to get back together. Ultimately it didn't work out , but the first time I broke up with him it had been just too painful to keep up and I really wasn't ready for it to be over for good.

So when mini-break-ups occur, does absence generally make the heart grow fonder, or do all the old problems just reappear more intensely?

In our case, sadly, the same unsolvable issues returned, but we also went on to have some very good times together. He still remains a very dear friend to this day. So, in my mind, those extra couple of years were not a waste of time at all.

When it comes to discussing mini-break-ups, people are pretty divided in their opinions. Some believe that if a relationship has turned sour once, then the old problems will eventually creep back like cancer, poisoning your relationship once more. They believe that when you meet 'The One' there will never be problems of this magnitude.

But I beg to differ. Of course there will. It's just different. Nothing is ever completely perfect, however perfect you are for each other. But the mini-break-up haters disagree. The reason you are sweating it, they say, is because the person wasn't right for you in the first place. So never go back.

A male friend recalls how he got back with a girlfriend only to realise it was over as soon as they went out for their reconciliation dinner.

'As soon as we started speaking to each other it felt really staid,' he remembers.

'We thought we could just pick up where we left off, but immediately I got irritated that we'd had to go to a vegetarian place for her and there was nothing I liked on the menu! The date consisted of two hours of hell, with both of us trying to spark up random conversations. It didn't work.

'When we stumbled home that evening, I couldn't resist looking at her phone messages (I know, I know, cardinal sin, but we all do it!) and discovered the added bonus was that all her friends hated me.

'There were dozens of texts from her mates saying "You can do better", "He's not worth it" . . . Blah, blah, blah . . .

'I bloody well was worth it! So I woke her up and confronted her and next morning I moved back to my old place.'

While I felt sorry for him and did earnestly believe his protests of suitability, I could also sympathise with the friends who sent the texts. That's one of the worst perils of on-off relationships. Your friend finally discards that deadweight of a bloke, so naturally you assume the days of tongue-biting are over. Elated, you unleash the venom, launching into a no-holds-barred character assassination.

'I never really warmed to him,' you rant. 'I didn't like the way he talked down to you.'

You pause for a second, but decide you might as well let rip.

'He was always very arrogant, I thought,' you blurt out. 'I mean what's with all that bragging about how much everyone loves him at work?! Yeah, I find that hard to believe. And the stories about the time he got lost in the Lake District! Change the blinking record!'

All this time your friend is listening, kind of half nodding and with a slightly puzzled look on her face.

'It's a shame he didn't cark it from exposure really!' you then add for good measure. She looks a bit shocked. Is it sinking in? Does she agree? Hmmm. Best shut up then.

A week or so passes and she's been strangely quiet. There's a sinking feeling in the pit of your stomach. You just know she's back with the little toad. So the next time you see her, you're forced to retract everything and claim that at the time of your outburst you were just drunk or pre-menstrual or something.

Then she'll pretend she believes you and everything is cool, but really the shutters are closing. Now she knows you don't like him, she won't tell you anything, for fear you'll judge him *and* her! So Toad Features has finally come between you both. Won't he just love that?

However, you could just take a leaf out of the book of

a straight-talking Geordie pal who doesn't believe in mincing her words.

'When my friend got back with the snivelling, pathetic excuse for a human being she called her boyfriend, I told her I stood by all my previous comments,' she said matter-of-factly. 'I thought then that she deserved better and I still do. She's still with him now, but when he breaks her heart again, I'll be there for her.'

Well, thank the Lord that friends' odious long-term boyfriends are on the whole few and far between. Which is why most of the time you can openly and honestly support your female friends in their times of need. And if they're in the midst of a mini-break-up, they're about to get really needy.

As they desperately try to decode a mad scramble of different feelings and emotions in order to decide which route to take, they may end up crying on your shoulder. A lot. All the while infuriatingly veering between different levels of indecision.

They may even make barmy decisions you completely disagree with, but sometimes you just need to let these moments of temporary insanity run their course. There is a method to the madness.

As a friend astutely observed, when you split, the pressure dissipates and if you are still in touch with the old partner, all of the attraction and comfort is still there, just without the baggage.

He added: 'But, if your girlfriend is driving you nuts, then a week off won't change that and she will drive you nuts again at some stage.'

When I split from Tom, my boyfriend all through

university, for almost two years I found myself looking back wistfully, wondering if I'd made the biggest mistake of my life. These fears were only more heightened when Tom met 'The One' and once again I was left on the shelf.

The truth be told, we were never a perfect match. I was too high maintenance for him to stomach and he lacked patience, at times deliberately winding me up. Our arguments, on occasion, had been awful. But I wasn't able to truly acknowledge that I was better off without him until I'd found love with Adam.

I think it is often the case that you never really get over an ex until you fall for someone else. After all, it's not too easy to tell yourself you did the right thing when you are sitting curled up on the sofa alone on a Saturday, the traditional cosy couple's night in.

If things were always black and white with relationships, then breaking up would be easy. But in reality, with numerous shades of grey to colour your judgement, it's pretty normal to encounter that niggling feeling at the back of your mind questioning whether you've done the right thing. But this in turn can lead to going back again, and again, and again for more emotional make-ups, break-ups and tears before bedtime.

A male friend had a succession of splits with his girlfriend, each time agonising over his decision. He did love her, but couldn't live with her or without her.

She was so much a part of his life, but he felt she cramped his style with her strong views and her inability to let go and have fun. He asked her to meet him halfway, but there was no happy medium. Eventually, after yet another break-up, he had to go it alone, but it took a long, long time for him to get over her.

So often I've seen friends repeatedly go back to dysfunctional relationships, only to put themselves through the same torturous experiences over and over again.

Just when you think they are making a good recovery and have safely gone cold turkey for a while, a moment of madness comes over them and back they trot for another fix of misery.

Like sadists, they keep on running at full speed into a brick wall. They fall down, dust themselves off and do it all over again, until one day the only thing stopping them from repeating the same mistake is that they are too weary to get up.

Sadly, sometimes you need to get to your lowest point to finally see the wood for the trees.

A female friend recalls how she journeyed for miles to Edinburgh to give it yet another go with her troublesome ex-boyfriend, only for it to end in disaster.

'He flew me up as a grand romantic gesture and it all went horribly wrong very quickly when he sheepishly admitted he was seeing another girl,' she recollects.

'I was horrified and furious! Luckily my best friend also lived in Edinburgh so she picked me up, took me out and got me horrendously drunk.

'We then sat in her car outside his flat, eating cheese, chips and coleslaw and looking for signs of "movement", for a good twenty minutes before I came to my senses and said, "Can we go home, pass out and never tell anyone about this please?" '

Another friend admits to getting back with her ex-boyfriend just so she had a roof over her head.

'We lived together and a few days after we broke up, I totally got the fear,' she owns up.

'I honestly remember thinking, "If this is really it, I'll have to find somewhere else to live!" Lame, but I was young and lazy.'

But it's not all bad! There are mini-break-up success stories too. One chap I know first fell in love with his now wife at university. Over the years, they were as on/off as Joan Collins's marriages, but he always knew deep down that she was 'The One'. During their periods of separation, he dated other girls, but always went back to her. If anything, the 'off' episodes only strengthened his feelings for her. She was the benchmark girl, the goddess no other fling could ever live up to.

Likewise, when a friend split from her long-term boyfriend, I always thought they'd get back together. They'd been separated for a year when they finally decided to give it another shot. Instantly they were both so much happier and now say they feel so much stronger for it.

Having originally met at work, at first they didn't really put much thought into how working, living and sleeping together might affect them. In fact, in the beginning it was just lots of fun – sneaky looks across the office and counting down the hours until they could fall into each other's arms.

But, as both were workaholics, their jobs began to take over.

'In the end, we were just getting up, working together, coming home, talking about or doing work, going to bed but not having sex,' the girl admits.

'We also began arguing loads, and I cried most days and thought I was going crazy. When he said he wanted to split up, I was devastated. I loved him so much, but our relationship seemed impossible.'

Working together as exes was a nightmare, but as the months went on my friend got strong because she had to. She knew her former boyfriend was dating other people, which made her feel physically sick, but every day she hid her torment from her colleagues. She then embarked on a wild fling with a total cad, which, although disastrous, was just what she needed to distract her.

But she and her ex never fully let go. They remained on friendly terms throughout it all and every now and then, they would fall back into bed together. When the passion subsided, my friend found these trysts agonising. Afterwards, she was left lonely and confused.

So after yet another fling with her ex, she was relieved to go on holiday to South Africa. She pinpointed the moment she stepped on the plane as the time to begin to forge a new future for herself. Only problem was, she began to miss her ex terribly while she was away.

'I was kicking myself for being so weak,' she says, 'but before I came home, I called him. He sounded so pleased to hear from me and we both started crying and asking each other what we were going to do.

'When I flew back home, he met me, and we didn't really say a great deal about it, we just kind of started seeing each other. This time, we put a lot more effort into doing our own things and seeing each other one night a week and at weekends. It made our working relationship much better and we are stronger than ever a year on.'

So mini-break-ups (or even lengthy ones) can help put things into a much clearer perspective. Indeed, as well as convincing you that Mr Right was under your nose all along, they can also give you the clarity to end things for good.

When Tom and I left university, we had a kind of unspoken mini-break-up. Off we departed to take up demanding jobs in different cities. But although we both knew it was the beginning of the end, neither of us acknowledged that fact. Instead, the truth remained unspoken. We both knew the score. We were hanging on a little while longer, being each other's back-up. We were apart, but had the security of not having publicly declared so.

It was surprisingly easy.

Although we missed seeing each other every day, we didn't miss the arguments and sulky silences. Our relationship hung by a thread as we met up for fleeting weekend visits every month or so.

For months we were stuck in limbo. Going out, but not really going out, but neither of us acknowledging that fact. I knew deep down that Tom would be seeing other people and I also went on a few dates.

Psychologically, I guess, we were both dipping in our toes and testing the water before wading in gently, rather than enduring the sudden shock of hurtling off a diving-board into icy-cold water. When The End finally came in an emotional phone call, it was upsetting but bearable – by then we were both well used to the water temperature.

As break-ups have come and gone over the years, I've come to the realisation that it's very easy to take people for granted and it's naive to think that a relationship is always going to be perfect. You'll always have ups and downs and if you constantly bail at the first sign of trouble, then perhaps you are sabotaging your own chance of happiness.

Indeed, one chap who broke up with his girlfriend about a year into their relationship reveals that parting only made him realise how much he wanted to be with her.

'In that way it was good,' he admits. 'However, it was also incredibly horrible and painful and it took several years to really put it behind us. So tread carefully.'

In a happy ending, after overcoming all their emotional obstacles, they are now married, blissfully happy and realistic about love.

Another friend revealed she and her future husband decided to have a two-month break from the day to day drama of their relationship to focus on whether or not they wanted to spend the rest of their lives together. The rules they laid down were one weekly phone call and no seeing anyone else (including snogging), and it did them the world of good.

'We were really young and he had five years of navy service ahead of him, meaning we'd be long-distance for much of it,' she explains. 'We needed time and space to see if the hardship was worth it. Time apart made us see that we did have something special that was worth the hardship of long-distance. We got married after being together for seven years, so it all worked out for the best.'

It was a canny, and admittedly brave, move on her part to risk going for a break and laying down the rules.

Sometimes a mini-break-up can actually do more harm than good if people have different agendas, particularly if one person thinks it's an excuse to go out and pull while the other uses the time to get their head together and work out their feelings.

As anyone who has watched that infamous *Friends* episode where Ross and Rachel are 'on a break' will know, if the rules aren't spelt out, terrible things can happen!

'WE'RE ON A BREAK': THE RULES

1. Give it a time limit. Give yourselves a month or two to work out whether you're better off with or without each other and to get some perspective.
2. Don't change your whole lifestyle when you break up. If you're suddenly going out six nights a week, it's not really a good indication of whether you'll be better off that way in the long run. You can't keep that up.
3. Be honest. There's no point lying at this stage; you both need to know why it's happening and what you want to happen at the end of it.
4. Someone has to make the first move. If you realise you want to be together – or not – you have to say so, even if you're the one who caused the break-up in the first place.
5. Be prepared to grovel if you were the one to finish things. You'll probably be kept waiting a while as punishment and if you do get back together, you'll then be constantly questioned about whether you are having second thoughts.
6. Don't be too hard on yourselves. Just because you had a break doesn't mean the relationship is tainted. You really can wipe the slate clean.

When Adam and I had our mini-break-up, one of the hardest things to stomach was not the other girl he dated, but the news that he'd pulled one of his female friends, who seemed to be his between-girlfriends stand-in of choice.

Although they clearly didn't want to go out with each other, I knew they'd had 'moments' on and off during the time they'd known each other. It had happened before and it was happening again. When we got back together how could I not be paranoid about their 'special' arrangement?

In a similar scenario, another friend revealed her boyfriend kissed a girl they both worked with, who'd clearly had a crush for years, while they were on a break. Although they weren't together at the time, in her mind it was on a par with cheating, not to mention the public humiliation of people at work knowing. She didn't forgive him for a good while and there was a lot of grovelling.

As I said before, no relationship or marriage is without its highs and lows, so perhaps it's best to press the pause button before you abandon all thoughts of your dearest and head off to pull someone else.

Arguments can often be resolved almost as quickly as they flare up and a bit of bickering is perfectly normal – it's the ones who don't fight that you need to watch.

In fact, I'm always a little bit suspicious of couples who boast, 'Oh, we've never had a cross word.' Either they are very boring or complete liars and, strangely, according to my mother's mantra, these are the couples most likely to split up.

'Those that openly have a good row and sort out their differences are often the happiest,' she asserts. 'How often do you think someone has the perfect marriage, only to discover they are divorcing?'

Recently, after a series of silly bust-ups with The Beau (all quickly resolved and forgotten I might add) that ranged from who would do the washing up to the fact that I sometimes crack my elbow in bed (I know, it's gross), I brought him home a newspaper article I'd found.

It claimed that having a blazing row with your partner could help you live longer. Apparently, husbands and wives who suppressed their anger were likely to die earlier, while those who let rip were better off in the long run. Vocalising your grievances, no matter how explosively, cleared the air and was much better than bottling up tension.

The Beau read the article and rolled his eyes, but didn't say a word (probably to avoid another argument).

Of course, a few days later we were quarrelling again, after The Beau went AWOL on a night out when he was supposed to be staying at mine. His phone battery was dead and I didn't sleep a wink as all sorts of awful scenarios raced through my mind: The Beau getting so drunk he'd passed out in the gutter or being beaten to a pulp by hoodies who'd nicked his MP3 player. I tried not to be neurotic, but although 99 per cent of my common sense told me he'd be fine, a nagging one per cent of doubt was enough to make me crazy.

By the time he crawled in at 2 a.m., I was fraught, but also so relieved to see him that I didn't have the heart to reprimand him. That is until the next morning, when I deprived him of his usual cup of tea and deliberately switched the light on and banged around to disturb him from his heavy post-session slumber. I kept up the cold-shoulder treatment until after lunch and a few apologetic text messages, but then, of course, forgave him – until next time.

It is dramas such as this, when regrettably played out in front of some of our closest friends, that keep them amused. Indeed, if I were asked to describe most of our spats in three words, I'd choose trivial, ridiculous and, er, trivial.

'I listen and you both get the wrong end of the stick,' a mutual friend laughed. 'Sometimes I want to bash your heads together!'

'I can always tell if you're cross with him on the phone because you get "the tone", where you sound like a teacher telling off a naughty child, before hanging up,' she added. 'You do it when you're telling off friends for being silly too.'

As I blushed, she kindly added that a lot of her other female friends do the same thing with their boyfriends. And, thankfully, there were a lot worse examples than The Beau and I.

'I once went for dinner with some friends who had had a fight just before I met them,' she revealed. 'They then threw snippy comments at each other throughout the meal and whinged at me about the other one whenever the other went to the loo! Note to friends: this is not the way to make people feel included!'

But, anyway, we digress. Back to that no man's land that is the mini-break-up.

Here's a notable lesson for the more demanding ladies among us (and yes, that includes me). Sometimes, when the whistle blows and you've been the dominant one in the relationship, you might assume you'll get extra time in the form of a mini-break-up to sort things out. However, to your bewilderment, your long-suffering partner may have decided on a permanent transfer, leaving you reeling at the own goal you've just netted.

One girl had a fantastic career, lots of friends and a real party lifestyle. Although she lived with her fella of three years in her swanky city pad, he was pretty much an afterthought.

Eventually, after being overlooked for one final time, the poor chap decided he'd had enough and told her he was leaving. Because she'd always been able to walk all over him and he'd pretty much done whatever he was told, she simply shrugged off his words.

He moved out, but still she thought he'd be back for his dinner, back for *Corrie*, back for Christmas . . .

Suddenly the penny dropped. He wasn't coming back at all.

Her world fell apart as she realised that she hadn't exactly been marriage material. Instead, he'd gone looking for the real deal. He moved away and she even drove hundreds of miles to his new home to beg him to come back to her, but he wasn't having any of it.

Newly single, the heartbroken girl was lavished with male attention, but just wasn't interested. Instead she had a complete crisis, quit her high-flying job and decided she was going travelling in the hope that he'd see she was a reformed character.

But then, about eight months later, she had to attend a mutual friend's wedding. When she turned up – horror of horrors – he was there with a fiancée in tow. All those years she'd taken him for granted and now all hope was lost.

Likewise, an interesting pattern emerged with my quiet friend Jane, where each relationship ended in tears (hers). A succession of boys ditched her, whereupon she eventually moved on, only to discover the original boyfriend desperately wanted her back. It turned out she had been their quiet support system and now they were like ships without an anchor.

Although she fleetingly went back on occasions, she soon discovered she was over them and enjoyed the triumph of being in charge of the situation. It seems that often you don't miss the water until the well has run dry.

So why do all these different types of mini-breaks-ups keep happening?

Usually there is a serious problem or destructive elements smouldering under the surface, which regularly erupt and cause arguments.

If you are always the underdog in the relationship, it might not seem worth pursuing. It's not good if you feel undermined and unloved when you need to feel special and valued.

For many couples, money issues can cause serious strains on a relationship, particularly in a live-in situation. If one person squanders their wages while the other works hard to pay the rent, it can be a recipe for disaster and resentment.

While opposites attract you also need some common ground. If you like to dance all night and your man is happy with a book and his slippers, you may have a problem and end up passing like ships in the night.

But even if you are spending loads of time with your lover, nobody likes a control freak. If your partner constantly tells you how to live your life, then no matter how many times you go back to each other, there will always be trouble.

If you find yourself criticising endlessly, then perhaps it's time not just for another mini-break-up, but to actually move on. On the other hand, even if you don't constantly complain, but are permanently irritated by the tone of your other half's voice or the way they slurp as they eat their cornflakes, then things are not great.

And finally, of course, there is the ultimate problem of lies and deception breaking up your happy home.

Lying or cheating on the part of your partner can naturally leave you doubting them and if ultimately you can't trust a person, you could be wasting part of your life by hanging in there expecting changes. In fact, the hardest decision on whether to break-up or mini-break-up is when you discover that a third person is involved.

One friend's world fell apart when, suspicious of her long-term boyfriend's behaviour, she followed him to Fulham Broadway Station. Watching from a safe distance, she witnessed her man engaging in an illicit meeting at the top of the escalators.

She later stalked them to his new girlfriend's flat, before finally collaring the cheating rat and bellowing seven shades of abuse at his floozy. She left with an overpowering temptation to fling a brick through her bedroom window, but sanity prevailed, as she did not fancy a stretch in Holloway.

Although he later tried to make up with her, she knew she could not trust him. Good job too – he eventually married the trollop and disappeared to Canada.

During a heated debate, a pal once raised an interesting infidelity theory. As some upstanding individuals in our group got very judgmental about one girl's decision to continue seeing a guy who already had a girlfriend, she made the following point: 'Most people have experienced each side of the cheating triangle at some time,' she mused. 'Whether you have cheated on your partner, gone after someone who isn't for the taking or been cheated on, you should be careful not to judge.'

Infidelity is always a highly emotive subject. If you've been cheated on, it's absolutely horrible. The thought of the person you love sharing intimate contact with another person is one of the most sickening feelings in the world.

Then there's what to do. Do you finish with them for good? Do you take them back? Do you leave them to stew for a while? What if they're leaving you for the other person?

It can often take iron resolve on both sides to get things back on track again and even then all sorts of destructive scenarios can crop up.

I know of one man who was so badly burnt by a cheating ex-girlfriend that he saw no point in being faithful after that. 'Why wait to get hurt?' he reasoned. So, sadly, for a while he didn't think twice about infidelity – that is until he'd got it out his system and met the right woman. Now he wouldn't even think about straying, so 'once a cheat always a cheat' isn't necessarily true.

Unless you are one of those disturbing people who are

able to justify their actions to the extent that they feel no remorse, then if you cheat, you are likely to feel wracked with guilt about the unsuspecting person you've betrayed.

As you agonise over your romantic future, the grim reality of your actions is likely to keep you awake at night, hating yourself for being so disloyal and weak. On the other hand, if you decide to confess to your crime, then watching the sheer misery you have just inflicted on someone who cares deeply for you should be enough to put you off being unfaithful for life.

It's also obvious that how you treat a person could shape them, relationship-wise, for the future. Psychologically, the fallout from your little bombshell could make them suspicious, unhappy and jealous for many years to come.

Having discussed the urge to stray at length with people, it seems that infidelity occurs for many reasons, including boredom, feelings of being neglected, too much alcohol or maybe because deep down you know the relationship is already over.

At times everyone feels restless in relationships, but being with someone long term isn't a ride on a permanent love train; instead, it veers off like a rollercoaster. There are heady highs and gloomy descents. But as you travel through the low points, most likely there'll be another exhilarating twist round the corner. So perhaps it's best to resist the opportunity to bail at the first hurdle.

When there's someone else paying you attention, it's easy to magnify the object of your temptation to a God-like status. But this utopian vision is probably best left as just that — the reality rarely lives up to the fantasy.

A friend detailed how from the age of 14 she believed she was head-over-heels with a lifeguard, a few years older than her, at her local leisure centre. She constantly went swimming or to aerobics in the hope of catching a glimpse of him.

When she started university some years later, she bumped into him and was delighted when he showed an interest in her as well. This even developed to a few one-night stands, but the circumstances were never right for them to get together.

Still, he was never far from her thoughts. Once she'd graduated, they arranged to go on a date, but to her disappointment he didn't turn up. That night she met the man she was to date for the next four years. When they broke up, lo and behold, she bumped into her lifeguard once more.

But something about her crush was different, or, more to the point, exactly the same. While over the years she had matured, the man she thought she'd always obsess over was still exactly the same – hideously drunk and being blokey with his mates. In an instant she realised she'd outgrown her crush.

As much as I love to read 'long-lost love' stories, I think my friend's admission proves it's best not to get too carried away with your romantic aspirations.

At work recently, I was editing a story about a couple that had started courting aged 16, only to separate and marry other people. Neither of their marriages lasted and over the years, as trials and tribulations came and went, they always wondered about the great love they'd lost.

Finally, 60 years later, they were reunited and married.

It was the perfect love story – it had tragedy, an enduring love that time never forgot and a happy ending.

'This story is making me cry,' I gushed to my workmates, flapping my hands in front of my eyes as they rolled theirs.

I am an absolute sucker for a soppy story. When it comes to films, give me some sentimental pap any day of the week. While film critics were generally not that enamoured with the Kirsten Dunst and Paul Bettany movie *Wimbledon*, I loved it. I even have it on DVD. (Possibly, I may also be the first person in the world to admit that Mariah Carey's howler, *Glitter*, left me a tiny bit choked.)

But the main reason I loved my wrinkly love story so much was because it had that element of 'the one that got away'. Every girl has one: a chap who the dreamer in you has decided that, at a different time, in a different place, would have been perfect for you. You would have been together forever, probably doing lots of charity work and raising a cute 'rainbow' family like Brad and Angelina.

However, I was alarmed to read some astonishing statistics recently that said that almost twice as many women as men wished they'd married someone else. Apparently, more than one in five married women (22 per cent) said that if they could have their lot again they would change their husbands.(Bradford & Bingley commissioned the survey of over 35s, where 1,250 men and women were asked to name their biggest regrets.)

How very depressing. Could it be that these unsatisfied women were still hankering over 'the one that got away'? The thing is, if they did actually leave their husbands and pursue the sweethearts they'd always wondered about (assuming that they could actually find these long-lost loves and that they'd be on the market), what would the end result really be? Would there be a passionate reunion with a hunky Cary Grant type who would be ready to whisk them off for the love affair of the century?

Or would they find an ageing, more weathered version of the boy they used to know, with just as many annoying habits as the poor abandoned husband and a whole host of shattered dreams? I'd hazard a guess that in 95 per cent of instances it would be the latter.

A couple of years ago, a friend was left completely devastated when her father walked out on her mother after 30 years of marriage. His head was turned by a younger woman at work, but it was only after he'd left his wife, hurt his children and left a trail of heartache in his wake that he realised the grass wasn't greener. But it was too late to go back. He is now facing up to the reality that he made a massive mistake which just cannot be undone.

I blame this reckless behaviour on Romeo and Juliet Syndrome. When it's clandestine and you're snatching stolen moments, it's easy to see yourselves as two star-crossed lovers risking everything to be together.

However, once you *are* together, will that passion fade? It's quite likely that the enormous sacrifices you've made to pursue the affair will leave you feeling pressurised to make it work. Can you really withstand that pressure, not to mention the fallout and criticism from the people you hurt and disappointed to get together?

Going back to the infidelity triangle, I've been cheated on for definite once and there were other occasions when I suspected as much.

One boyfriend had mystery scratch marks on his back, but couldn't offer a plausible explanation. Another was spotted holding hands with a girl by a friend, but denied all knowledge. Frustratingly, without any hard evidence or admissions – despite some FBI-style grilling – I had no choice but to give them the benefit of the doubt.

They didn't give me any reason to suspect them further, so I had to let it go. The problem was that without suddenly developing mind-reading skills or humiliating myself with lie detector tests on a trashy talk show, how would I ever know? In all honesty, I'm not really sure how I would have reacted if my worst fears had come to fruition. I would have gone to pieces, I imagine.

When one partner is playing away, things can get very ugly. It takes a strong woman to dismiss all the desperate appeals of a caught-out boyfriend and move on. However, I did hear the most amazing revenge story from one woman scorned. It is a tale that will surely deter even the most philandering of men from straying.

On discovering that her boyfriend was playing away, the apoplectic miss didn't sit down and weep. Instead, she went round to his home, let herself in and furiously trashed the place.

After pulling down all her love rat's wall-to-wall shelving and smashing his beloved stereo, she then let down his tyres. Then she called his mum and told her exactly what he'd been up to and why she wouldn't be able to go on that year's family holiday.

Next she paid a visit to her love rival's home and smacked the little trollop in the face. At this point, you'd think it was a job well done, but, oh no, there was more to come.

Keeping a focused mind, she set about tracking down the girl's unsuspecting boyfriend. Knowing that he worked as a chemist, she went to the public library and painstakingly looked up pharmacies in the area, calling them all until she found him and revealed just what his girlfriend had been up to.

Explaining her wrath, she said: 'It felt brilliant and cathartic and I would recommend it to anyone in the same situation. The weirdest bit was that despite this totally unhinged behaviour, the ex still wanted me back and sent letters, emails and jewellery. I told him where to go.'

While it can be pretty counterproductive to pry into your fella's affairs, sometimes a little bit of snooping can save you from a lot of heartache. One friend checked out her new chap's Facebook profile, quickly discovered he was also dating someone else and was able to bin him before she fell too deeply.

If you have been cheated on but decide to give it another go, finding forgiveness can be easier said than done. It's all down to whether you can regain the trust.

A straight-talking pal, Fiona, once had a row with her best friend, only to go to a party and discover her in bed with her boyfriend. She stood there, speechless, looking at two of the people she cared about most in the world writhing around naked, before running out the house.

The worst thing of all is that while the boyfriend begged for her forgiveness, the former friend, who had clearly bedded her half-cut bloke to get back at her for the earlier argument, remained unrepentant. Instead, she was completely bitchy and smug about the whole thing, until she got a deserved belt round the chops.

Although Fiona eventually allowed the boyfriend to worm his way back into her affections, unsurprisingly it was never quite the same and, unable to trust him, she soon broke it off for good.

If you are going to try to rebuild a relationship following an infidelity, then two things have to happen: one, the cheater has to prove they are worthy of their partner's trust, and two, the wronged party has to eventually stop holding onto the hurt and using it as ammunition in arguments. Only then can you really move forward and be happy again.

Which brings me to whether or not you can be friends with an ex.

Obviously, if you've been badly burnt, it's difficult to remain friends if you are angry, heart-broken and want to kill his new girlfriend. It will always be difficult to remain friends if one person is bereft, but sometimes it does seem a shame to discard such a strong friendship while keeping others going with less important people.

But at the other end of the scale, things can be surprisingly civilised. Given a decent interval of time and with both sides willing, friendship can be re-kindled (new partners permitting, of course!).

One girl reveals how her ex-boyfriend married her best friend and she remained friendly with them both, even becoming godmother to their first-born. Her relationship with the guy had truly run its course, and there were no real regrets. In fact, she was very happy for them.

It often all depends on whether the dumper has

dumped the dumpee with dignity and kindness. You will be loath to be friendly with someone who has left you feeling angry and trampled on. But often someone who has shared your life for months or years is the perfect listener when you have a problem. After all, they know you inside out, the good and the bad, and can often give you advice you would not accept from anyone else.

But there are limits. When I first started seeing Tom, I had framed photos of me with my ex-boyfriend Jack up on the wall of my university accommodation. When he asked me to remove them, I stubbornly refused, claiming we were still good friends so I could hang his photos up if I wanted.

It was only when Tom's dad came to visit and asked who the guy in the picture was – he thought it could be my brother – that I found myself acutely embarrassed. I really should have known better.

But it can be tricky to know where to draw the line. Often you've formed close bonds with members of your ex's family and want to stay in touch, but how much is too much? Do you now have to do this by stealth, to avoid upsetting his new bit of crumpet?

A friend recently ranted that she wasn't allowed to her ex's wedding as it would 'ruin the bride's day', but then again, if the shoe was on the other foot, she might feel just the same.

Another girl who got married last year has all her exes on her Facebook friends' list and regularly communicates with them. When one former love discovered that her mum was ill, he turned up to visit while the girl and her husband were there! Her spouse went ballistic and she thought he was being ridiculous – until his ex-fiancée got in touch and the tables were turned.

But then we've all read too many 'reunited after 20 years apart' stories, haven't we? No one really likes an ex on the scene. So although it's nice to be friendly with your ex, your (and their) new relationship should really come first.

I'm well aware that I've been scathing about territorial female friends who make life difficult for the new girlfriend. Yet, in the past, I myself have committed some howlers, including being far too needy with an ex-boyfriend.

A good while after Adam and I parted company, the environmentalist Steve Irwin was killed by a sting-ray. This news upset me greatly. I was a big Steve fan. I'd even been to his Australia Zoo in Queensland and marvelled at the man himself in action. So when I woke up one tragic morning and saw that Steve had died, I was distraught.

I called The Beau, but his mobile was switched off, so in a moment of impulse, I decided to call Adam, who shared my Irwin obsession. When he answered the phone, I immediately started sobbing.

'What's wrong, babe?' he asked, concerned.

'Steve Irwin died,' I howled.

It was only as Adam tried his best to comfort me over the phone that I realised how sleepy he sounded.

'Are you in bed?' I asked, sniffing.

'Yeah, I'm at Molly's,' he said. Suddenly I pulled myself together.

Apologising profusely, I hung up. I was mortified.

Visions of him snuggled up in bed with his girlfriend

flashed through my mind. What on earth must Molly think? What sort of psycho ex calls your boyfriend at 7.30 a.m., when you're still in bed, crying over a man she's never met? I instantly hated myself.

I always joke with The Beau that Life BC (Before Charlotte) does not exist. But here I was crowbarring myself into Adam's new girlfriend's bedroom at stupid o'clock in the morning.

I don't really know why I did it. A long while before then I'd accepted that Adam and I hadn't worked out for many good reasons and, while we were able to be good friends, he no longer belonged to me.

And I didn't belong to him either. I was content out of the relationship and we were both very happy with other people. I had to leave him be.

Now I was with The Beau, I wasn't really in a position to phone Adam up crying about weird celebrity deaths and sharing shock at headlines and life events. That was now The Beau's role. Lucky old Beau.

Chapter Eight

Starting Again

When Adam and I broke up for good, I suddenly found myself out on the street.

Not that he chucked me out, but living with my ex-boyfriend – echoing the events of two years previously when we had taken a break – was now completely untenable. It hurt too much, so I couldn't stay with him for a minute longer.

Plus, let's be honest, who splits with their bloke then carries on doing the weekly shop with him?

So, as quickly as possible, I began to pile my belongings into boxes and Adam helped me load them into my car. I kept it together until halfway through this process, when Adam's best friend and his girlfriend arrived to meet him for lunch.

Suddenly the demise of our relationship was out there for all to see. All I needed was a loudhailer: 'Roll up, roll up! My broken heart is being publicly flogged!'

'Look!' I wanted to bellow manically. 'What a waste of three and a half years of my life! It's over! We're finished! I've got to start all over again! And, best of all, you're here to share my downfall.'

Of course, Adam's friends weren't there to laugh at me. Actually, they looked sad, sympathetic and embarrassed to be there. I'm sure they felt as awkward as I did. But seeing them completely floored me.

So, like the Littlest Hobo, I packed up my stuff and set off to a new life.

Thankfully, after a couple of nights of uncontrollable sobbing, I was able to hold it together. I think the fact that our break-up had been on the cards for so long made it a lot easier to deal with. I was well aware of how lucky I was to feel I was able to cope. There is nothing worse than feeling completely broken and like you'll never find happiness again.

WHAT BECOMES OF THE BROKEN-HEARTED? A FORAY INTO THE MIND OF THE FORSAKEN

1. Shock/denial

'He said it's over, but it can't be the end. I'm not going to even try to fathom it out. Just another glitch.' Lots of knee-clutching and rocking and lying in the foetal position.

'Everything will be fine. We'll get married and have babies. He'll want me back. He can't live without me – he knows that. Nothing to get upset about. If he's broken up with me for good, it's his loss. Feel strangely indifferent, empowered even. He's going to phone and apologise any minute now. You'll see . . .'

2. The floodgates open

Shaking, hyperventilating disbelief is shuddering through body.

'Think I'm going to be sick.' Cue breakfast disappearing down toilet.

Eyes prickling and tears coming. Great big sobs splattering down toilet bowl mixing with muesli. Still retching, but nothing coming out.

Three hours later have phoned in sick.

'How can one person cry this much? Will end up like that scene in *Alice in Wonderland* where she nearly drowns in a sea of her own tears.'

Lying in bed where pillow is completely soaked with salty tears and drool from howling.

Cue the howling: 'Noooooooooo! This can't be happening to me.'

Stagger back to bathroom and splash water on face. Eyes so swollen can hardly see them. Two little bloodshot peepers stare back at me from mirror.

'Is it possible to go blind from crying?'

Every muscle in body aches. 'Feel like I have flu. What's he doing right now? Probably at work being big man like nothing's happened.'

Brief interlude of exhaustion.

3. Anger

'Hate him! How could he do this to me? What a wanker! Who does he think he is? I wonder if next girl will notice he has stretch marks on his back?

Hahahahaha.' Slightly deranged laughter.

Phone Laura and rage for hours about crap characteristics he has.

'He hated animals! Best off out of it,' rant manically.

Constantly looking at his page on Facebook. Why's he written on her wall? What is his status? Single! Didn't take the little shit long to advertise he's back on the market. Every female friend he has is the enemy.

4. Drunken sorrow

Have downed bottle of red wine and watched *Casino Royale*. Not even sight of Daniel Craig emerging from the sea in tight trunks cheered me up. More sobbing.

'If he saw me trapped in a cage drowning, then maybe he'd caaaaaare.'

Grab picture taken on holiday in Australia, with him smiling carefree in front of Sydney Opera House and rain tears on it.

Look at phone. No messages. Maybe just send text? NO! Put it down again.

'Why aren't I good enough for him?' Pitiful sobs. Too drunk/exhausted to manage proper wail.

Grab phone and type in text: 'Plese cant we just meet up and takl about git [a Freudian slip?] Love you.'

For half an hour pace flat, agitatedly re-reading text and swigging wine, until finally phone bleeps. From him!

'Hi. I don't think that would be a good idea, Charlotte [clearly patronising use of name].'

'NOOOOOOOOOOO!!!!' Photo hurled at wall. Cut finger picking up shattered glass.

Type in text: 'I self-harmin now. Hope ur happy.'

Brief interlude of anger/crying, then pass out.

5. Depression/self-loathing

Wake up. 'Not sure why feel sad. Hold on, something important to remember…Uggghh.' Sudden memory of heartbreak comes back and thumps down on already fragile head like sledgehammer.

'He left me. No one will ever love me again.'

Look at sent items on phone. 'Oh God, bad texts. Can't believe he didn't reply to last one. Heartless, clearly.'

Cancel phone call from concerned friend. No one can help me now.

'Maybe I'll run away and work for charity. Could get a job at an elephant sanctuary in Africa. Then perhaps I'll get bitten by a mosquito and get malaria and then he'll hear about my plight and come out and rescue me? No he won't. He haaaaaaates me. Why am I so pathetic?'

Open packet of ginger nut biscuits, take one out and eat slowly, then put rest back in cupboard. Go back two minutes later, pick out packet and eat another three. Go to put back in cupboard. Ten minutes later finish ginger nuts. Feel sick, but can't stop eating. Look in freezer for cake or ice cream.

Repeat stages 2 to 5 several times over.

6. Leave house. Friends crack jokes. Don't even try to smile. 'No one understands my pain.'

Walk into club and have panic attack. 'All these people trying to get laid. Stupid fools.' Tell Laura am going home.

'But you just paid ten quid to get in,' she says. 'Try to stay, you might have fun.'

'Can't. I'll never be same again. Going home.'

Repeat stages 2 to 6 several times over

7. Acceptance
'I actually feel OK today. Found myself laughing and caught fit IT man at work looking at me. Smiled back too. Am having a break from men though. Maybe I'll become a lesbian?'

When a relationship has ended for good, whether it was your choice or the decision was taken out of your hands, there's a lot more to contend with than merely getting used to life on your own.

Suddenly there are a million things to think about.

If you rent together, will one person move out? Will you both leave? Or will you have to keep the tenancy on for several months, coming to some kind of arrangement where you both spend alternate weeks at the flat while the other stays with friends?

If you have a mortgage together, the situation can seem unbearable. After all, you spent months finding the perfect home, somewhere you put your heart and soul into. The place is riddled with memories and poignant keepsakes – the fun you had painting the walls, the ornaments on the mantelpiece that he hates but you love, the kitsch fridge magnet he brought you back from a stag do in Dublin.

It was a home in which to build a life together. When you have a really honest moment you remember you even allowed yourself to wonder where you might put a cot. Now one of you has to leave. How can life ever be the same again?

Of course you hear stories of people who split, but still have to live together. Their love may have died, but because they're tied into a mortgage or there are financial obligations, leaving is just not an option.

One young lady had the dilemma of splitting with her boyfriend almost three months before their tenancy agreement was up.

'The worst thing was that I wanted to break up with him ages before, but I couldn't afford too,' she reveals. 'I couldn't lose my deposit, so had to stay put.'

But unable to stand keeping her feelings suppressed any longer, she finally ended it and now has six weeks until they can finally part company.

'It's hell,' she says. 'We live in a small apartment and I sleep upstairs and he sleeps downstairs. The fact that we're still living together makes it so much worse, as he hasn't accepted that I don't want to be with him.

'I'll come home and he's bought me flowers and made me dinner and when I say I'm going out, there's a big row. He's still in denial and even talks about planning trips for our anniversary.'

With her ex unable to truly accept the finality of their

split, she reveals she often wakes in the night to find him climbing into bed to hug her.

'Because he's like Jekyll and Hyde, if I ask him to get out, we have a big argument and I don't get to sleep until four in the morning,' she sighs. 'So I've found it better to pretend everything is OK and humour him like a child before reiterating that it's all over in the morning.'

She says she lives in constant fear of what her ex will do next as he struggles to come to terms with their break-up.

'I've found the best way to calm him down is to say nothing at all. One minute he's telling me he hates me and that I've ruined his life, the next he's going through Facebook, convinced I'm having an affair with all my male friends – even though most of them are gay!'

Her experience sounded like hell on earth, so I realised I'd had it easy. When Adam and I split up, we'd conveniently been living on the top floor of his parents' home. I didn't have to serve them notice or part with a hefty deposit – I could pack up my stuff and leave and that would be the end of it.

Of course, I was suddenly homeless overnight, but fortunately help was at hand. Thanks to a guardian angel in the form of my friend Clare, I had another option to roughing it in the underpass with the tramps at Waterloo Station.

Like a true pal, Clare actually allowed me to sleep on a mattress on the floor of her room in a shared house for a whole month. It must have been the longest 30 days of her life.

Amazingly, this didn't put her off cohabitation with me and when the month was up, we found a lovely, spacious flat to rent and we moved in with another pal.

I'd landed on my feet. When a relationship goes sour, finding somewhere nice and affordable to live at short notice is arguably the most daunting thing. Another friend of mine wasn't as lucky.

Recently single, she suddenly found herself abandoning the comforts of Coupledom for a room in a shared flat. Knowing full well that she couldn't afford to rent on her own and that getting onto the property ladder was not an option, she reluctantly moved into a flat occupied by two other girls.

At face value, everything seemed perfect. Her flatmates were nice, the room comfortable and the rent reasonable. But having been used to keeping a shipshape home with her ex-boyfriend, the chaos of a shared house soon began to get to her. Not least because of a couple of extra hangers-on spoiling her domestic bliss.

Turns out the landlady, who lived in the flat below (I like to imagine she was a bit like Simon Pegg's weird landlady, Marsha, on *Spaced*), had a senile and mangy old moggy that, for some reason, had taken up residence in their flat, crying and howling twenty-four seven.

The only way to shut it up was to feed it, which was happening about 58 times a day. 'It just needs to be put down,' my friend whined. 'I'm so fed up.'

Complaints to the landlady had fallen on deaf ears. In fact, she was more interested in throwing impromptu parties in THEIR living room. My friend would come home to find several people she didn't know listening to music and clogging up her front room.

'Maybe if I were 21 and straight out of uni I could cope with this,' my friend despaired. 'But I'm not. I'm 29 and a young professional. I shouldn't have to be living like this.'

It was true; why should she have to encounter such problems?

But journey into the world of shared accommodation and you soon realise that there are a lot of strange people out there.

Not only are their cleaning standards often far inferior to your own, but they are selfish, food-stealing, note-leaving mentalists who make you so angry that after another bog-roll no-show you find yourself actually imagining that you are maiming them as you viciously grate parmesan in the kitchen.

Some of my best friends are former housemates, yet I believe I have also had the misfortune to live with some of the dirtiest, dodgiest and weirdest people in Britain.

My back catalogue of abodes is riddled with horror stories: the married landlord who came on to me and put my rent up; the sweet but haphazard chum who almost gassed me as I slept; and the shifty housemate I saw on the local *Crimestoppers* (interestingly, this was a few months after my room had been broken into and my belongings swiped).

I've also endured the frosty silence of a housemate who walked round the house ignoring me for days on end because I dared to watch telly in my own bedroom at the lowest possible volume at 11 p.m. on a Friday night.

I had one with more than a keen interest in jazz mags and sex lines. Then there was the sad tale of the homesick young lady who became mentally ill and imagined the rest of us were poisoning her food and gassing her.

Shared accommodation is an absolute minefield.

So I had nothing but sympathy for the friend who, in her late 20s and with a lack of funds, had no choice but to move into a shared house.

The three male students she'd met on a website were in their final year of uni, so she assumed they'd be knuckling down. They seemed nice and she needed somewhere to live straightaway, so she threw caution to the wind and decided to go with it.

It was never going to be the best – her box room was so small you couldn't swing a dead cat in it – but her main grievance was the thinness of the walls, which ensured she was regularly blasted awake at all hours by pumping music.

The students' generous university timetables meant they rarely had to clamber out of bed before 11 a.m., so often returned from the student union with friends in tow and proceeded to hold impromptu parties. In their drunken state, they gave little thought to their exasperated flatmate, who had be up at 7 a.m.

She asked them nicely to turn the noise down, bought earplugs and tried sleeping remedies, but every night she was plagued by yet more broken sleep.

Although the party always disbanded as soon as she complained about the noise, it was like a real-life *Groundhog Day* – if they weren't inviting mates round, they were cooking noisily in the kitchen (leaving her terrified they'd leave the gas on or burn the house down) or laughing out loud to *Family Guy*.

Too embarrassed to go down and make a scene yet again, she vowed to find a new place to live. But then something amazing happened. One of the students got a job!

Suddenly this young man was on the same schedule as her and she had an ally. When the other two headed off to the union, he stayed in with her watching *Location, Location, Location* and the nocturnal habits of his friends, who were also beginning to temp, began to peter out too.

Strangely enough, as they bonded over property entertainment shows, she and the student actually fell for each other. He was about five years her junior, but, surprisingly, it just worked. Six months later they moved into a one-bed flat together.

Three years on, they are still an item and as happy as Larry. Sweetly, whenever we playfully joke about how his sleep-deprived girlfriend was about to craft a voodoo doll of him out of toilet rolls, he looks mortified and still apologises profusely.

I myself was almost driven to distraction by the people who lived above me, whose voices and footsteps on their wooden floors would resonate down after midnight, just as I was trying to drift off.

I eventually penned them a slightly overemotional letter explaining what sleep deprivation was doing to my sanity and gingerly posted it through their door, hoping I hadn't just started World War III.

Actually, they turned out to be thoroughly decent. Mortified by the disruption and extremely apologetic, they did their best to keep the noise down and are still friends of mine to this day.

So once you've got your living arrangements sorted, everything else should fall into place, right?

Um, sometimes it does.

When you're single after a long time off the market, it can be a massive shock to the system. There's that first post-break-up bonk to clumsily navigate your way through. It could be a heady one-night stand, it could be the best thing ever, it could be the start of something beautiful, it could be a complete disaster – that's just the way the lust lottery goes.

A newly single friend told me an excruciating tale last week.

Shame-faced, she recalled how she'd pulled a guy and stumbled from one faux-pas to another.

After finishing with the man she lived with, agonisingly and to his complete devastation, my friend needed some light relief. So she got plastered and ended up going home for some fun and games with a lad she'd been introduced to at a party.

But the next morning, as they lay in bed and she asked him question after question about his life, he eyed her suspiciously.

'Don't you remember anything I told you last night?' he enquired.

Later, as she went to leave, he asked her for her phone number. Taking his phone, she threw him a smouldering smile.

'Well, at least I can remember my number!' she joked.

But later that day, as she lay half dozing on her bed back home, she sat up with a jolt.

Alarm reverberated through her like an electric current as she recalled the digits she'd keyed into his phone. In a horrific flashback, she realised that in her sorry state, brain addled by alcohol, she'd actually given him her heartbroken ex's number.

Panicked at the thought of the worst type of text he could compose, she desperately called her friends, until one managed to give her the guy's number. Then she had to go through the humiliation of composing a 'nutty' message admitting to her crime.

'He must think I'm so weird,' she cringed. 'I still can't believe I did it.'

Although the man did text back, dubbing her 'a drunken moo', he didn't mention meeting again.

'Oh, the shame!' she exclaimed, her head in her hands. 'And we live in the same area too, so I'll probably have the embarrassment of running into him in Tesco Metro.'

As the full realisation of being single again sets in, you may find yourself compulsively agreeing to dates with anyone who asks, just to get yourself well and truly back in the saddle.

When I heard Tom was getting serious with 'The One' after we split, I panicked. So I agreed to a date with an OK-looking guy who worked in the office next to mine. I don't know what I was thinking. He was rough as anything and as thick as two short planks. Within minutes, I knew it was a terrible idea and cut the date short as soon as I could. You forget just how much you need to have your wits about you!

If your self-esteem is bruised from your break-up, you may fall for the first load of old flattery heaped on you from a seemingly charming man at a party. But it pays to do your research – could be he's worked the rest of the room first! There are some real sharks out there.

Being single also radically changes the way people react to you. If you are the only single person in a group, your well-meaning friends will probably try to fix you up with just about anyone they can think of.

And if you venture out socially with a friend and her long-term boyfriend or husband, you may find yourself being treated like a younger sibling. They constantly check on your wellbeing, as if they assume something is wrong with you and imagine you spend all your time at home alone, crying into your microwaved meal for one.

Then there are the assumptions of complete strangers. If you're at a party and you chat to a man for anything longer than five minutes, then you must be fully prepared for a horror lunge. If you haven't name-dropped a boyfriend and have taken time to chat to him, then in his eyes you are fair game. This can be very frustrating and embarrassing when in reality you were doing nothing more than indulging in friendly conversation.

If you do like the man, you can guarantee there is the drunken friend who thinks you are unable to make the transition to swapping numbers on your own. Thinking she is being helpful, she steams in there like Cilla Black on speed and demands he take your number, scaring the poor man half to death and thus ensuring he will never call.

When out with one of my closest single friends, The Beau and I are actually really bad when it comes to this type of behaviour. After a few beers, we get a bit overexcited, grinning at each other if she talks to a guy for five minutes or unsubtly leaving the group conversation ('Shall we go get a drink?' Nudge, nudge, wink, wink) so she can talk to him one-on-one.

In the sober light of day, I've often been forced to sheep-ishly apologise for my un-sisterly crimes. After all, it's not as if I don't know what being in this situation is like.

As I unsuccessfully attempted to chart the waters of Singledom, I can remember going to a very couple-y party where I couldn't have felt more isolated. All around me were pairs (loved-up/engaged/married) swooning over each other, and then there was me – the spare.

At first things had been looking up. I chatted to a gorgeous man for ages, but then I discovered he had a beautiful fiancée elsewhere. We were well into a flirty 40-minute chat and lots of top-ups of my drinks when one of his female friends wandered over and rather unsubtly dropped his other half into the conversation.

Suddenly I felt like some kind of predator for even indulging the thought that he was attractive. What's more, I could see friends of his fiancée watching me out the corner of their eyes. It seemed like every girl in the room had morphed into a beautiful gazelle, their ears pinning back as they eyed me. As the token single girl, I was being viewed as a cheetah, prowling round ready to pounce.

Predicting danger, the herd closed ranks. Leaving me to slope off, hungry and despondent.

One of the hardest things about being an unattached girl really is the ridiculous way other women sometimes get threatened by you when you genuinely pose no problem to them at all.

Now, I am not going to pretend I've never acted like this because the truth is I once did. I've always been highly strung, but as a teenager I was dynamite, threatening to explode at any moment.

Let me take you back, oh, a good 13 years (blimey) to when I was 17 and had all the emotional maturity of Paris Hilton. Every Friday night, I would join hordes of friends from college and the supermarket where I worked on the delicatessen and queue up for the lamest nightclub in the West Country, where being underage was almost a necessity.

I would often go with my teenage sweetheart, Jack, but being a volatile force at the best of times, having access to countless Hooches and Bacardi Breezers (actually about three was enough) and my boyfriend in the same vicinity as, God forbid, OTHER GIRLS was never a recipe for tranquillity and calm.

On one particular night, I remember being outraged because I could see the back of my boyfriend's head on the dancefloor and he seemed to be very near A GIRL. Thinking he was about to kiss her, I ran up to him and slapped him across the cheek.

If I'd bothered to investigate properly, or even asked, I would have found out that he was in fact talking to a girl he used to go to school with. She was perfectly nice and in no way after my boyfriend. But in my immature and hammered mind, I could see no such logic.

Instead of apologising, I glared at my shocked fella and then turned on my heel and stormed out the club.

Bless him, my harassed and red-faced boyfriend followed loyally behind me. Shamefully, the high drama I created as I flounced out the club was observed by a policeman, who, taking pity on Jack, asked, 'Do you think you can handle that?' He nodded wearily and hurried after me to find me hyperventilating with outrage a little further down the road.

I'm not proud of this story, but I think it is not unfair to put it down to my misguided youth and my inability to handle alcohol. The point is that, looking back now, I am ashamed by my behaviour and would never again conduct myself like that in front of people.

Over the years, I've learnt that airing your dirty linen in public and being that aggressive about other girls will get you nowhere. So the older I get, the more shocked I am to find myself on the receiving end of jealous behaviour from women who frankly should also be old enough to know better. Whether you are genuinely single or just a girl who is not visibly attached to a man, you are often unfairly targeted by insecure women.

One of the more recent incidents was at Glastonbury, when I was with a female friend watching The Killers. The downpour which had besieged us all weekend had at last stopped for a short spell and, clasping our beakers of pear cider by The Other Stage, we were feeling pretty high-spirited.

As anyone who has been will know, generally, the atmosphere at Glastonbury is infectious. You find yourself being jostled and knocked every second as you try to make your way through the crowds. But rather than drowning in the icy stares and unspoken tension you'd experience on London's Northern Line in the height of rush hour, you find yourself revelling in Glasto's air of camaraderie. People feeling jolly and being nice to each other. In fact, random conversations with complete strangers are often the highlight of the whole experience.

So there we were, myself and Clare, happily supping our cider, when a group of revellers squeezed into a space in front of us. One of them was a very tall man wearing a flat cap and holding a mascot.

In true festival spirit, he started to proudly tell the tale of how his mascot was captured forever in cinematic glory, in footage of the audience during the festival two years previously. Wow.

It was all very mundane, but suddenly a crazed-looking young lady pushed through the crowd and stood in front of him.

'Hello,' she barked with a sarcastic smile.

'Hi,' I replied, puzzled. Glaring at me, she pulled the guy round so his back was to us and then proceeded to do an impression, which was clearly meant for my benefit.

'I'm a stupid bint,' she squealed in a sickly voice, while swaying her hips and grinning inanely. She then launched herself at her man and started snogging his face off.

Outraged, I barged up to her, grabbed the silly cow by her anorak and headbutted her.

Actually, I didn't. In reality, I seethed silently, too furious to enjoy the Killers' set, as dozens of brilliant comebacks swarmed my thoughts. But I'd missed my chance and, if I'm honest, I was actually a bit scared of the psychotic look in her eye.

They'd moved along the crowd and I could just about make out her smug face as she jumped up and down to 'Mr Brightside', possessively clinging on to her man.

'But I've got The Beau,' I thought to myself. 'Why would I even be remotely interested in your stupid man and his boring story?'

And even if I hadn't been with The Beau, the fact is I would still have been chatting innocently with Mr Flat Cap.

I always think it's quite a similar situation when straight men (who can be slightly homophobic) are in the company of a gay man. I once watched a boyfriend squirm with discomfort when we were sitting in a bar with a gay friend. I wanted to tell him: 'Give it up! Just because gay men fancy men, doesn't mean they automatically want to shag you!'

It was the same with that girl – not everyone in the world is after your bloke, love!

Going to the other extreme, there are times when you are clearly not the slightest threat – in fact, you might as well not be there at all. Welcome to the world of the gooseberry.

You join your friend and her bloke for a day out or evening in and suddenly feel like a spare part.

'I can't tell you how many times I've been in this situation,' said one fed-up friend. 'If the couple are really touchy-feely, you begin to feel really uncomfortable.'

Another friend, who loathes PDAs at the best of times, recalls the hell of being trapped in a front room with her pal and her new eye-candy.

'We were watching an action film, but it was impossible to concentrate due to all the slurping and fawning that was going on in front of me. I was sorely tempted to pour a bucket of cold water over them, but instead I just sat there silently seething.'

Although being a gooseberry when your mate is in the first flush of romance with her new bloke is pretty awful, fast-forward to the permanently 'together' stage and it can be even worse.

'We're getting married!' they declare. While you're

pleased your friend is happy, a part of you begins a mourning period. It's the realisation that from now on your friend is part of a package. For a while now, you've noticed that when you invite her out for a drink she announces she's bringing her man too.

Not that you don't like his company, it's just that sometimes you want your best friend to yourself. While he is happy to listen to your girlie chat and offer you well-meaning advice on your love life, there's something a little bit humiliating about sitting in Starbucks pouring your heart out about the latest chap who hasn't called back to your best friend AND her ideal husband.

As they smile sympathetically over their cappuccinos, all the time entwining their fingers under the table, it's enough to make you want to stab yourself in the heart with the plastic knife you picked up for your blueberry muffin.

Likewise, if she's brought her offspring and is trying subtly to breastfeed, pacify the ear-splitting wails with a dummy or chase an out-of-control toddler around the table, you feel a bit silly for burdening her.

How you long for times gone by, when you were both blissfully unattached and spent duvet days on the sofa verbally dissecting unsuitable men, watching trash telly and gorging on your own body weight in chocolate, crisps and Haribo sweets.

One single friend declares that the rapid rate at which most of her friends are getting married, having babies or settling down with the person they're likely to spend the rest of their lives with has left her very alarmed.

'I want to get married and have kids too and sometimes that manifests itself in a proper panic attack that my biological clock is whizzing along,' she says.

'It's not helped by the fact that last Christmas I realised most of the cards I get are not just signed by couples anymore. Now they add their pets and children too.

'It was bad enough when I was getting cards from pairs of people, but now they have to emphasise their cosy home life with their cats and dogs as well, just to really rub salt in the wound. Meanwhile, my cards only ever have one name on them.'

She was also left reeling when seven months before a wedding, her friend wanted to know whether to put her down with a 'plus one'.

'As I didn't have a boyfriend at the time, she has put me down as single,' she sighs. 'I can't stand the thought that I've been consigned to the singles' bin that far ahead.'

And if the pressures your friends put on you aren't enough, there's also your family.

A good friend revealed that visiting her parents at weekends is now right up there with trips to the dentist because she is so sick of being made to feel like a complete freak for being single at 29.

'When your mum's face has sympathy written all over it and she has tears in her eyes, it's pretty hard to stomach,' she said. 'I haven't got a terminal illness, I'm just single!'

She added that she longs for reprieve from the incessant suggestions that she goes on dates with the geeky/monosyllabic/simple sons of her parents' friends.

'The final straw was when my mum started suggesting I meet up with the ex-boyfriend she knows full well cheated on me!' she says. 'How desperate does she think I've become? Hell will freeze over before that happens!'

CONVERSATIONS BETWEEN
MOTHERS AND DAUGHTERS

Mother showing off a bag of Disney videos she purchased from a charity shop

Mother: I bought them for when you give me grandchildren.

Daughter: Really?

Mother: Mind you, VHS will probably be phased out before that happens.

Daughter: I saw a psychic last week and she said I'd have a baby before I was thirty-four. Will that do?

Mother [smiling]: Oh, that's only four years I've got to wait!

Mother and daughter out shopping

Daughter: You think I've got terrible taste in men, don't you?

Mother: No I don't!

Conversation interrupted by a sports car screeching past, with the young man driving it checking out the daughter.

Mother: You know what sort of man is driving that car?

Daughter: No.

Mother: Irrational and erratic. Look at the way he's driving. A yobbo. You need to stay away from men like that.

Mother and daughter on the phone

Daughter: I'm in love.
Mother: Has he got a girlfriend?
Daughter: No.
Mother: Is he wealthy?
Daughter: Yes.
Mother: Does he polish his shoes?
Daughter [sighing]: Don't know, I've only seen him in trainers.

Mother and daughter having a Christmas discussion

Daughter: Can I invite a friend over for Christmas Day?
Mother [getting excited]: Yes, of course! What's his name?
Daughter: Actually, she's called Sarah.
Mother: Oh. [Puts on a serious face] Are you a lesbian?
Daughter: No. Both her parents are dead and she's just been dumped by her boyfriend.
Mother: Oh.

Mother and daughter having a boyfriend chat

Daughter: I really like Jamie. I hope he never does anything to hurt me.
Mother: You tell him that if he does, I'll get him with knives.

Mother and daughter discussing old school friends

Daughter: I went to Wendy's thirtieth last night.

Mother: Is she married?

Daughter: No.

Mother: Has she got a boyfriend?

Daughter: No, she's single.

[Long pause] Mother: Any other school friends there?

Daughter: Yes, Carrie Kennedy.

Mother: Is she married?

Daughter: No!

If you think your mum is bad for passing judgment, then don't even stop to think about what the youth of today think about you.

As I recalled earlier, when you're 18, being 30 seems like another lifetime away. A fact my pal discovered after breaking up with her long-term boyfriend and jetting off to a Greek island for a much-needed break.

One night she and a friend were sitting in a bar when an 18-year-old girl skipped over and started talking to them. She had just flown out to work there for the summer and after excitedly revealing everything about herself in two minutes flat, she enquired how old they were.

'Thirty,' they both chirped.

'Really?' the teenager responded. 'Wow! That's so cool! I really respect that. I hope that when I'm thirty I'm still out there partying, man!'

It seemed that in her eyes, at their ancient age, they were more likely to be tottering around on their zimmer frames than letting their hair down in a holiday resort bar.

With this type of prejudice towards us 30-somethings,

clearly the pensionable citizens of the dating world, it's no wonder that getting back on the singles' scene is daunting.

You'd assume there would be some benefits. Perhaps this time you'll all be a bit older and wiser. Surely the men you'll encounter will have sown their wild oats by now, be more mature, easier to read, nicer . . . Yes, well, dream on.

If you're back fishing in the deep, dark waters of the dating pool, it's extremely easy to come a cropper. There are often hazards at every turn, as you wade into the murky waters, completely clueless.

After breaking up with Adam, I quickly managed to freak out a guy by indulging in far too couple-y behaviour when chatting to him on a date down the pub.

I can recall the exact moment he changed from being relaxed and chatty to clearly wishing he'd never met me for a drink in the first place. It was when I grabbed his hand affectionately and squeezed it.

In all honesty, it was just instinctive behaviour that I'd been used to in my previous relationship. I'd done it without even thinking, but as far as dating etiquette went, it was too much, too soon. I could actually see the whites of his eyes bulging with fear as he snatched his hand back.

We never progressed to another date.

In another story, a friend, in a genuine accident, missed her last train home after a barbecue at her new man's place. It was about date four and she was all for getting a taxi when he kindly offered to put her up, in his bed (yeah, and the rest . . .).

Yet the following week he had the audacity to complain to a mutual friend that she'd deliberately orchestrated circumstances in order to stay the night. Then, like a complete arse, wrapped up in his own ego, he didn't call her.

Men can be brutally unforgiving and, as the story above illustrates, ridiculous when it comes to finding reasons to be put off a girl – and that isn't necessarily something that changes with age.

Convinced that forewarned is forearmed, I asked my male friends to compile a list of 'ladies to avoid' and the behaviour they exhibit, so that at least we can gauge some idea of where we're going wrong. While some make sense, others will no doubt enrage you . . .

WHAT <u>NOT</u> TO BE LIKE

The money piranha

'I've always been pretty shocked that there are girls who are obviously out for one thing, and that's rich men. It's like the idea of equality goes completely out the window for the sake of a posh car or nice suit. Hanging out in City bars just because they attract bankers with big bonuses (regardless of whether or not they're bores or, worse still, arrogant pricks) is not an attractive quality.'

The try-hard ladette

'Mostly, the loud and "laddy" girls are the ones I (and most of my mates) steer away from. They talk nonsense about football and beer in a desperate bid to make you love them. While good-fun, pint-drinking girls tend to be popular with lads (even for a random shag), they are not girlfriend or wife material. Underneath it all, men want a lady.'

The uptight feminist

'This is very clichéd, but I think most men like their woman to be just a little bit girly, and militant feminist types are off-putting. She can still be feisty and independent – those are great qualities – but she should retain her femininity.'

The baggage handler

'Women who are obviously screwed up by previous relationships, overbearing mothers and so on. Yes, I know that's most women, but at least some have the decency to push the feelings deep down inside.'

The boring cow

'I hate mousy little women with no opinions, no zest for life and no interests beyond going shopping at Next or watching the next shitty chick flick starring Colin Firth. Expand your horizons, ladies . . .'

The oompa loompa

'I avoid girls like the plague if they look like they've bathed in a tub of Tango. If a girl is going to take that long making herself look like she's auditioning for the role in *Charlie and the Chocolate Factory*, imagine how long she'll take getting ready when you go out.'

The bride-to-be

'They have the dress, they have the church booked, all they need is a groom that fits the tux. Then the babies can start!'

Psycho chicks

'A bunny boiler who rings you a thousand times or a stalking weirdo. Had one bird who used to turn up on nights out with my mates and even scored a few of my friends in an effort to get back with me. Strange girl! Then there was the one who tried to read my palm . . . I swear to God. She was an actual model. Stunning, stunning girl, but I ran for the door. All I could think was "WEIRDO!"'

And finally . . .

'Bad smells will usually do it, talking about their pets for too long, laughing like a pig, having pictures of their dog in a denim jacket on their phones, and the following sentence: "I want to be treated like a princess."'

Regardless of whether or not you're back dating again, coping with the kick in the teeth that is your most recent ex being smitten or – God forbid – now betrothed to someone else can tend to overshadow everything else.

There is also nothing more likely to prompt full-scale panic in your head than the unwelcome news that your ex is bringing his new fiancée to a wedding or mutual gathering.

You might not give a stuff if you're with him or not, but the last thing you want is him or his smug new fiancée thinking you look anything but your best.

Plus, of course, female pride dictates that everyone else at the event must naturally think you are so much hotter than your poor dowdy successor. It doesn't matter how you do it – crash diet, botox, a full face-lift – you HAVE to look better.

As one lady put it: 'I defy any woman not to look out feverishly for her ex and his new bint, spot them, then immediately march off to the loos to fluff her hair and apply more lipgloss.

'He could be the biggest dirtbag on the planet, but there's always a moment of satisfaction to be had from making him realise what he doesn't have any more. Or is this just me?'

One girl went to great lengths to wreak the ultimate revenge on her nasty ex-boyfriend and his new dollybird at a friend's wedding.

Knowing full well that he'd be there with his new girlfriend and she didn't have a date, she went on holiday the week before and got tanned and gorgeous. She then spent days finding the perfect fabulous outfit and turned up on the big day smug in the knowledge that she looked better than she had in years.

At the wedding reception, she bowled up to her ex and his new strumpet first and early on, so that it was on her own terms and she wouldn't have to feel intimidated all day. After being polite and lovely, she asked them when they were going to get married and then watched them squirm. She left the conversation feeling fantastic and they were the ones feeling awkward and uncomfortable.

A brilliant and well-executed operation, missy.

Shame it didn't go quite as well for my aforementioned friend, Amelia, with the ex with the Red Rum fiancée. She recalls how she once had to endure the torturous experience of hanging out with them at a fancy-dress party.

'As Lindsay Lohan correctly says in *Mean Girls*, fancy dress is an excuse for girls to dress like sluts and get away with it, which is something I always forget,' she rants.

'That night I'd made myself look absolutely ridiculous as a butch bearded lady.

'The ex was dressed as the Dalai Lama and Red Rum was dressed as Cinderella, although I don't remember the real Cinderella's neckline being so low you could almost see her nipples.

'Anyway, Red Rum decided she wanted to be my best friend that night and wouldn't leave me alone. So I hid.'

The mortified bearded lady stowed away under a bed in a dark room where a viking and a cowboy had passed out and were snoring loudly above her.

'The Dalai Lama and Cinderella came in to look for me, but didn't find me, thank goodness,' she continues.

'It was at this point that I decided it would be a good idea to phone the guy who was messing me around at the time because he hadn't replied to a text I sent the the day before. It was three in the morning, I was hiding from my ex and his slutty fiancée under a bed, dressed as a bearded lady and phoning my current commitment-phobe who clearly couldn't be bothered to talk to me. Surely my finest hour?'

Another friend recalls the horror of meeting her bloke's new girlfriend at a party.

'I knew she'd be there with him, so I deliberately dressed up,' she confesses. 'I couldn't help myself.

'Although we were introduced to each other at the start of the evening, I gave her a wide berth until towards the end of the night, when I spotted her dashing in my direction to talk to her friend, who was standing right next to me.

'To my utter shock, she proclaimed, in a stage whisper, "Hey, my luck's in! Went to the late-night garage and got some condoms!"

'I had no idea if she did it on purpose or not, so I let out a nervous laugh, but I was mortified. The last thing I wanted to do was go to that party and think about my ex's genitals, but as soon as she said that, images flashed into my mind of them having sex. Yuck.'

Indeed, thinking about your ex with someone else is never comfortable.

As the months passed after Adam and I split for good, I knew there was no going back – but that didn't mean I was ready to hear he'd found love again.

Having moved in with my friends, I'd been revelling in my clean break. Living at opposite ends of London ensured there was no chance of bumping into each other.

Still, at times, I did feel a bit melancholy. As well as my

boyfriend, Adam had been my best friend and that was what I missed the most. Whenever I was feeling sad, in need of reassurance or just wanted to hear a cheerful voice, he was instinctively my first call. But the transition from cosy phone calls to our first meeting was not as easy as I'd expected.

As I gave him a big hug, I found myself having to desperately resist the urge to perch on his lap and nuzzle into his neck. Not because I wanted to get fresh with him or anything, but because the warm familiarity of his embrace and his scent (including, admittedly, a faint aroma of Marlboro Light) was reminiscently comforting.

Clearly a heady mix of Adam's pheromones and the familiarity of his smell were triggering natural behavioural responses in me. It reminded me of how he'd been my companion. In his arms I'd felt comforted and I missed that feeling.

Incidentally, just to go off at a tangent for a minute, I once road-tested some pheromone-laced perfume for a magazine article. The 'perfume', and I use that title lightly, smelled rank, a bit like mouldy flower petals. However, in the name of science, my friend Anna and I headed out coated in the stuff.

On the plus side, it seemed to work. The men swarmed to us like flies to shit. But on the negative side, we had absolutely no control over the type of men who lavished us with attention. There wasn't a handsome chap in sight. Instead, the scent largely seemed to attract Neanderthal Man's most un-evolved descendants.

I decided to call it a night when an overzealous giant of an Eastern European man nearly floored me as he grabbed my face and started trying to lick it, all the time slurring, 'Yawuu aw beuu-oo-tiful.'

Anyway, back to Adam. As I affectionately studied his welcoming face for a minute or two, I had a wobble.

While my relationship with Adam hadn't been destructive, I'd felt it clearly wasn't right, but had we given up too easily? What if I never met anyone else who came near? Would I now go through life regretting my decision and referring to him as 'the one that got away'?

A vision flashed into my mind of me dragging my feet through life, tortured by my foolish decision. Until one day, in my 70s and a bitter recluse, I'd lie too close to the fire in the dirty, moth-eaten, white Coast frock Adam had once bought me and meet my end in a flaming fireball like Miss Havisham in *Great Expectations*.

But if I was having a wobble, it was too little, too late. Adam had some news. Adam had met someone else and was smitten. Adam was dating a girl who sounded far prettier, cleverer and more successful than me.

'That's great news!' I smiled, with gritted teeth. 'I'm really happy for you.'

We finished our drinks and, after another warm embrace, headed off our separate ways. But as I walked numbly to the tube, I began to question my reaction. Was I really overcome with jealousy?

Well, once I got over the initial shock – not really.

Instead I realised that I was just being ruled by a self-centred part of my brain that always wanted to be top dog.

I recalled how when we'd first broken up, Adam had sweetly told me he'd been so happy with me that he was going to be very choosy about his next girlfriend in the hope that he could experience even a little of what we had had. Now a little churlish voice inside me was complaining about how I'd been trumped so quickly. I'd done lots to shape him up, why should I lose my spot as number one?

But I've already slated men who deliberately mess with girls' heads after they've broken up with them as part of some twisted desire to still monopolise their minds. It shouldn't happen the other way round either. In reality, it's a bit like being a clingy mother, isn't it? It would be weird not to let go and try to smile as you wave them off.

Conclusion

Recently, when my father was sitting at home reading the newspaper, I heard my mother calling his name. He didn't move.

'I'll tell you what the secret of a great relationship is, Charlotte,' he mused, without even looking up from his paper. 'Selective hearing.'

I think perhaps The Beau may soon adopt the same strategy with me. At times when I exhaust even myself with neuroses and occasional hormonal madness, I think The Beau is the most saintly man in Britain.

Now and then, after a high-maintenance episode, I find him staring out the window, gazing into space with the look of a man who's been psychologically broken at Guantanamo Bay.

Is he just one step away from a permanent orange jumpsuit?

But when I ask The Beau if he thinks I have terror-ised him into changing, he reminds me of my fondness for a bit of drama. In fact, he asserts, beyond trying to make him keep a diary and have a more structured social life – a quest I soon abandoned – he could not think of anything too heavy-handed that I have tried to impose on him.

Perhaps that is because I can actually pinpoint very little about The Beau that I want to change.

Yes, he is laid back almost to the point of narcolepsy, but he is also sharp and intuitive. At times he knows my own mind better than I do, which drives me to distraction.

Maybe the temptation will always be there to try to whip him into shape, but just finding something will be a chore in itself. Although, like most men, he leaves his socks on the floor and deposits the washing in crumpled lumps on the clothes horse, I'm not going to read him the riot act. You win some, you lose some.

But I know I'll always be high-maintenance.

When I ask The Beau if he thinks he'll ever lose patience with me, he kindly says he foresees his influence will encourage me to be calmer and think before I speak. He also claims that being with me will make him less apathetic to things and that it's nice to feel someone is devotedly looking out for you at every turn.

'Your short fuse is, in fact, the reason our relationship is never boring,' he revealed. 'I couldn't think of anything worse than being with a dullard.'

Well thank the Lord for that! It seems that some men find 'nicely a bit bonkers' birds endearing.

Indeed, I could have hugged the male friend who stated that there's nothing more boring than being with a woman who's practically perfect in every way.

'Our ideal women are attractive, but we don't seek perfection, so don't be neurotic about the odd lump or bump,' he insisted. 'The women we adore are confident, strong-minded, independent, fun-loving creatures who we want to share our lives with, but who also have a few interests of their own outside the relationship.'

Thankfully, the majority of the time, The Beau and I get on swimmingly. He's my favourite person in the world and I'm never happier than when I'm walking round Hampstead Heath hand-in-hand with him.

When it's just the two of us, brushing the stresses of everyday life to one side, I feel completely content.

Yes, at times a silly argument causes us to drift slightly off course, but despite the odd heated or complacent detour, we always get back on track again.

I recently asked a gay friend where he thinks women go wrong when it comes to dating.

'Women project a lot of expectations on to men,' he said. 'They have a utopian vision of what love should be like. They think men will change, but often they can't. They are too idealistic.'

He had a point. Gaggles of girls seemed to coast through young adulthood believing they'd simply bump into the man of their dreams and live in peace and harmony for the rest of their days.

And why not? There are fabulous romantic stories in the paper all the time to inspire us. They feature elderly lovebirds proclaiming the virtues of love at first sight and revealing, with their wrinkly, toothless grins, that the secret to a happy marriage is 'never spending a night apart'.

Then there is the escapism of women's fiction and Hollywood films, which have since our teens brought us sweet love stories of women just like you and me, who net 'The One', who also happens to be devoted, ridiculously good-looking and loaded.

They walk off into the sunset, with their perfect hair and Tiffany engagement rings twinkling – leaving the rest of us stuck in real life constantly striving to find a flawless man.

So no wonder the passing of time begins to install panic in the very heart of the late 20-something.

The ultimate romance has always been packaged as easy and attainable. You're allowed to have a dream and a career and all the expectations in the world. But many young women find they are not quite living the dream. All around them their peers are settling down, creating fear and panic.

Boyfriends are found and lost, with the pressure and coaxing applied to help them tick all our ideal boxes ironically shaping them up for the next girl. Suddenly it is she they've got engaged to, or married, or had a child with – or all three.

Girls today are from a generation that says, 'You can have it all,' but has being so spoilt for choice left us running round in circles? When we meet a man with potential are our expectations too heavy-handed? Do the man makeovers we lovingly dish out actually leave our boyfriends feeling so ineffectual that once they've finally broken free of the apron strings they rush to find happiness in the arms of someone else?

Some girls clearly like to exert power over their boyfriends to feel a sense of one-upmanship. But is this 'my way or the highway' attitude just a one-way route to self-destruction?

As one man asserts: 'Unfortunately, there are girls out there who push their men around, running them with a very strict regime, beating them with the big stick till the particular mutt in question either does the off or throws a fit of rage.

'Perhaps they got off on it, perhaps there is a jewel of pleasure to be taken from the mire of depression which they work themselves up into every time a man dares to do what he has been told not to. But it's not a balanced way to conduct a relationship.'

His comments reminded me of the friend who ended up cheating on his girlfriend after being constantly emasculated. It made me think that I ought to be careful with my own temper tantrums. Like the controlling men I described earlier, there can be equally controlling women and neither are particularly nice to encounter.

One man I know dated several girls who were, as he himself described, 'proper nutters'. They wouldn't let him move without their say so and chastised him about the slightest thing.

On the one hand, you could see they were infatuated with him – they bought him amazing gifts and were loyal and devoted. But, ultimately, they got their kicks from pushing their fella around until the relationship became more like a dictatorship.

It is telling that none of these girlfriends ended up with a ring on their finger. In fact, the girl who eventually did land the diamond was a gentle, easy-going girl who offered him support and partnership without constantly belittling him.

It seems that if you want a man to transform, and ultimately commit, rather than trying to control him, a more subtle approach of gently showing him how his life could benefit from small changes is a more shrewd approach. Even better, let him think it's all his idea and be open to his suggestions and help too.

When it comes to netting a keeper, or even a marriage proposal, it often seems to depend on at which stage in his life (and yours) you became intertwined. In many ways, it seems to be like a solar eclipse – all the elements need to be right. For a solar eclipse, it is crucial that the moon is the correct distance from and in alignment with the sun in order to perfectly obscure it from view. You also need to be in the perfect geographical spot, with the right weather conditions and protective eyewear to catch a breathtaking view.

When all the elements are right, from time to time solar eclipses do happen – just like meeting 'The One'. But just like the sun and the moon, women and men are vastly different. Is it this stark difference that means no matter how far equality goes, the two sexes will never think in the same way?

Rather than expecting the world from a man before you consider him to be husband material, perhaps the princesses among us should think beyond the assumption that our needs as women take priority. Would it hurt to take into account men's wants and needs – rather than constantly criticising them for their shortcomings?

Could we lay the foundations for a long-term future without being so rigid in our demands and with a mix of love and compromise?

'I think there is a definite point in every woman's life when she realises that it's really very easy to get a man's attention,' asserts one friend. 'Flattery and a bit of tits and arse and they will always lap it up.

'BUT that doesn't really mean anything at all. I see it a lot of the time at work. The guys are older and married and a lot of the girls are young and giggly. They surround the guys and laugh at all their tired jokes and make them feel all masterful and interesting, and all the while their words are slurring, their beer bellies are growing and then there's always the odd burp . . . nice.

'Perhaps this is a lesson for those of us in long-term relationships: don't be complacent, keep up the flattery, be interested in their lives and make them feel sexually attractive. Otherwise, if there's a bad patch, someone else could be waiting in the wings to steal your man.'

When I started doing research for this book, I sent out a list of questions about relationships to groups of male and female friends. I'd hoped that by doing this I'd really get an insight into the minds of the two sexes. I wasn't wrong! I also got dozens of brilliant stories which made me realise I'm in good company when it comes to slightly silly behaviour.

Sometimes, if I was up typing too late into the night, I'd lie awake until the early hours, my heart pounding and feeling panicked about my subject matter. I'd feel painfully embarrassed by my most cringeworthy dating antics and wracked by guilt after flashbacks of regrettable, selfish and thoughtless behaviour raced through my mind.

But in my darkest moments of paranoia, I was able to find some comfort in the fact that, thank goodness, most people have got a back catalogue of horror.

Interestingly, many of the women I emailed replied almost instantaneously. Smoke seemed to be coming off their keyboards as they rapidly responded to each question and quickly fired their answers back.

Also, quite a few of the girls passed the list of questions on to female friends and colleagues. I started to get very candid emails out of the blue from women I'd never met. They seemed to find sharing this information therapeutic. There was a sense of camaraderie.

Meanwhile, the men remained very quiet. Just when I assumed I was going to have to make do with next to no responses from menfolk, they started to filter through. After thinking about the questions for a good week or two, the guys were beginning to reply. Their answers were also very honest, but it seemed they'd procrastinated for some time before eventually pinging them back.

So the women responded feverishly, while the men were much more methodical. But why this extensive difference in reactions?

A few weeks ago, I went to meet a friend I hadn't seen for ages in a bar in Waterloo.

'There's always been that "don't touch a woman in her thirties vibe", she exclaimed, on a roll. 'It's like we're damaged goods. Obsessed with marriage and babies . . .'

As she paused for breath, I suddenly heard a snippet of conversation coming from the next table, where two men were sitting having a pint.

'So what about the football?' one said.

I had to laugh.

For me, this pretty much summed up why the girls fired back their answers so quickly, but the boys took their time. For many women, it is almost second nature to discuss relationships, men and marriage – and sharing seemed to be part of the healing process. But on the other hand, men seemed more likely to broach such subjects only when they felt they had to.

With this imbalance of the elements, no wonder those solar eclipses are so hard to come by!

Perhaps this went some way to explain why when boy meets girl there can be such discrepancies in protocol when it comes to texting, calling and when you progress to boyfriend and girlfriend.

But you can't just rely on solar eclipses, sometimes you really do need to do yourself a favour and make the decision to stop pursuing unsuitable men. Yes, occasionally you can tame a wrong 'un, but how much easier would life be if you just made the decision to banish the cads and opt for a good 'un instead?

If you're getting the runaround it's normal to want to do something about it, but sometimes it's also worth sticking around to see if you've bagged yourself a slow-burner.

While at the beginning you should be able to expect a certain amount of respect from a man who wants to prove his worth as a suitor, give him a chance to get there. Sometimes that imperfect caterpillar needs a little bit of time to transform into a beautiful butterfly. On the other hand, if your butterfly steadfastly refuses to leave its chrysalis, don't wait forever. I met a stunning girl again recently who was with her new fiancé at a party. She told me she'd got engaged quickly after a whirlwind romance. At first sight physically, you might not have put them together, but there was no mistaking the look on her face – it was clearly that of a woman in love.

'We just understand each other,' she smiled. 'We're so right together.'

Looking at her beaming, relaxed face, I remembered the last time I'd seen her, draped over the arm of her handsome ex-boyfriend. They'd made a striking couple. At the time she smiled, but her eyes looked sad. She seemed on edge, weary from a tempestuous relationship with an unsuitable man.

Another friend wasted many a month with a handsome but cruel chap who hurt her terribly. When I asked her to list his redeeming qualities, she struggled, before admitting wistfully, 'But he's so beautiful . . .'

'But he's ugly inside,' I replied.

Don't get me wrong, I am not saying that handsome man are all bad and ugly men are good. But beauty often does only go skin deep. It's far too easy to get wrapped up in looks, and if someone's physical appearance is the only silver lining of a dark, heavy cloud of misdemeanours, then questions need to be raised. If that is the only thing someone has going for them, then alarm bells should ring.

I've found in the past that the most physically fetching of men can quickly lose their appeal as the rot from within starts to seep out.

Then there's the unexpected realisation that someone is becoming more and more attractive by the day as you grow to love them as a person.

When my friend continued to announce that she wanted to marry her cold-hearted Adonis, I asked her if she thought he'd stand by her if her face was maimed in an accident.

'No,' she replied, without any need to pause for thought.

Yet when I questioned my married female friends at length, so many of them seemed to be happy with men who'd won their love with both a physical appeal and a big-hearted nature within.

There also seemed to be an overriding theme that their husbands-to-be had been very kind to them when some mishap or other had occurred very early on.

Bizarrely, in at least three examples, in the early days of courtship, the young ladies in question had got so drunk they were sick, prompting their caring chaps to look after them.

As one friend asserts about her own 'puking' first date: 'I knew very quickly that we were right. I could do no wrong in this man's eyes. Apart from the obvious sexual attraction, he was just so kind and protective.

'On our first proper date at a friend's very smart flat, I got horribly drunk and was sick on myself, in his lap and on my friend's fax machine!

'Then, on another occasion, I passed out after drinking one too many vodkas, and when the fire alarm went off in our seaside B&B, he had to dress me and carry me out of the hotel. I was unconscious throughout and to this day have no recollection of the night's events.

'It seemed no amount of bad behaviour could deter him.'

She also revealed that while she'd done things to change her spouse over the past ten years, he'd also sparked transformations in her too.

'He's made me less selfish and spoilt,' she admitted. 'And he says I've given him stability and confidence.'

After years of attempting to change boyfriends, many

of whom seemed only too happy to be malleable, I recently found myself in a strange dilemma.

Although The Beau has battled to get past my plethora of split personalities – often manifesting themselves in times of stress, sleep deprivation and menstruation – it seemed I, like my friend, had mellowed a little, had become a calmer, nicer person to go out with.

Perhaps he has secretly been slipping Ritalin in my morning tea? Either way, for the first time ever, the urge to have my usual Mary Poppins moment, clicking my fingers bossily then launching my umbrella to make a sharp exit, is strangely absent.

I have also been reflecting on my past relationship behaviour. If I was honest, I could clearly dish it out, but had I ever really accepted criticism myself? The answer was no.

So recently I have been attempting to undergo an epiphany of my own. While I still occasionally treat The Beau, to quote the man himself 'like a whipping boy', for the first time I'm taking on board constructive criticism and ironically it's me that's now being whipped into shape.

The Beau's chief concern is my ability to work myself up into a frenzy over things which in the grand scheme of things don't really matter.

Recently, one fraught morning as I sat angrily on the tube, I discovered a *Little Book of Calm* which had mysteriously appeared in my handbag. The thoughtfulness of it almost moved me tears. It was at that moment that the realisation hit me that perhaps I'd found 'The One'.

Reflecting on past relationships, I would be sad to

think my exes thought I was a control freak. Instead, I sincerely hope my efforts to change boyfriends, for what I hoped would be to their benefit, have contributed, even a little, to happiness elsewhere. But I also hope to break the chain.

However, my marriage and baby Tourettes continues to flourish. On one occasion, as I walked round the supermarket with The Beau, I mentioned 'our future children' for the umpteenth time and he rolled his eyes.

'Sorry,' I whined. 'But talking about it makes me feel happy.'

'I feel happy,' he replied, deadpan. 'As happy as an orange.'

'In a juicer,' he then added for effect.

Unfortunately, this didn't discourage me.

During the course of writing this book, I questioned dozens of people on their views about finding 'The One'. Out of the hundreds of great insights and brilliant comments I received, one stuck in my mind: *'One day you'll meet a man who's already been shaped up by someone else, and you'll become "The One".'*

So I'll leave you with one last story.

Recently, The Beau and I were at a wedding when the bride appeared with the bouquet. As she prepared to throw it, he looked at me with mock horror. Then, as I pulled a determined face, he pinned my arms to my side in a vicelike grip.

But as the bouquet hurtled above my head, I summed up the strength of the Bionic Woman. Struggling free just at the crucial moment, I launched up and caught it. As I held my prize triumphantly, The Beau looked at me, his eyes wide. But then the corners of his mouth began to twitch and a slow smile began to escape.

Afterwards, I couldn't stop grinning and neither could The Beau.

Could the worm finally be turning?

THE TRUTH ABOUT MEN (BY MEN)

- 'Don't let him go on a lads' holiday when you're together. It will only end in tears as he will be with single lads who will push and push until he ends up getting so drunk, he WILL pull.'
- 'When he says he'll be five minutes in the loo, that means he's only on page 4 of the paper and has another 36 to read, so leave him be and put the kettle on!'
- 'If you're wanting a man for keeps rather than just a brief thing, then you need to be a "lady" for as long as possible. That means no swearing and definitely no farting! You also don't want to be the girl that all the blokes already "know". No one wants to be second. I bet even Buzz Aldrin wishes he'd stepped onto the moon first.'
- 'We hate calling. Texting is alright, but it's not just a power struggle, sometimes we just don't think we should contact a girl, otherwise it reflects badly and appears slightly desperate. Guys always think about girls – that's pretty much how I fill my day.'
- 'We're all bastards. Well, that's what you want us to say, isn't it? The fact of the matter is that for every ten

bastards, there's probably one nice guy. Your job is to find that one in ten, rather than settling for one of the other nine.'

- 'We don't think a girl is a slapper if she puts out too early, but, and this is a cliché, if a guy is made to work for it a little then we tend to appreciate it more.'

- 'In our post Spice Girls and *Sex and the City* world, women have become a bit unapproachable. The cosmopolitan-drinking covens are hard enough to crack, but the abuse you get from her and her mates when you try to talk to a girl would put you off. If girls were a little more approachable, then they would get approached more.'

- 'We just want to stay in our caves but go out once in a while with mates to play or watch sport, socialise and ogle ladies. But there's no harm meant – it's just a release!'

- 'Give us space and we will come. That is a mangled version of the *Field of Dreams* quote "Build it and they will come," not some mucky innuendo. Ha ha!'

- 'Men are very simple creatures. The good ones (which is most of us) don't have codes, or play games, or have five-year plans, or any of that bullshit. We're not all as emotionally bankrupt as you give us credit for!'

Acknowledgements

Right, deep breath!
A massive thank you to Caroline and Suzy for getting this whole bizarre process started – clear proof that the best ideas are conceived down the pub.

Carly Cook, my fabulous editor, you claim you stalked me, but in fact you gave me an incredible opportunity to fulfil a burning ambition and for that I can't thank you enough. Many thanks to my literary agent Amanda Preston and Emily and Josh at Headline.

To Fitzsy, ta for being a true friend and sedating me with red wine when I became my most manic as the deadline loomed. Thank you for taking your time to painstakingly read my work for me and for offering me encouragement as I typed away manically on the Jubilee Line and 189 bus. Likewise, thank you to Laura for always being on stand-by to cycle over at times of crisis for tea and sympathy.

Thank you to all my beloved pals, including Claire D, Heather, Sunny, Anne, Lucy, Alex, Becky, Sophie, Claire N, Emily, Stef, Leah, Neil, Claire H, Victoria, Trudi, Miki and all Sparklettes for your amazing support and ideas.

To all the brilliant boys and girls who, like complete troopers, entrusted their wonderful tales of woe, wickedness and wanton behaviour to me, I never imagined you'd be so forthcoming – you are all ace. Fear not, your secrets are safe with me!

Adam, you are a legend. Thank you for being incredibly tolerant and allowing me to be so honest. And big, big cheers to Tom and Jack.

Mary and Peter, your son is the kindest and most chivalrous person I've ever met. Thank you for everything.

To all my family who supported me, thank you dearly.

To my grandmother Mary, thank you for allowing me the privilege of including a true love story. You are the most elegant lady I know. Thank you also to Grandma Lily, and the Aussie/Kiwi rellies for all the encouragement.

To my younger siblings Ben and Sofie, you are much more sensible than me. At the risk of making you cringe, I love you and am very proud of you.

To Mum and Dad, your support, dedication and kindness know no bounds. Mum, if you hadn't talked me into sitting my English A level when I was full of self-doubt, this would never have happened, and your guidance with the book has been invaluable. I am eternally grateful to both you and Dad. I love you very much.

Last, but by no means least, thank you to my beloved Beau. I'm never happier than when I'm with you.

More Non-fiction from Headline

Jane Austen's Guide to Romance

LAUREN HENDERSON

Pride and Prejudice, Sense and Sensibility, Persuasion

Jane Austen's witty, perceptive and romantic novels have delighted readers for two hundred years. With common sense and good judgement, she observed the hits and near-misses of her heroes and heroines in love. Relationships certainly haven't got any easier since then and Lauren Henderson believes that we could all use some of that Regency wisdom.

A fun and insightful book, full of sage advice and wise strategies, JANE AUSTEN'S GUIDE TO ROMANCE also includes an original quiz so that you can work out which Jane Austen character you are most like and most suited to:

- If you're a lively Elizabeth Bennet in love with a flirty Frank Churchill, will your relationship last?

- Can a playboy like Mr Wickham ever settle down?

- And how does a shy Anne Elliot find the confidence to snag her man?

Whether single or in a relationship, an Austen devotee or a newcomer, this original and audacious how-to guide is an absolute must for anyone in love with romance.

NON-FICTION / GIFT 978 0 7553 1463 8